D1292336

LANDS OF THE INNER SEA

BOOKS BY W. ADOLPHE ROBERTS

Biography:

SIR HENRY MORGAN: BUCCANEER AND GOVERNOR
SEMMES OF THE ALABAMA

History:

THE CARIBBEAN: THE STORY OF OUR SEA OF DESTINY
THE FRENCH IN THE WEST INDIES
THE U.S. NAVY FIGHTS
LAKE PONTCHARTRAIN

Travel:

LANDS OF THE INNER SEA

Novels:

THE MORALIST
THE POMEGRANATE
ROYAL STREET
BRAVE MARDI GRAS

Verse:

PIERROT WOUNDED AND OTHER POEMS
PAN AND PEACOCKS

INVITATION TO TRAVEL SERIES

UNDER THE DIRECTION OF LOWELL BRENTANO

ASSISTANT EDITOR, RALPH HANCOCK

Lands of the Inner Sea

THE WEST INDIES AND BERMUDA

By W. Adolphe Roberts

Barry University Library

Miami, FL 33161

COWARD-McCANN, INC.
NEW YORK

COPYRIGHT, 1948, BY COWARD-MCCANN, INC.

All rights reserved. This book, or parts thereof, must not be reproduced in any form without permission.

Published simultaneously in the Dominion of Canada by Longmans, Green & Company, Toronto.

Manufactured in the United States of America

F
1611
.R6
1948

217750

DEDICATED TO

PAULINE BROOKS CRAWFORD

Contents

Foreword

THE Tropic of Cancer runs between Florida and Cuba, Key West being some seventy-five miles north of it and Havana twenty miles south. This dotted line on the map has always beguiled the imagination of Americans. Beyond it they sensed glamour and romance, a wilder beauty and a climate more languorous than could be found in their own country. Two separate worlds exist on either side of the straits. Yet the parallel of terrestrial latitude called a tropic is not a sharply defined frontier between the temperate and warm zones. Elsewhere around the globe it would be hard to put one's finger on the spot where the change begins. It is very apparent here, because southern Florida and the Antilles are of different physical formation, have different climates and a flora and fauna that show wide divergencies.

Florida is as level as a table, except for the low hills in the central Lakeland district. The Everglades occupy the better part of the toe of the peninsula, and on either side of this giant marsh the coastal strips are of sandy soil. Plenty of beauty there, but the winter temperature is manifestly subtropical. Key West on its island is the only Florida town, the only town in the United States, that never is nipped by frost. Ubiquitous coconut and other palms, brilliant flowers, and a few birds common to both zones create an illusion.

The moment one sets foot in Cuba, however, he is conscious of two things: that he has come to a new geographical region, and that he has reached the genuine tropics. The West Indies are mountainous, with the exception of the Bahamas to the northeast in the Atlantic Ocean and scattered coral islets that are in the process of emerging. The main arc is a chain of volcanic origin, probably forced up from the bottom of the sea in prehistoric times and modified by later convulsions. The countertheory that it may have been a range that sank until only its taller peaks remained above water is tenable, though fossilized shells and other aquatic relics are found at great altitudes. This spur of the Andes, as it is believed to be, may well have foundered and re-emerged not once but several times.

Pico Turquino in eastern Cuba exceeds 8,300 feet and Pico Trujillo in Hispaniola 10,300. The smaller island of Jamaica has its famous Blue Mountain Peak, 7,388 feet above sea level. Little Dominica in the Lesser Antilles, twenty-nine miles long by sixteen miles broad, soars sheer from the beaches to its Morne Diablotin, over 5,000 feet.

The prevailing loam of the Antilles is a rich ferrous red, or a black laden with decomposing vegetable matter. Even where the soil is gray and poor it is astonishing what water will enable it to do. Soaked by streams and dew, or steaming after the fury of the rains, it responds with a riot of unfading green, and fabulous blossoms from the orchids of the high woods to poinciana trees with every twig ablaze, bougainvillea vines, cannas, and hibiscus of the most vivid colors. There are drought areas, but irrigation is all that is needed to make these lushly productive.

Fruits offer still greater surprises than flowers. Oranges, lemons, and limes grow throughout the region, but they are of Mediterranean origin and do equally well in the far southern tier of the United States. Americans know the banana and pineapple as being tropical, since these have long been imported in quantity, and have a vague idea about some other species. They have tasted the papaya and the avocado, inferior specimens of which are grown in Florida and California; they have heard of the mango. As a list this is woefully limited. To begin with, the bland yellow banana that Americans eat is not the only one below Cancer. There are at least half a dozen popular varieties, just as there are three or four sorts of pineapples and a dozen popular kinds of mangoes. The avocado in its native climate often attains a length of eight or nine inches, is big around in proportion, and weighs more than a pound. The fruits that are never sent north commercially include the subtly sweet *níspero,* or naseberry, with a taste like candied honey; the star apple, like a peach to which the cream has already been added; the *guanábana,* or soursop; the sweetsop, the custard apple, the guava, the cashew, which bears the familiar nut as a pendant to its pulp, and many others.

Packed to overflowing in handcarts, or spread on long counters in the markets, the fruits delight the eye and give off a medley of aromas. Nothing is more characteristic of a tropical market than this faint sugary yet tangy smell.

The birds are no more brightly hued than those of Florida, but the majority are different. In natural history the Antilles form a subregion that ends, by the way, with Grenada; Trinidad and Tobago are offshoots, in this respect, of the South American mainland. The hummingbirds are numerous and glittering; one species peculiar to Jamaica is the smallest bird in the world, no bigger than a bumblebee. The little green todies with scarlet throats, second cousins to the kingfisher, though they live in woods and feed on insects, are exclusively West Indian. The fruit finch, or orangebird, with its incredibly golden breast; the green and rose-pink trogon; the satin-black tinkling grackle, parrots and parakeets, the pugnacious tyrant flycatcher called the petchary, doves with iridescent plumage; these are the typical birds that animate the scene.

The reptiles have the double merit of being pretty and harmless. Poisonous snakes are unknown in the Greater Antilles. In the Lesser Antilles, one venomous species, the fer-de-lance, is found only in St. Lucia and Martinique. Lizards of jewel-like beauty abound. The large arboreal Venus lizard is jade green in a normal state and darkens to a muddy brown when frightened. The geckoes, with their topaz or agate eyes, range from a birch-bark white to patterns of black and orange stripes.

All the senses combine to create the magic with which the traveler is bemused in the tropics. The total goes beyond that of colors and odors and the luscious flavors of fruit, beyond the sound of palm fronds clashing in the trade wind. Touch plays its part, and in a seductive manner. There is nothing quite like the feel of balmy air stirred to a scarcely perceptible breeze, which caresses one's body as if the skin were being stroked with the fringes of a swan's-down fan. Only between Cancer and Capricorn can this gamut of sensations be perfectly experienced, and notably in and about the Caribbean Sea.

The history of these lands exercises its fascination, too. The atmosphere may seem indolent, but it has not deterred explorers, soldiers, and liberators from performing arduous feats. For three centuries Spain, France, England, and Holland waged a succession of wars for the control of islands where sugar could be grown and which commanded the approaches to the treasures of Mexico and Peru. Buccaneering, which had much claim to romance, and piracy, which had little or none, flourished here with extravagant violence. In Cuba and Hispaniola independence was won after bloody revolutions. The belief that good government would follow automatically proved to be but a dream. Civil strife rent the republics time and again. It cannot be said that a final political structure has evolved in the region. There are nations yet to be born, and unions that may be achieved.

No wonder that the salient monuments of the past are either cathedrals or fortresses. The Spaniards raised the former as Te Deums in stone to celebrate their conquests. The frowning piles at the mouths of havens, such as the Morros of Havana, Santiago de Cuba and San Juan, the stone castle of Diego Columbus in ancient Santo Domingo (now Ciudad Trujillo), and the ruins of Fort Augusta, Kingston, were designed to protect important cities. Brimstone Hill in St. Kitts and Diamond Rock off Martinique were unique strong points, of which more will be said. The surf of battle dashed against most of them. Few escaped being captured at least once. Consistently enough, the newest development of regional scope has been the building of naval and air bases by the United States during World War II from the Bahamas to Trinidad.

The first North American visitors to the West Indies were Yankee traders, subjects of the Crown then, who evaded the stupid rules against intercolonial commerce that all governments were trying to enforce. The European theory was that colonies existed for the benefit of the mother country and should deal with one another through her as the broker. From running goods between ports under the English flag, the Americans soon branched out into smuggling operations in the Spanish, French, and Dutch possessions. They came for molasses, rum, and turtles. They carried back unforeseen emotional baggage in the form of enthusiasm for the harbors of the sun. Every youth with seafaring ambitions wanted to make a West Indian voyage. The traffic swelled after the Revolution in the face of British hostility to the young republic's shipping. It lived through the hazards of the War of 1812 and at last found freedom in the terms of the treaty that ended that struggle.

Today American commercial air lines dominate the Caribbean, and American surface craft are fast resuming the network of routes that they maintained prior to World War II. Planes and boats have been hard pressed to accommodate the tourists eager to follow the lure that laid a spell upon their ancestors.

The present book is a record of intimate impressions by one who was born and raised in Jamaica and knows some of the other islands almost as well, who has swung around the circuit several times and has just completed a vagabond trip to virtually all of them. The object is to tell the prospective traveler not only about the things he cannot very well miss, but those that he should go out of his way to see. Postwar conditions affecting lodging, food, and amusements are set forth, in so far as permanent changes appear to have been brought about.

For the purposes of travel guidance, the Guianas—British, Dutch, and French—are included, though they are on the South American continent. These three colonies are governmentally tied in with the West Indian holdings of the European powers in question. Their money and their postal arrangements are similarly controlled. Furthermore, the Guianas can be most conveniently reached by the extending of a Caribbean journey through Trinidad. Their coastal cities are on the Pan American trunk air route south, but their hinterland is linked with the adjoining Latin countries, Venezuela and Brazil, only by forest trails.

Bermuda lies in the Atlantic at about the latitude of Savannah, Georgia, several hundred miles east of the coast and north of the Bahamas. It is in no sense West Indian, yet the tourist planning a voyage associates it in his mind with the other warm-weather islands and very often chooses it over the rest because it is so easy of access. Bermuda, therefore, receives a special section in these pages.

If forewords are to escape being skipped, they should be short. So enough of this one, and let us get on with the story.

LANDS OF THE INNER SEA

CHAPTER 1

HAVANA: SIGHT-SEERS' PARADISE

BEFORE the late war an overwhelming majority of pleasure seekers left for the West Indies on excursion liners, the ships of the fruit companies, or the freighters that enticed with their "tramp trips" to out-of-the-way ports. During the conflict those who could get visas and priorities went, perforce, by plane. The ordinary person's timidity about the air vanished for good. When travel was thrown wide-open once more there was a shortage of vessels that is still being felt. The sky clippers really came into their own; a habit was fixed that will give them a permanently large share of the business. But the flying tourist will feel at times a nostalgia for the old ways, for the space aboard ship, for a slanting deck, and long, lazy hours leaning on the rail or stretched out in a canvas chair. Myself not least.

I knew that, once in the islands, every major connection of my tour would have to be made by plane. In order to preserve a sense of proportion and not yield wholly to the modern cult of speed—yes, and for my own pleasure—I decided to start out from the United States on a ship. It was far from easy to arrange. Ships were few and crowded. A maritime strike suddenly tied up all American ports, and it was no sooner ended than the stevedores of Havana struck. Departure was twice canceled, because the owners would not take a chance on cargoes that might spoil before they could be unloaded. However, at noon on a June day I at last sailed from New Orleans on a fruiter that had survived the German submarine campaign.

The Mississippi delta is a curious and attractive gateway. Aided by the current, a steamer makes fast time down the 110 miles of winding river, skirting first on the left the Plain of Chalmette, where Andrew Jackson defeated the British in 1815, then passing between

1

fields of sugar cane that merge into jungles of water cypresses and endless expanses of reeds. The closer one gets to the mouth, the more complicated the topography becomes and the greener the vegetation. Levees thrown up on either bank support occasional houses that otherwise would have to stand on stilts, as well as long rows of orange trees in single, double, or at the most triple file. Land created of silt brought by the stream from upcountry is scattered in islands and shoals, of which the reeds take quick possession. There are so many bayous and false channels that the layman is bewildered before the ship reaches Head of Passes, where the pilot is taken aboard. One understands why an early Spanish name for the Mississippi was the Escondido, meaning "hidden" and having reference to the difficulty of realizing that a great river lay beyond the maze at its outlet.

The bar crossed, we rode steadily on the Gulf of Mexico, a summer lake at that time of year, but capable of going on terrible rampages in the hurricane season and when the northers blow in winter. The run from New Orleans to Havana is a straight course, and even a ship of moderate speed covers it in less than two days. Landfall was to be early on the second morning, after only one full day at sea. Many of the passengers were simply starved for travel, having had none except by train or bus since Pearl Harbor, and they spun out that day till long past midnight. Most were not booked beyond Havana, but the entire cruise is worth bearing in mind if you ever want to get off the beaten track. The ships of this line (the Standard Fruit Company) are primarily interested in bringing back bananas. They go on to small Haitian ports to load and make a round trip of it, returning to New Orleans direct. The United Fruit Company has recently inaugurated similar tours, from New Orleans to Havana, and back by way of Central America.

Havana unfolds ideally if you come to it along the coast from the west. In that case you pass the imposing Organos mountain range, then a series of foothills and valleys, the pretty bay of Mariel, savannas merging with the suburbs of the capital—and suddenly you are off the Malecón, the paved drive that follows the gulf shore for miles within the modern city. At La Punta fortress you round into the channel with Morro Castle on the opposite point. Vessels from the United States usually approach the channel southward in a straight line. Either way the view of the old city from then on is unforgettable.

The Morro, familiarized by prints and postcards, has scarcely slipped past when you see the presidential palace a few blocks from the water front, the stunning Máximo Gómez monument, and La Fuerza fortress with perhaps a glimpse of the cathedral behind it. The ordinary buildings have flat roofs and narrow balconies. They are tinted in various pastel shades, the prevailing color being a yellowish umber. The effect is that of southern Spain with a strong Moorish influence.

You are looking at the original Havana "within the walls" (*intra-muros*), as the term was, that huddled on its harbor behind strong defenses. The aspect of things down here decidedly is not French. It will emerge, however, that for various reasons Havana today merits the sobriquet "Paris of the West Indies."

The Cuban immigration and customs officials are liberal with American tourists, and the doctor not fussy unless some contagious disease happens to be epidemic in the port of origin or in Cuba. The only health certificate that it is necessary to carry is one showing a recent vaccination for smallpox. Any document proving nationality will be accepted, but the wise traveler carries a passport because that is the perfect evidence and ensures against delays. Also, if you should decide you'd like to go to some other foreign country from Cuba it will be impossible to do so until you have obtained a passport. The system of issuing landing cards is the best I know of. A questionnaire was filled out at the time you bought your ticket, and the immigration man bothers you with no more red tape. He gives you a card good for six months. The customs examiner notes on the back of it whether you brought in a camera, a portable typewriter, or other object for your private use on which a resident would have had to pay duty. The card is an identification that serves all purposes. It guarantees that you will have no trouble when you are ready to leave.

Cuba wants the tourist. So do all her Caribbean rivals. But some of these, as I shall show later on, are not so shrewd and reasonable as Cuba is in making the tourist feel from the beginning that he is a welcome guest. That may explain, in part, why before the war more visitors went to Cuba than to the rest of the West Indies put together and why the first new tide has taken the same direction.

There are hotels of every sort in Havana, starting with the smart Nacional and Sevilla-Biltmore, at either of which it would be hard to get by, room and meals, for less than fifteen dollars a day, even in summer. Both are excellently run, and the choice is one of location. The Nacional is rather far out on an elevation facing the sea, at the juncture of the city proper and the residential section called Vedado. The Sevilla-Biltmore is on the Prado, at the heart of things. Typical of a Caribbean republic is the fact that the Nacional, although less than twenty years old, has already played a sanguinary role in history. Army officers stood a siege of a month there during the revolution that overthrew President Machado in 1933. On the final day the hotel was shelled and stormed, with a casualty list on both sides of sixty dead and more than two hundred wounded.

Some twenty-five other comfortable hotels offer rooms ranging from ten to two dollars a day, the winter rate being in each case about one third higher than the summer. I shall not list them all, for this book seeks to avoid the statistical dullness of a Baedeker. Suffice it to mention a few that I especially like, or that the average American seems to prefer.

I am fond of the Inglaterra, that proud and ancient house on the Parque Central which Joseph Hergesheimer celebrates so gracefully in his *San Cristóbal de la Habana*. It has lost much of its splendor, having yielded ground-floor locations to commerce and thus reduced the size of its lobby. But the bedrooms are still spacious as those of a palace, with lofty ceilings, jalousie screen doors of carved wood, and tiled floors. An atmosphere of cool and leisured dignity results. The Inglaterra is now moderate-priced, and that is true of another old hostelry that appeals to me, the Ambos Mundos. The latter is situated not far from the harbor on the *calle* Obispo. From the upper floors there is a superb view of historic buildings near by and the Morro across the water. Ernest Hemingway and the late Thomas Barbour, naturalist and lover of Cuba, are among those who have praised the Ambos Mundos.

The Plaza, on Zulueta and a corner of the Parque Central, is no doubt the favorite among tourists who want to strike a medium between the swank and the economical. It opened the first roof garden in the city, and catered successfully otherwise to American tastes. The Lincoln on Galiano, the Royal Palm on Industria, and the Parkview at Morro and Colón are also popular with northerners. The Ritz on Neptuno is more Cuban, as is the Presidente far out in Vedado. The old Pasaje on the upper Prado is completely native.

A word about Havana street names. I have given those that are commonly used, and I shall continue to do so. A remarkable state of affairs exists between a municipality with a passion for renaming and a public that absolutely refuses to accept the new appellations. Thus, the Prado has long since become officially the Paseo de Martí, and though there is no more venerated figure in Cuban history than Martí, it remains the Prado in everyday parlance. Zulueta was changed to Agramonte, Neptuno to Juan Clemente Zenea, Galiano to Avenida de Italia, Monserrate to Avenida de Belgica, O'Reilly to Presidente Zayas, etc. But try to get anyone to admit the changes, the street signs notwithstanding. Newcomers are forced to learn by a trial and error system how to find addresses on the disputed thoroughfares. Luckily, some maps give both the old and new names.

The general plan of the city is not hard to grasp, and a person with any sense of direction can orient himself in a day or two. The main artery is the Prado, which divides roughly the most ancient section from the streets that sprang up "outside the walls." It runs from the sea to the Parque Central, then in front of the Capitolio and the Plaza de la Fraternidad. Between the water front and the park it is a magnificent avenue, broad, with a raised central walk paved with marble and shaded by trees that meet overhead, while on both sides there are roadways for traffic. Beyond the park it changes its character. There are no trees to obstruct the view of the Capitolio and the latter's grounds, but on the opposite edge the excess space of the Prado is given over to a sidewalk lined with open-air cafés.

A European atmosphere that constitutes one of the charms of modern Havana is created by these cafés. The first was launched as an experiment nearly twenty years ago on the urging of Don Gabriel Camps, a great man about town of his day. I chanced to be present at his inauguration of the second or third one, I forget which. It was the occasion of many speeches on the virtues of open-air drinking and the opportunities it furnished for watching the world go by. The idea caught on. There are six or seven of the resorts now, always crowded in the cool of the afternoon and on fine nights. Some of them feature music from raised platforms in the midst of the guests. I was amused to note that a female orchestra composed of comely lasses was enclosed in glass, except on top. This device reduced flirtation with the talent to a minimum. Vocal solos were rendered over a loud-speaker.

As you face away from the sea, the old town lies to the left of the Prado. Its streets are narrow, but do not do much twisting and turning. The two narrowest among the important ones are Obispo and O'Reilly, where the awnings on opposite sides almost meet, and in which cars of any breadth find it hard to pass each other. Yet fashionable shops have always lined both streets, and they are busier than ever today. In this quarter are located the presidential palace, the cathedral, the city hall, most of the government departments, the national museum, and the national library.

To the right of the Prado is the newer, but by no means the newest, Havana. Its fairly evenly spaced streets are utilitarian in the international manner, rather than picturesque and colonial. Here are the department stores, a couple of American five-and-ten-cent stores, and an infinity of little shops on the ground floors of apartment buildings. Southeastward is a sprawling district of poor dwellings occupied by Cuban workmen, Negroes, and Chinese. Along the shore to the west, the city becomes more and more residential, and modernistic structures begin to appear. Finally we are in Vedado, where the homes are semisuburban and for the most part nineteenth century, standing back in their own gardens. The blocks of apartments are highly modernistic, with curves of glaring white wall, much glass, and shining, undecorated balcony rails. Beyond Veldado, across the Almendares River, is Marianao, a separate municipality.

Transportation is popularly by trolley cars and some thirty bus routes, the fare being still five cents. It is impossible to exaggerate the crowding on the busses, which are small, have narrow seats and jumpy springs, and are driven at breakneck speed. The Havanese call them in affectionate derision *guaguas* (pronounced wah-wahs), a word that is slang in Peru for a baby and in Mexico for an insect that destroys fruit. Why it should mean an omnibus in Cuba, who can tell? The passengers are generally amiable about their discomforts, so the guagua is not a bad compromise if one wants to cover a long distance cheaply. Taxicabs are numerous, but the twenty-cent fare that prevailed before 1939 has been more than doubled.

Before we go sight-seeing, let us dwell a little upon the romance of Havana's early history. I am of those who hold that the enjoyment of a beautiful or noble place is heightened by a knowledge of the deeds that created it. If there are sensitive travelers who do not share that view, I have yet to meet them.

Don Diego Velásquez, who had come to Hispaniola with Christopher Columbus and had made himself the richest man in the island, was commissioned in 1510 by the second admiral, Don Diego Columbus, to conquer Cuba. The expedition was largely financed by Velásquez himself in return for the appointment as governor. His chief lieutenant was Pánfilo de Narváez, an erratic captain who had been fighting in Jamaica. They landed at the eastern end of Cuba and subdued the Arawak Indians easily enough, though opposed heroically by the cacique Hatuey. After a false start at Baracoa, the first capital was established in 1514 on the landlocked harbor of Santiago. That same year Narváez pushed through to the west and chose a site on the bay of Batabanó where the island is narrowest. Velásquez visited and approved it in 1515. A town was founded there under the name of San Cristóbal de la Habana. But it proved not to be a good site for a port, the water being too shallow.

Years before, Sebastián de Ocampo, the first man to circumnavigate Cuba and prove that it was an island, had found a harbor on the north coast where he had repaired his caravels. His glowing report on it had been forgotten. In 1517 some ships belonging to Velásquez rediscovered it, and two years later Havana was transferred there across the thirty-odd miles of isthmus. It had reached its true location. A mass was sung under a towering ceiba tree on the shore where the chapel called El Templete now stands. A central square, or Plaza de Armas, was laid out near by with two of its sides reserved for an administration building and a church. Not long afterward a fort with a tower was erected, to be succeeded by La Fuerza, the oldest Spanish fortress in the New World that is still intact and utilized.

The books tell that Hernando Cortés, defying the last-minute attempt of Velásquez to displace him as commander of the expedition to Mexico, fled Santiago and completed the refitting of his ships at Trinidad on the south coast and Havana. This was in 1518, and departure into the unknown did not occur until the following February. The Havana he visited was the original town at Batabanó. The gold and other treasure, however, that soon began to pour out of Mexico made the new port's fortune. It would have been a roundabout route from Vera Cruz via Santiago de Cuba to Cadiz, Spain. But Havana was on a direct, short course. Cargoes could be held there until a fleet of galleons had been assembled for the dangerous Atlantic crossing. No one had so far challenged the Spaniards in American waters.

Presently there appeared on the scene the brilliant, lordly figure of Hernando de Soto. He had been with Pizarro in Peru, where he had been the one to lay hands on Atahualpa, the Inca monarch, and had obtained for himself a large share of the riches of Cuzco. He had returned home to live like a grandee, had married the beautiful Isabel de Bobadilla. This measure of success was not enough for him. He wanted to equal, if not surpass, the exploits of Cortés and Pizarro. To do that he would have to discover and conquer an Indian empire. From rumors he had heard, he believed that such a one existed in the interior of the North American continent. So he got the king to appoint him governor of both Cuba and Florida.

De Soto spent part of his fortune in the equipping of four ships with all the necessary arms and lavish supplies. He enlisted 120 mounted men and 620 foot soldiers. Priests joined him as chaplains and several Dominican friars went along as missionaries. The venture attracted scores who paid their own expenses in the hope of being accepted as minor partners. The flotilla, which sailed for the West Indies in April 1538, had swelled to some twenty ships.

The reception given De Soto, inspired by his fame and the glamour of his known project, was of a sort that inflates the ego. He landed at primitive Santiago and took over the executive power. But the merchants and planters feted him as no mere governor would have been feted. Bullfights and horse races, banquets and dances were held in his honor. The sports mimicked the ceremony of a medieval tournament, with the bestowing of handsome prizes on the winners. A number of fine horses was presented to De Soto, and at that period there were few things more valuable in Cuba than a horse. Young colonists riding their own steeds clamored for places in the cavalry.

After lingering a few weeks, the commander sent his ships loaded with troops to Havana. His wife and household servants were aboard one of them. Then, at the head of his knights and squires, he made a triumphal march through the island and established headquarters at the fast-growing port at the western end.

It was precisely at this juncture that French sea raiders had begun to be a threat in the Caribbean, and that Havana had its first experience with the pirates that were to plague it for decades to come. In 1537 and 1538 coastal villages in the islands and on the mainland had been looted and ships at anchor seized. The governor at Santo Domingo reported in alarm that the hostile actions of the French were "shameless, bold, and continuous." Early in the first year a vessel flying the banner of François I had appeared a mile off Havana and driven the shipping to cover. The privateer had then retired to the bay of Mariel, where three local craft pursued him to their sorrow. The winds had proved favorable to the Frenchman, who destroyed two of the Spanish ships, took the third as a prize, and swaggered back into Havana harbor itself to taunt the citizens. He left at the end of a few days without having attempted a coup ashore.

But shortly before the arrival of De Soto's flotilla an unnamed corsair, after having been repulsed at Santiago, dashed to Havana and was lucky in finding no warcraft there. He landed his men, and the inhabitants having fled to the woods and hills, the town was combed for treasure. Little of worth was found, so in a rage the looters burned the church and almost every other building except the fort, which was too tough for them to storm. Construction with wattle, mud, and thatch was a simple problem, and the dwellings were quickly restored.

The presence of De Soto and his armament naturally intimidated the pirates. If he had devoted all those resources to Havana he could have made the city great in a generation. But the Golconda that was to be his very own glowed brightly for him. He proceeded with apparent caution, sending two scouting parties ahead to find a good landing place in Florida. They returned with the most discouraging reports—and he closed his ears against them. In May 1539 he sailed north with martial pomp and fanfare, leaving Doña Isabel to act for him as governor of Cuba. Her apartments were in the tower of the fort, from the windows of which she watched the horizon in vain for longer than five years.

De Soto's debacle in the wilderness, his discovery of the Mississippi and burial in its waters, is an oft-told tale. A remnant of his force struggled through to Mexico toward the end of 1543. The news, which sent the stricken wife back to Spain (incidentally, she did not weep herself to death, as the legend goes, but lived to be an

old woman), affected Havana's security. While there had been hope
of getting in touch with De Soto, armed ships had cruised periodically to the Gulf Coast. These now departed, and the way was again
open to the foreign raiders.

Jacques de Sores, a Huguenot, had come to the West Indies as
chief lieutenant of François le Clerc, the celebrated peg-leg French
privateer, when war broke out between their country and Spain in
1552. The pair practiced some lively deviltries together, then divided the territory. Cuba was assigned to Sores. He was the first to
master the bottleneck harbor of Santiago and sack the town, which
had grown imporant enough to yield eighty thousand pesos. He
burst on Havana in July 1555 with two ships, of which one carried
twenty guns. The affair of seventeen years before was repeated on a
larger scale. Men landed to the west, marched in, and occupied all
buildings except the fort. The latter was subsequently bombarded
by the ships and assaulted on every side until it surrendered. Sores
was inclined to be clement until the small booty that materialized
spoiled his temper. A counterattack from the interior was repulsed,
but he chose to regard it as treachery, butchered twenty-five prisoners in reprisal, and let loose his hearties on private homes and the
church. A fanatical Protestant, he roared with glee as corsairs decked
themselves in the priests' vestments and desecrated the holy images
by stabbing them with bloody daggers and parading them among
the ruins. This Lutheran travesty, as it has been called, was not forgotten or forgiven by the Spaniards for many a year.

Sores held Havana for eighteen days—some accounts say twenty-
six days—and then sailed, leaving the vendetta behind him. When
Huguenots from France founded a settlement on the St. John's
River, Florida, in 1564, the fact was noted with horror by Admiral
Pedro Menéndez de Avilés, a really great captain and at the same
time as intense a bigot as ever lived. He asked Philip II for a man-
date to scourge the impudent heretics, descended upon the latter,
and announced, "I am come to hang or behead all Lutherans [to a
Spaniard every Protestant was a Lutheran] I may find." Menéndez
was the victor in the fighting that followed. He strung up his first
fifteen prisoners with placards above their heads, "Not as Frenchmen, but as Lutherans." He massacred the remainder with less ceremony and stamped out the colony, thus collecting an installment on
the score, as he saw it, for the excesses in Havana ten years before.

One could go on indefinitely with anecdotal history of this kind; it would be pure gain in getting the feel of how and why the original city was laid out as one finds it today. But lack of space forbids. We must restrict ourselves to the highlights of the next century or two.

La Fuerza fortress, replacing the old fort with the tower, was completed in time to baffle Sir Francis Drake, star among the English privateers, who now outshone the French. The Spaniards never feared anyone more than Drake, whom they called El Draque and pictured to children as a half-mythical monster. After ravishing Santo Domingo and Cartagena early in 1586, he appeared off Havana with a fleet of thirty ships, which he kept arrayed in battle line, just beyond gunshot, for a week. Then he turned rightabout-face and was gone to the easier exploit of destroying St. Augustine, Florida, the town Menéndez had founded.

Drake was the immediate cause of the building of Morro Castle and of La Punta fortress opposite. They were both completed by 1597, and Havana, which meanwhile had been made the capital instead of Santiago, was regarded as impregnable. Such it proved to be for longer than a hundred and fifty years. In 1628 the Dutch admirals Pieter Pieterzoon Heyn and Pieter Adriaanzoon Ita menaced the city, then withdrew and achieved the far more profitable feat of capturing seventeen vessels of the autumn plate fleet from Mexico, with plunder valued at between twelve and fifteen million guilders. The most notable of the buccaneers, Henry Morgan, came with twelve ships in 1668 and passed the harbor mouth in slow defile, perhaps consciously offering a variation of Drake's threat. He scared the populace into digging trenches to link the forts, but his real designs were against another place. L'Ollonais, a French buccaneer, often boasted that he would take Havana; the Morro never even sighted him, though once he slew eighty-nine of ninety men who had been ordered to capture him and sent back the sole survivor with a braggart message to the Cuban governor.

In 1727, Spain and England being at war, an English squadron blockaded Havana. The admiral had failed to take into account that the port had been for some years an active shipbuilding center. The defenders had a constant flow of craft from the stocks to launch against the enemy, and at the end of a month the British were forced to withdraw, their commander so mortified that he is reputed to have

died of "grief and shame." Twenty years later, during the War of
the Austrian Succession, six Spanish and six English warships fought
one another to a draw within musket shot of the foreshore now improved as the Malecón.

The day of abasement against which it was believed the Morro
forever guarded became a reality during the Seven Years' War. Spain
had kept out of the struggle until January 1762, when she was
drawn in on the side of France under the curious terms of the treaties of the Family Compact. A great British expedition was immediately got ready in Jamaica under the Duke of Albemarle and
Admiral George Pocock. Fourteen thousand regulars had been sent
out, and these were reinforced by Jamaican and North American
troops, the latter commanded by Colonel Israel Putnam. Landing in
open country on both sides of the harbor, the British invested Havana in June. The wall enclosing the city on the land side had recently been completed. It was clear that frontal attacks would be too
costly, and the ships could do little while the Morro stood.

But Albemarle and Pocock had an eye for the weak spot. The
Cabaña heights on the harbor front behind the Morro had not been
properly fortified, and if siege guns could be dragged up there they
would command both the castle and the city. At the end of three
and a half weeks the heights were carried. The bastion facing Cabaña was reduced in another week, and on the forty-fourth day of
the siege a mine breached the south wall of the Morro. The British
poured in and successfully stormed the huge fortress for the only
time in its history. The city itself held out for two weeks longer,
though its food supplies had been cut off and it was being mercilessly shelled. It capitulated on August 13, and all Cuba was declared to have been annexed by England.

By the Treaty of Paris, which ended the war the following year,
the British took Florida and that part of Louisiana which lay east of
the Mississippi, except the city of New Orleans, and gave Cuba back
to Spain. The latter acquired from France the rest of Louisiana, including New Orleans. The invaders had been in control of Havana
eleven months when they marched away. There came the Conde
de Ricla as governor, or captain general as the title was thenceforth,
and the Conde O'Reilly as chief of the military forces. They had
orders to perfect a defensive system. The small Atares Castle was
at once built at the southwest end of the harbor, and twelve years

later the stupendous Cabaña Castle covered the length of the heights that the foe had turned to such deadly account. O'Reilly, a gifted Irish adventurer, briefly interrupted his mission to take over and pacify New Orleans, which had revolted against its first Spanish administrator.

Havana was never again attacked in war. Paradoxically, the English occupation had worked out as an advantage, because it rudely broke up an era of contented provincialism and caused Spain to take more interest in Cuba. O'Reilly went beyond military needs in improving the capital. Most of the captains general for the next century were tyrannous but energetic men with ambitions to build an imperial city. The population increased rapidly after 1763, overflowing the walls and founding seven new suburbs within thirty years. In 1810 a reliable census showed that it had swelled to 96,114, an impressive figure for the period in America, and only 259 less than New York then contained. The main factor in holding the port back was Spain's perverse devotion to the theory that her colonies should trade only with her. In 1778 a liberal ministry gave Havana the privilege of receiving the ships of all nations; almost immediately this was restricted and then withdrawn. After the Napoleonic Wars mercantile freedoms were obtained one by one, largely through the efforts of the Cuban-born Francisco de Arango.

Modern Havana has a population of about 800,000, but in the midst of this enormous growth the best monuments from the past have been preserved. That is a reason why the traveler finds it so rewarding a city.

The first church on the Plaza de Armas was no doubt intended to develop into a cathedral, but after it had been burned several times the site was shifted. In 1674 a small church was built on a square two blocks distant, enlarged in leisurely fashion during the next fifty years, and completed in 1724. It became fashionable, was favored by one bishop after another, and in 1789 was created the cathedral. Officially it is San Cristóbal, named for the patron saint of Havana. Ordinarily it is called the Colón Cathedral, because when the Spaniards yielded their half of Hispaniola to the French they insisted on removing the bones of Christopher Columbus from Santo Domingo City to Havana. In 1796 these were held to have been deposited ceremoniously in a niche in the left wall of the chancel.

They were again transferred—to Seville—a century later, when Spain lost Cuba. Yet there is good reason to believe that a mistake had been made at the beginning, and that the right bones had never left Santo Domingo. Neither Havana nor Seville is willing to admit this. I shall discuss the point in treating of the Dominican Republic.

The cathedral is not an imposing building architecturally, but its low mass, especially on moonlight nights, evokes to perfection the atmosphere of Spanish colonialism in the eighteenth century. A rococo altar gleams with gold, marble, onyx, and carved woods. The sculpture is varied, of historical value, and often artistic. In addition to the empty Columbus tomb, note the memorial to Pierre le Moyne, Sieur d'Iberville, the founder of Louisiana, who died in Havana of yellow fever in 1706 and was buried here. American, Canadian, and French residents join every year in placing a floral wreath below his tablet. The treasure room of the cathedral may be visited. It contains antique vestments heavy with gold embroidery, a celebrated monstrance of solid silver, plate, jewelry, and paintings.

El Santo Cristo is the oldest church that still functions as one. It is pure sixteenth century. The chapel of the Santa Clara convent is probably older, as is the rest of that fine building with its ancient walls of *mamposteria* (broken stone and sand enclosed in plaster) and its exquisite patios. But the convent, acquired by the state twenty-five years ago in a deal that reeked of graft, now houses the Department of Public Works. San Francisco Church, about two hundred years younger, is occupied by the Post Office and Telegraph Department; it lost some of its sacred aura while the British ruled Havana, for they used it as a barracks and stable part of the time, and then irked Catholic sentiment even more seriously by holding Protestant services there. Beautiful La Merced is rich in ecclesiastical art.

The *casa del ayuntamiento*, or city hall, on the Plaza de Armas, is not so old as it looks, for it was completed only in 1780. The captains general of Cuba made it their official residence. The first two presidents of the republic did also. After that it passed to the municipality. Its patio is spacious and magnificent, and in this secluded spot the Spaniards chose to raise the city's statue of Columbus. But the discoverer is honored in many places; in the cathedral, as we have seen, and in El Templete, where there is a large canvas protraying his landing. There is a street called Colón, a Colón market, and a Colón cemetery.

To the right of the city hall and facing the Plaza de Armas is the former palace of the Spanish lieutenant governors, a venerable limestone building where the Supreme Court now sits.

For a city of Havana's size and prestige, both the library and the museum seem inadequate. The former possesses some quarter of a million volumes and many precious manuscripts, most of which are in storage. The two or three rooms open to the public are located, of all places, on the upper floor of La Fuerza fortress, a romantic setting of narrow windows cut through immensely thick stone walls, dark woodwork, and crumbling steps leading from one level to another. But it is limited for the purposes of reading and study. Plans for erecting a building for the national library have long been afoot; virtually every president has referred to them optimistically at the start of his term, and then failed to do anything about them.

The museum is in a stately old mansion on Aguiar. A museum in the outdated sense of being a repository for curios is precisely what it is. The modern conception of exhibits organized to aid research workers and teach the uninformed is blithely ignored. Personally, I enjoyed browsing there, because the emphasis is on history and there is a thrill in coming upon the most unexpected relics of men and events that have a meaning for me. The skeleton of the favorite war horse of the generalissimo Máximo Gómez, and the rowboat in which General Antonio Maceo crossed the bay of Mariel during the War of Independence, may take up inordinate space in a small room, but they do strike a note of reality. Weapons and clothing of every period abound. The Latin penchant for the macabre is evident in such items as a photographic close-up of Maceo's skull, made when his bones were disinterred from their temporary grave near the battlefield, and in the many gruesome death masks of other heroes. There are also charming bits of ironwork and stone from demolished sections of colonial Havana. Two rooms are given over to Cuban paintings, some good, some bad.

A little house at the corner of Paula and Egido, opposite the Central Railroad Station, should not be missed. It is the birthplace of

José Julian Martí, leader who made the dream of national independence come true, and of course contains objects of interest associated with him.

The above does not exhaust the roll of places that should be seen in the old city. Take it as an indication of the "musts," and find the rest for yourself. Work from a list if you like—the Cuban Tourist Commission will give you one—but it truly is more fun just to wander about, poke into the public buildings and courtyards that attract you, sit on the benches in the squares, and check up later on the significance of the spots that forced you to linger.

I must add that a visit to the Cabaña and the Morro across the harbor is necessary to complete a survey of the old as against the new. Few overlook this, anyway. It is one of the best advertised trips. Launches leave several times a day from two points on the water front. At whichever castle you land, it is practicable to pass on foot from one to the other. The Morro has become mainly a national monument, a show place, yet part of it is reserved as a school for army officers. Soldiers on duty supervise the visitors. The pile is somberly impressive, with its battlements, its outer galleries protected by breast-high bulwarks several feet broad, its watchtowers, corridors, and succession of vast rooms buried deep in the masonry; the more so since from each exterior window you look out upon an azure sea. There are chambers where the condemned were held until the time came to throw them, living or dead, to the waiting sharks; and farther down there are dungeons cut in the rock below the level of the water.

The Cabaña is considerably larger than the Morro, if less overwhelming, as the sight-seer will discover after he has walked miles to cover its ramparts, passageways, and courtyards. All of it may not be seen, except by special permission, for a prison is maintained within its mass. For almost a century it has been the favored place of detention for political offenders. Cuban patriots were held and tortured there during the two revolutions, 1868–78 and 1895–98. Many died before firing squads in the Ditch of the Laurels, a sunken enclosure that had been a moat, one wall of which is pitted by hundreds of bullets that pierced the condemned. An ancient tradition of discharging a blank cannon shot from the Cabaña every night at nine is still observed. This is no longer a curfew, but the citizens would feel lost without it as a signal to set their watches.

Now for the newer Havana.

The Prado has buildings that belong to both periods. The Teatro Nacional, elaborated from the structure erected by a famous captain general of the 1830's, Don Miguel Tacón, and originally named after him, is as ornate as any nineteenth-century opera house. Early newspapers lauded "such accommodations as have not hitherto been found in the Western World." Unhappily, it has fallen on degenerate days, motion pictures and vaudeville having almost wholly superseded the drama on its stage. Offices and shops have impinged on its magnificent foyer.

Up from the theater, on the same side of the Prado, is the Capitolio, the latest and by all odds the biggest and most expensive of the city's public structures. It was built in the flush 1920's under the tyrant President Gerardo Machado, as a somewhat vulgar flourish to mark Cuba's sense of importance, and as a scheme for lining the pockets of Machado's gang. The republic did not need a capitol second only in size to the United States Capitol. Even so, it could have been completed for eight million dollars and it cost twenty millions. The difference evaporated in graft. Gold leaf bedecks the dome, beneath which stands a huge female statue of the tutelary deity of the country, heavily gilded. A twenty-four-carat diamond was embedded in the floor to mark the zero kilometer of the roadway system, but this was pried out and stolen in 1946, a crime so sensational and seemingly impossible of achievement that the cynical have bluntly labeled it an "inside job." The diamond was returned, anonymously of course, by registered mail from Miami, Florida, in the summer of 1947.

There is splendor and much aesthetic merit in certain aspects of the interior of the Capitolio. The exterior is true enough to its model, which stands in Washington. But I find it a pity that a Caribbean state should have shown so little originality as to imitate the Greco-Roman style of architecture that eighteenth-century America associated with republicanism, and that afterward was adopted by stock exchanges and banks. It would have been more to the point, more native, to have drawn inspiration from Spanish colonial or even from Indian buildings—Mayan or Aztec—though as regards the latter it is true that they were of the mainland and that the aborigines of Cuba were too primitive to employ stone.

The presidential palace, completed in President Mario G. Menocal's time, is a curious hodgepodge, sort of Italian Renaissance and sort of Moorish. Its dome of glass tiles, predominantly yellow, has often been compared by facetious observers to a wedding cake's crowning glory. The furnishings and mural decorations were governed by Menocal's personal tastes, which ran to the court of Versailles and especially the Louis Quinze period. This results in another incongruity. The palace, however, has a bizarre elegance, and I prefer its individualism to the standardized bulk of the Capitolio.

Mutual aid societies form an integral part of Spanish life and function on a scale unknown in other countries. They were brought to Havana by Spaniards, who organized according to the province from which they had come; several of them are richer and more powerful than ever today. Their own buildings, which are run as monster clubs, give their members cultural benefits and full medical attention. The most prominent are the Centro Asturiano and the Centro Gallego, both on the Parque Central. Stop to think that the first-mentioned has a membership of about forty-eight thousand and you can form an idea of its social significance. A tourist cannot get in without an invitation. It is worth angling for one, just to see the ball-room, to which you mount by marble stairs, the luxurious tiled bar, and the many recreation rooms.

The University of Havana, founded two and a quarter centuries ago, has a cluster of comparatively modern buildings on a hill in the direction of Vedado. Near by are the Botanical Gardens, the former Quinta de los Molinos, an estate used as a summer residence by the Spanish captains general. The site is described in Hervey J. Allen's *Anthony Adverse*. There are superior botanical gardens elsewhere in the West Indies, but a day passed in these is well spent.

Finally, in Marianao, just outside Havana, is the Casino Nacional, a Monte Carlo of the West where the standard games of chance are played through the winter months. Its loveliest feature is the marble fountain by Aldo Gamba with the figures of eight nude nymphs dancing around the rim of the basin. The smaller summer casino in the grounds opens when the large building closes for the season.

CHAPTER **2.**

THE PARIS OF THE WEST INDIES

NJOYING Havana, after you have covered the important "sights," is a matter of temperament. Some persons
come for the night clubs, the bars, dancing to rumba music, gambling at the Casino, and such-like forms of amusement in a tropic
setting. Others are devotees of sports, from the typically Spanish
game of *jai alai* and the lowly cockfight common in all warm countries, to international horse and boat racing. Still others want the
outdoors as exemplified by bathing beaches and automobile trips
in quest of the exotic. Quite a number, women for the most part, are
interested chiefly in shopping. And there are many who, like myself,
seek a little of all these things, but if asked to analyze their basic enthusiasm would reply that it was for getting beneath the surface,
perceiving the beauty and the rhythm that is the secret of Havana's
charm.

Frankly, I shall pay a lot of attention to the approaches that delighted me. This method will be followed in connection with all the
cities and lands portrayed. I do not think the reader would wish to
have it otherwise.

Havana is a great eating and drinking town, though in the latter
respect, among natives, the emphasis emphatically is not on hard
liquor. The cuisine is of Spanish origin, modified and in my opinion
improved by Creole inventions. French cooking also has a following,
and American dishes are served in hotels and restaurants that have
a tourist clientele. Cubans love sea food, and their favorite meat is
perhaps pork. The wonders they achieve with these stand-bys de-
serve to be celebrated by a Charles Lamb. They cook chicken, too,
in a dozen admirable ways. Their dependence on rice is almost Oriental, either as a component part of innumerable dishes or served

19

separately. The banana and its coarser variety, the plantain, are used in several forms as vegetables throughout the West Indies and notably in Cuba.

Here are a few delicacies, their merit gauged by the fact that they immediately come to mind: *Cangrejo Moro,* or Moro crab, a name that has nothing to do with Morro Castle, as some tourists imagine; Moro means Moorish. This huge crustacean with heavy claws has a singularly toothsome meat. *Langostino,* or fresh-water prawn, also a giant of its species, at its best cold with mayonnaise or other dressing. *Paella,* a rice dish with various sorts of sea food, diced pork, and spicy flavorings steamed together in a casserole. *Lechón asado,* or roast suckling pig, good in any country but superb as the Cubans cook it. *Patas a la andaluza,* or beeves' feet, baked or stewed, which Thomas Barbour calls "succulent beyond belief." *Embuchado de la Sierra,* an imported pressed meat made of the flesh of Spanish wild boar and eaten as an appetizer before the soup.

It may be assumed that none of the dining rooms in the smart hotels will disappoint. But certain restaurants with a tradition behind them are the eating places that should on no account be overlooked. La Zaragozana, on Monserrate, is famous for its sea food. Tourists patronize it because it is close to the center of their beat, and because it publicizes itself judiciously without yielding to the temptation of lowering standards and going all-out for profits. On the other hand, El Palacio de Cristal, Consulado and San José, seems known only to the most discriminating Americans. Here is a restaurant from vanished Lucullan days, large yet unassuming in appearance, tranquil, offering perfect service, and with a fastidious pride in its cuisine. Every one of its specialties is worth the waiting for—and worth the price, which is seldom modest. La Cosmopolita, on the Parque Central; La Floridita, Obispo and Monserrate; and El Patio, Prado at Genios, are all of a high order.

The Café de Paris, in a former mansion on the cathedral square, offers French cooking, as its name implies. It has the reputation of being the leading restaurant in the city, but people who ought to know say that it is no longer as good as it was. Nevertheless, French cooking being by and large the best on earth, it is impossible to go wrong in this fine old place. The selection of wines is of the first order. Ambos Mundos, at the lower end of Obispo, features all the sound Cuban dishes as well as some of German origin. The Miami,

Prado and Neptuno, has an American tinge, while enjoying the reputation for a good native cuisine. Its prominent corner site is only two or three blocks from either the Sevilla-Biltmore or Plaza, and few tourists fail to try it.

The classic Cuban cocktails and punches are made with rum. Strictly speaking, the familiar Bacardi product is a sugar-cane brandy, for the method used in distilling it is different from the one followed in making the true rums of Jamaica and other West Indian countries. But we'll not cavil at an accepted name. The most popular cocktail is the daiquiri, invented shortly after the Spanish-American War and named for the seacoast village near Santiago where United States troops first landed. Few recipes are as simple: pale Bacardi rum, lime juice, sugar, and crushed ice, thoroughly shaken. La Floridita and the Ciro bar connected with the Plaza Hotel are famous for their daiquiris. But I find it hard to explain why their mixers and many local rivals concoct so seductive and stimulating, so perfect a drink, whereas a cocktail of the same ingredients in even the best American bars is markedly inferior. Call it the Havana touch in judging the proportions and timing the electric shaker, for there seems to be no other answer.

Just as the daiquiri may be called the opposite number of the Martini, though not so dry, the Cuban *presidente* cocktail bears a vague resemblance to the Manhattan. Popular with tourists and adopted by some natives is the Cuba libre, a mixture of rum and Coca-Cola with a squeeze of lemon peel; for my part, I do not endorse it. A *mojito* is made with Bacardi rum, aerated water, powdered sugar, and a sprig of mint. Punches, hot or cold, call for a darker rum.

The Havanese have a taste for wine, but as it is not manufactured on the island and the customs duties are high, it is drunk regularly only by a few. Three or four types of excellent beer are brewed, and the people have become fond of this northern beverage. However, the country's favorite drinks—using the word in its literal and not its alcoholic sense—are the *refrescos* made from tropical fruit. It is commendable to be lyrical about these. There are some two dozen varieties, beginning with the cosmopolitan orange, lemon, grapefruit, and pineapple juices. The Cubans prepare the pineapple in two ways, from fresh fruit crushed right under your eyes; they strain the pulp, in which case it is called *piña colada;* or they serve it unstrained and topped with shaved ice, as *piña sin colar*. The second style is the more novel and captivating to the palate.

Foremost in popularity among the refrescos never seen in the United States are the tamarind and the *guanábana,* or soursop. The former is subacid and uniquely thirst-quenching. The latter has a virtually indescribable flavor, something like that of a peach kernel mingled with that of a very ripe banana. Whipped with milk, sugar, and ice, it attains an individuality so remarkable that it has been given a special name; it is a *champola*.

The common watermelon is diced, placed in the electric mixer with ice, and whirled until it comes out a frosted marvel, the pulp disintegrated. The same method is employed with the musk melon, papaya,* *níspero,* and other fruit with soft, watery pulp. Milk is added to the sweetsop, custard apple, almond, coconut, and several kinds of bananas.

To crown all, there are fruit and nut novelties, sold only in rare places, and exotic even to the Cubans: an *horchata de chufa,* for instance, an orgeat prepared of the white sap compressed from the tubers of a species of sedge; the grape verjuice of Seville, a semi-transparent, greenish drink made from the juice of unripe grapes and retaining a light and scented acidity. Crystals of fruit sugar are suspended in this verjuice, and they give the illusion of fermenting the moment they are swallowed.

Of night clubs and cabarets there are no end. At the head of the list for smartness and good entertainment when I last visited Havana was La Tropicana, which occupies a former private estate on the Avenida Truffin, out Vedado way. Its garden is magnificent and well tended. Vogues have a way of changing from season to season, but it is probable that La Tropicana will have a long, long run. The Sans Souci, in the grounds of the Country Club beyond the city limits, is older and solidly established in public favor, native as well as foreign. It operates wholly out-of-doors, and the luxury of its appointments among the subtly lighted shrubbery gives an air of the marvelous at night. Another first-class cabaret is the Montmartre, on Twenty-third Street, Vedado.

* It is improper to use the name papaya in Cuba, because the word has a vulgar connotation in the local idiom. One must say *fruta bomba*. This does not hold good anywhere else.

In the heart of town the Club Zombie, on Zulueta near the Parque Central, is open-air and amusing. The name probably causes strangers to expect it to be more bizarre than it really is, but they love what they get. The Panchín, the Tres Hermanos and the Pennsylvania, all near the beach at Marianao, are rated as second-line cabarets appealing to cruder audiences. Make no mistake about it, the entertainment value at the three last-mentioned places is high, if somewhat robustious.*

An outstanding virtue of nearly all Havana night spots is the fact that, although they offer a certain number of imported acts, they rely mostly upon native art. As I see it, that is what the visitor prefers, whether his artistic judgment is discriminating or otherwise. He wants on his return home to talk about the unique dancing he has seen and to hum strange, catchy tunes. It is a grave error to offer him the amusement fare to which he is accustomed and which he would applaud heartily on Broadway or at Miami Beach.

The rumba (spelled rhumba in Americanese, God knows why) is strictly an exhibition dance, a pantomime of sex desire and mating, which originated among plantation Negroes in slavery times. The man pursues and the woman gradually yields to persuasion. He struts like a barnyard cock when it is clear that his point has been gained, and she flees from the stage on a note of bawdy comedy. The tempo throughout is very rapid. That is what you see in a Havana cabaret when the true rumba is given. The Cubans consider that the ideal team is a sturdy, plump mulatto woman and a small, coal-black man. Rumba music has been adapted to social dancing by borrowing from the *son,* a fast-moving but dignified local ballroom measure.

Another curious exhibition number is *el papalote* (the kite). The girl is supposed to represent a kite, attached by an invisible cord to her partner. A nice effect is obtained on a large floor. The man makes gestures with his hands that imitate the playing out of a kite, and the girl retreats farther and farther from him. But when he starts to pull inward she must obey. At the finale they are breast to breast,

---

* Sloppy Joe's, on Zulueta, is the Havana bar best known to the general run of tourists, and so must be mentioned. It became a rendezvous in the prohibition era by catering to visitors who spoke no Spanish. But it was then, and still is, utterly commonplace.

the girl thrusting furiously against him in a vain effort to get closer.
A pattern of difficult steps is maintained throughout.

Very different is the purely social *danzón*, which in the days before
the revolution against Spain was said to furnish the only opportunity that well-bred young persons had for flirtation at a ball. It is
done to slow music, which quickens at intervals. Then, surprisingly,
the couples stop dead, to converse in whispers for perhaps one minute before a new quirk of the orchestra starts them going again.
Chaperons might see that the proprieties were being observed during
these interludes, but they could not hear what was said. Secret meet-
ings were arranged and elopements planned in the pauses of the
danzón. At the night clubs I have mentioned, at dances in the hotels
and at beach resorts, both son and danzón are frequently played.
So is the tango, which long since spread out from Argentina to become a dance that all Latin Americans love. Travelers from the
United States are charmed by these measures and pick them up easily.

Gambling is a mercurial subject, a star attraction, but one about
which one cannot be sure from season to season. Cuba permitted it
with almost no restrictions for many years, and collected a rich revenue in taxes for the indulgence. Clubs of every sort had their roulette wheels and other paraphernalia of Lady Luck. The government, however, felt that it could make more by leasing the gambling
concession to a syndicate, and the Casino Nacional was the result.
Play elsewhere was limited, so as to draw the big money into the
Casino. This did not work too well, for Cubans are inveterate game-
sters, and the law was widely evaded. The present administration
went a step further. It tried to suppress the practice as an evil, a visionary attempt in any Latin country. Now the Casino is being allowed to run again—as the only legal gambling house.

Nine games of chance were featured when I was last there. They
were roulette, baccarat, chemin-de-fer, electric poker, hazard, book-
maker, birdcage, wheel-of-chance, and craps. Roulette and craps are
too well known to need description, and some of the lesser games
are fads of the moment. Baccarat is open to any number of players,
usually eighteen seated against a banker for the house. The object
is to hold cards totaling nearer to nine than those of the banker.
Chemin-de-fer is a variation of baccarat, in which a bidder takes the

bank, playing against all the others until he loses, or until he cares to relinquish it.

Electric poker is simply a machine that drops cards into a display rack when buttons are pushed. You push five buttons and you get a poker hand. One pair entitles to another shot. The pay-off is on two pairs or better, at various odds. The game has a big following, though it has been shown that the edge in favor of the house is 10 per cent.

Every casino has its favorite story of luck. The Havana tale is unparalleled. I do not vouch for it, but I know that one hears it often and that in some circles it is taken for gospel. A quiet little American woman appeared one evening in the season of 1928–29, they say, hung around a roulette wheel for a while, and at last timidly took a dollar bill from her purse and placed it on a full number. The odds were thirty-five to one. She won, which was nothing extraordinary. But the woman let her winnings ride along with her original dollar, and she won again: $1,260. This was enough to attract a group of gamblers who urged her to pyramid, on the grounds that luck was clearly on her side that day. She trimmed nervously, dividing the amount and staking $630 on a third full number. When she cleaned up once more there was wild excitement. She cashed in her chips, hurried from the Casino with a total of $22,680, and never came back.

That is only the first and least astonishing part of the story. A few months later, another American woman entered the Casino, walked right up to the same roulette wheel, and successfully backed three numbers, one after the other. No one remembers whether these were the original bettor's numbers, but presumably they were. The new winner left as precipitately and finally as the first had done.

The Casino authorities conducted an inquiry to learn whether the two women were identical, and found that they were not. They were both schoolteachers, however, and came from the same state, though not from the same town. Their names were not made public. It is to be inferred that they knew each other, and that upon learning of the first teacher's luck the second had come to Havana for the sole purpose of trying to repeat the coup.

It is good business for a gambling establishment to encourage the spreading of such stories. So believe this one or not, as you choose.

The fact remains that the Casino is a highly agreeable place in which to dally with fortune, whether in the winter or the summer building. The ballroom, by the way, is excellent and one may be sure of seeing a good floor show there. Some of my pleasantest memories of *criolla* dancing and singing are associated with the Summer Casino. During the big season the management leans upon New York talent, particularly girls; it has its large Cuban clientele to consider.

The national lottery is but another form of gambling, and it is undoubtedly the most popular of all. Full tickets sell at $20 and up, but fractions can be bought for as little as twenty-five cents. The grand prize varies. Sometimes it is as low as $30,000, with a relatively large number of lesser prizes. Sometimes it is $100,000, and at the grand Christmas drawing it is $300,000. It has been calculated that there are 1,429 chances to win some kind of prize as against each 25,000 tickets issued. There is no other game in which the bank (in this case, the state) is certain of so high a percentage of the money risked. Yet its fascination for mankind, rich and poor, is unfailing. Hawkers of tickets swarm the streets of Havana. Little booths devoted to the traffic are everywhere. Yet there is also a lottery market, a long arcade on Galiano, where no other commodity is sold. Drawings are held on Wednesdays, when children from the city's oldest orphanage pick the winning numbers by a fraudproof method.

Baseball has in recent years become popular with Cubans. Despite the claims made for it, I doubt if it rouses as much enthusiasm among the spectators as does jai alai, the Basque sport also known as *pelota*. This incredibly vigorous game is played by dashing a hard rubber ball against the smooth cement walls of a court called a *fronton*, catching it on the rebound in the *cesta*, a long scooplike mitten bound over the hand, and sending it back with ever increasing speed until the human mechanism falters and the ball is missed. I am not sufficiently familiar with the rules to tell how the points are made. There are opposing teams of two and they battle with a frenzy that has earned for jai alai the reputation of being the fastest game on earth. The beauty of the gymnastic postures required of the players' bodies is not the least of its attractions. A favorite knows this and is as jealous of his grace as he is of his accuracy. Should he fumble badly, he is quite likely to bury his face in his arms for an instant or burst into tears; no Latin would scoff at this display of emotion, which is admired, rather, as proof of sincerity and artistic temperament.

Top-flight performers earn up to $2,000 a month. A few years ago a star of stars, Emilio Equiluz, made $7,000. There are two great frontons, one on Concordia and Lucena and the other on Padre Varela. Americans are ready converts to jai alai. The speed fascinates them, even if they are unable to grasp the technique at first. The sport has been successfully introduced in Miami. Americans also like the open betting that goes on both at jai alai and baseball games. An escape from the dreary morals of Podunk and Sauk Center is largely what they are seeking. When you recall how blue-nose even the large cities of the United States are getting to be, it is not surprising that Havana as a vacation resort grows more tempting each year.

Every form of amusement within reason is allowed and sensibly regulated in Havana, if it is clear that the people want it. There was for many years a nationalistic feeling against the bullfight as a Spanish institution. But in 1947 bullfighting was legalized, with the rules modified to forbid the killing of the bull. Cockfighting, on the other hand, is the sport of the Cuban masses, and you can see all the mains you want in the Jesús del Monte quarter, or suburban Guanabacoa and Marianao. Should you insist upon patronizing harlots and bawdy shows, you can find them. It is entirely a matter of taste.

From the standpoint of the variety of luxury articles and novelties to be found, Havana is a shoppers' paradise. Except for rums and a few other native items, prices are not a great deal lower than at home. But most tourists like to take back at least the $100 worth of purchases that the United States admits duty free, and to many half the fun of travel lies in bargain-hunting and picking up souvenirs. The following favorites merit the trouble and can be bought advantageously:

Perfumes and toilet waters. The French brands head the list; those manufacturers that do their bottling locally are able to sell more cheaply. The Spanish makes come next. There are also some good Cuban products, and at comparatively low prices.

Alligator leather. The wide selection of shoes, bags, etc., are fabricated from skins taken in the marshlands and river mouths of Cuba. The leather is both handsome and durable. It is fairly expensive.

Fans. Whether made in Havana or imported from Spain, these are better than any you can buy for the money in the United States. Cuban women really use fans and have good taste in them. The dealers meet that demand, and the wise tourist benefits.

Tiles. The products of an old Cuban industry. They are generally small and square, in scores of beautiful designs, and are employed in paving corridors, floors, and patios; sometimes as a facing for walls. I have known Americans who collected them ardently and hung a few of the most striking in lieu of pictures.

Mahogany. Cigarette and other boxes, candy and nut platters, bookends, etc., are made from this king of woods. All novelty shops offer a selection. Even in the public markets there are stalls that sell mahogany items.

Cigars. Irrefutably, Havana cigars are the best on earth. You can see them being made by hand in several factories in the city and get them on the spot, fresh, by the box. The managements welcome visitors. The superior brands, however, may safely be bought anywhere in town, for care is taken to maintain standards. The U. S. Customs limits the number of cigars that may be brought in under the total exemption to one hundred.

Rum. It can be had at close to one third the price charged in the United States, and grade by grade the quality is consistently better. So nearly everyone carries back the full quota allowed duty free: one gallon. In addition to rum, some of the native cordials are worth importing, and some French liqueurs can be bought cheaply.

The Havana I love and that I was seeing for the fifth time on this trip should be explored during the daytime largely on foot, with recourse to cabs and busses for making long jumps between centers of interest. No single day would be so crowded as the one I shall now imagine. Take it that I am telescoping half a dozen of my own days in order to give a rounded picture and recapture an atmosphere.

Let us suppose that you are staying at one of the less pretentious hotels on or near the Parque Central. You get up at seven-thirty and start out in search of breakfast. The streets are empty and clean-looking. It is too early for the office-bound crowd to begin to appear. The sunlight falls softly, and the air has the coolness of morning in the tropics, which penetrates from dew-drenched woods even to the heart of a city. You fear that it will not be easy to get breakfast, unless you are willing to eat the sparing meal that Cubans think proper at that hour. The big restaurants are closed. But people are sitting in barrooms and candy shops, nibbling rolls and drinking *café con leche* (coffee made with a small amount of strong extract in a cupful of hot milk). On the side streets are obscure Chinese restaurants you had not noticed before. They have signs in the windows announcing that they serve any kind of repast and at any hour. Trust the celestial caterers not to miss a bet. You conclude to try one of them and have a piece of iced papaya and an egg along with your rolls and coffee.

Outdoors again, you find the traffic becoming brisk. But it is still cool, and you stroll down the *paseo* of the lower Prado on mottled, reddish marble and under the thick canopy of the laurels. The benches at intervals are also of marble, with high curving backs and broad armrests. The stone is gleaming, newly swept, and watered with hoses for the day. This is the most gorgeous promenade in the city, and at the same time the favored of every class. Businessmen and beggars loiter there, servants with children, tired old women of mystery and a few belated girls at whose occupation it is easy to guess, and bohemian youths who might be artists or poets. There is a much greater assortment of types than would be seen on, say, Fifth Avenue or a Miami parkway. The aura is European, in spite of the large proportion of Negroid faces. It is too unconventional to evoke Madrid, too metropolitan for Seville. A Parisian boulevard: that is what it resembles in a strange, haunting way.

You reach the water front and have a superb view of the Morro directly opposite. To the left sweeps the Malecón, and to the right opens the square behind La Punta, the landscaped approach to the presidential palace and the beginnings of the old town. Both are alluring walks, but you circle behind the palace and go into the Colón market, which is something to see and especially in the morning. It is a huge, ancient, and dilapidated building occupying a square block. The glass dome at the center has gaps in it, and the plaster crumbles on the walls and winding stairs leading to the rooms of the caretakers. For reasons of safety—of hygiene, too, in all probability—it should be demolished and rebuilt, as has been ordered more than once. When this occurs a colorful link with the past will have been lost, for the Colón succeeds in being thoroughly mid-nineteenth century.

All things conceivable in a market, as well as many surprises, await the saunterer along those endless aisles. Packed stalls of fruits and vegetables, of course, more than it would seem possible to sell, considering the competition outside. Meat and fish counters at which it would be better for the stomach's sake not to look too closely. Live poultry, dairy, grocery, candy, flower, basket, hardware, woodwork, and leather-goods shops. Yes, and in addition to these a shop for religious objects, a retail liquor shop, booths for secondhand articles of every description, tiny bars, coffee stalls, restaurants for the market people, and even a billiard parlor. The medley of odors is agreeable, except in the vicinity of the meat and fish. Vivid nosegays adorn the counters. The place is loud with the singing of canaries and other caged birds, some for sale and some not. Cats arrest the attention, they are so numerous, the adults dozing on the counters among the goods, the kittens racing about or perhaps curled in baskets and bowls. A first thought that Cubans are great lovers of cats is revised. In so ramshackle a building, naturally the tenants are obliged to have some protection against rats.

In the market you have eaten fruit fresh from the ice: the cheeks of a golden, kidney-shaped mango, or a slice of pineapple. The tang has worn off, and thirst follows under the now blazing sun. It is too early in the day for alcoholic drinks. You begin on a long series of *refrescos*, the pure juices of nature that really refresh: *guanábana, níspero, piña, almendra* (almond); the very names are luscious in Spanish.

You roam in leisurely fashion along the fronts of buildings protected from the heat by either arcades or awnings. It is diverting to do window shopping among the narrow streets on both sides of the Prado. Noting the oddities on signboards is itself amusing. The Cubans, like other Latin Americans, run to the flowery and the lofty in their names for places of business. La Filosofía (Philosophy) is a general clothing and linen store, as is El Pensamiento (Thought). La Poesia Moderna (Modern Poetry) is a stationery and book store with little emphasis on poetry, and La Purísima Concepción (The Immaculate Conception) a grocery and bakery. Every tourist gets to know El Encanto (Enchantment), one of the principal department stores.

There will be time to visit a historic building or two before eating. Then, if you are prudent, you select a famous, high-priced place with its guarantee of elbow room, or else some little one away from the center of things. For the ordinary downtown Havana restaurant is terribly crowded at midday. After luncheon it will be well to go back to the hotel and take a siesta. The honoring of that old Spanish custom is plain common sense. The climate requires it.

When you re-emerge a long, varied afternoon is ahead of you, warm at first, but relieved occasionally by tropical showers that are over in a few minutes, and cooling as the hours lengthen and a landward breeze sets in from the Gulf. You ride out to the *playa,* or beach, in Marianao and spend a couple of hours, preferably at a private bathing club if you have a guest card, otherwise on the clean, orderly public beach. In summer the water is but a little lower than body temperature, and one swims languidly, rocked by the ebb and flow. It is more stimulating in winter. You have not come, however, only to bathe. Sky, sea, and sand, palms and gay costumes combine in an exquisite pattern, while few places are better for observing the beauty of the Cuban women. Ignacio Zuloaga, the Spanish master, so admired them on visiting Havana at the age of fifty-one that he said if he were younger he would move to the island and spend the rest of his life painting them, both whites and half bloods.

What should come after the playa? For contrast, you decide to go to the Colón Cemetery, on the route back, a short distance on the Havana side of the Almendares River. Modern memorials, the statues and tombs of the city, were not listed in the last chapter because they were being saved for a special tour such as this one. Most travel books in English say little about them, and that is a mistake. Cubans of the republican era have poured a singular passion into their monuments. Some are good, some merely grandiloquent or flamboyant, and some bizarre. The Colón Cemetery is a fine starting point. It has been called the most impressive of all cemeteries, outside those of Rome, and though it is a general burial ground, the large number of statesmen and heroes of the revolution who have been laid to rest here have given it a national character. Marble tombs, vaults, and towering memorials crowd one another in street after street of sepulchers. Here lie the generalissimo Máximo Gómez and many of his lieutenants, most of the presidents of the Republic, and nearly every other eminent Cuban of the past fifty years. Funerals have reached terrific proportions. When former President Menocal was buried in 1941, it was estimated that two hundred thousand persons followed the cortege to the cemetery, where five thousand mourners had already gathered, and still other thousands were forced to stand outside the gates.

The artistic merit of the mausoleums is not noteworthy, but some of the inscriptions are moving. Private vanity has led to some strange competing efforts. The monument to the firemen of Havana, for instance, is extravagant beyond words and is said to have cost $79,000; the angelic figure at its summit dominates the most historic section of the enclosure and thus strikes an absurd note. Graves are lavishly decked with floral tributes, and the open-air flower market a block from the main gate is a sight in itself.

On the shore below the hill crowned by the Hotel Nacional is the Maine Monument, commemorating the sinking of the battleship *Maine* in Havana harbor, the enigmatic outrage that led to the United States to declare war on Spain in 1898. It is elegant, restrained. Some critics have called it the best in the city, but it does not linger in the memory. Farther down, dominating two broad plazas, are first the Maceo and then the Máximo Gómez monuments. The old-fashioned yet always thrilling flourish of these is essentially Cuban. Both are immense, with equestrian statues above, a winged victory below, many supporting figures, and flights of steps leading to the monument proper. The Generalissimo was from the Dominican Republic, a fierce lover of liberty who offered his sword without price, and when they tried to make him the first president of Cuba he said: "No. Men of war, for war; and those of peace, for peace." Antonio Maceo was a Cuban mulatto, easily the genius among native-born generals. It can be no accident that while the Gómez statue faces the sea, that of Maceo has its back to it and stares into the heart of the land.

There is also a statue to Maceo's mother, but hers is not a glory solely reflected from him. The monument is entitled "The Mother of the Maceos." This black woman of the soil, born Mariana Grajales, had four sons by her first husband; when he died she married Marcos Maceo, to whom she bore seven sons. All these men, including the father and Mariana's sons by her first marriage, enlisted for the revolution and all died on the battlefield.

Behind the presidential palace stands an amazing statue. It is that of the fourth president, the venal Alfredo Zayas. He erected it to himself, having caused $36,000 to be appropriated for the park and monument, and he dedicated it just four days before he retired from office. The inscription on the base declares that it was raised "by a grateful people" to honor "the restorer of the liberties of his country." One marvels that it was not pulled down the following week. The Cubans take an ironic pleasure in it as a curio. They point it out to those whom they trust have a sense of humor. You turn from it with a shake of the head and wander up the Prado, where there are memorials to poets, into the Plaza de la Fraternidad to see the rather routine busts of Simón Bolívar and other Latin-American patriots, then back to the Parque Central to conclude your survey with the Martí Monument.

José Julian Martí, the Apostle, animator of the final and successful revolt against Spain, poet, journalist, and orator, who fell in the first skirmish of the war, is honored with a statue or bust in every town of importance. Havana has several, but this is the outstanding one. Martí is always represented as an austere man. His countenance with the heavy mustache broods, and this is true to life. Of the many photographs of him that exist, none wears a smile. The present portrayal of him is not remarkable, but the figures in high relief around the base are far more realistic than is usual on a monument. Here we see the Cuban peasants of the 1890's springing to arms; men of all ages, women and even children bearing archaic or makeshift weapons, a young lad in particular on whose face with parted lips there is both fear and pride as he lurches toward the perilous future.

The afternoon is waning. Soon the tropical twilight will darken swiftly like an eclipse. It is the cocktail hour, and you drop in at Ciro's or some other bar for a couple of daiquiris. The lure of the outdoors reasserts itself and you move to one of the sidewalk cafés mentioned in the previous chapter, where again you muse how like Paris this city can be. Mountainous clouds blaze above the Capitolio, the colors changing every minute or so as sunset marches to its finale, and suddenly it is night. Much pleasure seeking is in store for you before you go to bed; at the theater, in cabarets, maybe at the Casino, but certainly you will not make those rounds afoot. You return to the marble-paved Prado for a last look before dinner. It is densely packed now, the benches full, while countercurrents of eager, chattering people jostle one another in a good-humored way. What are the preoccupations of the crowd? Listening closely, you realize that over and above the human interests of everyday the master theme is politics.

Barry University Library

[Miami, FL 33161

CHAPTER 3

SOME PAGES OF MODERN HISTORY

ONRADO W. MASSAGUER is Cuba's cleverest cartoonist and a distinguished editor. He writes a column in one of the important daily newspapers. He is an authority on Martí, of whose memory he has made a cult. His private collection of books, prints, plaques, medals, photographs, and other material relating to Cuban history in the broadest sense of the term has few rivals. This busy and versatile man finds time to take part in virtually every aspect of the social life of Havana, and he does it in the spirit of the *bon vivant*. He attended Columbia University, speaks English fluently, and has many devoted American friends both in New York and his home city. Visitors from the States who have had letters of introduction to him have been fortunate indeed, for under his hospitable guidance they saw Havana as they would never have been able to see it without him.

I have known Massaguer for years. The Caribbean scene has been a lifelong study of my own. But I gladly admit that such grasp of recent Cuban trends as I may claim owes much to the clarifying talks I have had with Massaguer. Except where I cite him directly, he is not to be held responsible for the opinions set forth in this chapter. He plans soon to write his autobiography, by the way, when he will doubtless give a rounded view of events, public and secret, in which he has played a considerable role. No politician himself, he has dealt with most of the politicians of his time—and some revolutionists—at close quarters.

Ever since Cuba made her first move toward independence nearly a century ago, her relationship with the United States has been close. The average American knows this, but is a bit cloudy as to how it came about. A few pages of history are necessary to an understanding of why this country can never be indifferent to what happens in Cuba, why the latter's prosperity depends upon the good will of her neighbor, and why Americans and Cubans do not regard themselves as full aliens while visiting under each other's flags.

The initial serious revolt was led by Narciso López, a Venezuelan by birth, who operated from New York and New Orleans between 1848 and 1851. López did not believe that a Cuban republic could maintain itself. His plan, if the Spaniards were driven out, was to imitate Texas and apply for the admission of the island as a state of the Union. He made two landings in Cuba, was defeated both times, and was captured and executed along with fifty-two American volunteers who had served under him. The affair unleashed forces that Spain was not able to suppress. As early as 1848, President Polk's administration made a formal offer to purchase the island, and was told by Madrid that sooner than let any other power have Cuba, Spaniards "would rather see it sunk in the ocean." In 1854, after the death of López, three American ministers to European courts, including James Buchanan, a former Secretary of State of the United States, minister in London, and Pierre Soulé, minister in Madrid, took the amazing step of meeting at Ostend, Belgium, and preparing a document in which they urged their government to obtain Cuba by hook or by crook. This is known as the Ostend Manifesto.

"Immediate acquisition," it said, was of "paramount importance" to the United States. A new offer of purchase, not exceeding $120,000,-000, should be made. And then: "After we shall have offered Spain a price for Cuba far beyond its present value, and this shall have been refused . . . by every law, human and divine, we shall be justified in wresting it from Spain if we possess the power."

This ruthless policy was rejected by Washington. Had it not been, the friendship of the Cuban people would have been lost; for much as they hated the Spaniards and longed to be free, they balked at a shotgun marriage to follow. That was why they had not warmed to the López expeditions. Native leaders now arose and organized a purely Cuban revolution. The rich planter Carlos Manuel de Céspedes launched the Ten Years' War at Yara, Santiago province, in 1868. As a preliminary act he freed his own slaves, and the government he headed proclaimed general emancipation. Five years later he was killed in an ambush. Most of Cuba's lustrous military names made their first appearance in this struggle: Máximo Gómez, the Maceos, Calixto García, José Miguel Gómez, Agramonte, Menocal (the elder), Rabi the aboriginal Indian. It was a fiendish war, on the initiative of the Spaniards, who showed no mercy and forced the Cubans to retaliate.

American sympathy ran strongly for the patriots. In 1873 the *Virginius* incident almost caused intervention. Captain Joseph Fry, a former Confederate, was engaged in running guns through the blockade when his ship was seized between Jamaica and Santiago de Cuba, where a drumhead trial was held. Fry and more than fifty others, including many Americans, were shot by the Spaniards. Reconstruction still prevailed in Dixie, and President Grant appears to have regarded Fry as a sort of holdout troublemaker. He did nothing, despite the thousands of protests sent to him.

The Cubans were compelled to accept the Pact of Zanjón that ended the revolution in 1878. It proved no more than a truce. Guerrilla fighting was resumed for a while, to be succeeded by the unwearying, able, inspired work of Martí in preparing a new revolt that must not fail. He operated from various foreign countries, chiefly the United States. Though there were federal laws that if strictly applied would have strangled his effort, public opinion was with him and he was not disastrously hampered. He conducted a junta in New York and raised funds for *Cuba Libre*. He organized sixty-one clubs at Key West and fifteen at Tampa among the Cuban cigar workers and political exiles in southern Florida. Little by little, arms were smuggled through to waiting hands.

Even under the Spaniards, Cuba depended on the United States as her most important customer. In the 1880's she sold 75 per cent of her exports to the Yankees, yet could obtain needed American goods only at ruinous prices because of the customs duties imposed by her overlord. After long agitation by Cuban merchants and planters, Spain agreed to a broad reciprocity treaty with the United States in 1891, and trade boomed. But three years later Madrid arbitrarily canceled the treaty. Anti-Spanish feeling spread to the very conservatives of Havana. This is regarded by some authorities as the reason why the revolution occurred when it did. Martí was for unleashing it then and there, in 1894. But three vessels he had equipped were seized by the suddenly squeamish United States government and there had to be a brief postponement. It began officially at Baire, near Santiago, on February 24, 1895.

I reviewed the story of those days with Massaguer one evening in the book-lined study of his Vedado apartment. He had been too young to fight in the revolution, but his boyhood memories were tied up with it. A sense of contact with glorious and tragic events was created when he brought out his Martí scrapbooks and showed me pictures and documents. The official version of Martí's funeral, for instance; a drawing that showed the body conventionally posed on a bier, with a Spanish general beside it proclaiming that though this man had been a misguided rebel, he had been honorable and had died for his convictions. Then, next to the fanciful picture, a photograph of the corpse as it actually was, torn by bullets and in an advanced state of decomposition, with of course no Spanish general waving his arm above it.

This was what had happened: Martí had joined Máximo Gómez in the Dominican Republic, and they left for Cuba in the same small boat, landing near Cape Maisi. In May, after he had rallied a small army, the old generalissimo felt his way westward. Martí had been given the rank of major general, but the other leaders had unanimously urged him to regard himself as the political chieftain who must return to New York as soon as he had seen the campaign well under way. On the nineteenth a strong Spanish force was sighted at Dos Rios. Gómez felt he must attack. He warned Martí to fall back, "for this is not your post." The Apostle, who was riding a white horse, had often said he would never shrink from dangers he had asked the whole Cuban people to face. He ignored Gómez's suggestion, charged with the rest, and was shot dead. His body fell into the hands of the Spaniards, who took it to Santiago as a trophy, but gave it respectful burial.

The loss of Martí stirred the country to its depths, as possibly nothing else could have done. Men rushed to enlist. This revolution swiftly became more effective than the Ten Years' War had been, for in that war the fighting had been confined to the eastern half of the island. Gómez and his lieutenants now raided all over Cuba and fought at least one engagement on the outskirts of Havana. They usually won in the field. Spain's advantage lay in superiority of numbers, and under the new captain general, Valeriano Weyler, the

"Butcher," she practiced even worse atrocities than had disgraced her in the previous conflict. Many American soldiers of fortune joined the Cubans, including Frederick Funston, later a United States general and the captor of Aguinaldo in the Philippines. Winston Churchill, as a youthful war correspondent, rode briefly with a Spanish column.

Whether the Cubans could have defeated the Spaniards unaided is an open question. The killing of Maceo was a severe blow. There was always a shortage of ammunition. On the other hand, the enemy suffered crippling losses from yellow fever, and this along with the immense cost in money appalled the Madrid government. World opinion was against Spain because of the barbarities of Weyler, which were blazoned in every press but her own. She might have let Cuba go. Indeed, she made a halfway autonomy offer, which Gómez scornfully rejected, and seemed on the point of yielding further. But the argument became academic with the blowing up of the *Maine*. I shall not rehearse the familiar details of the Spanish-American War. The Cubans felt slighted in being given so small a share in the capture of Santiago, and took alarm when the Republic was not immediately recognized by Washington. They ended by accepting a period of tutelage under General Leonard Wood as governor and admitted that wonders were accomplished under him in the improvement of sanitation, particularly in the vital matter of the conquest of yellow fever.

However, they did not like the treaty under which the country was turned over to a Cuban administration on May 20, 1902. The United States got the naval base at Guantánamo outright and retained an ambiguous stake in the Isle of Pines. Tacked on to the treaty was the Platt Amendment, which limited the foreign relations and the public debt of Cuba, and provided that the United States might "intervene for the preservation of Cuban independence, the maintenance of a government adequate for the protection of life, property, and individual liberty," etc. The amendment was found humiliating. As we shall see, it was not mere verbiage. Cuba's political development was modified by it, and it was to remain in effect for longer than thirty years.

American industrialists who flocked to the island while Wood was in control have been called rapacious, but at that juncture outside capital was urgently needed, and they accomplished immediate good by building railroads, streetcar lines, and electric plants. Cuban sugar was the prize of prizes. The Americans saw that the crop could be increased by scientific methods until the island was truly the sugar bowl of the Western world. They bought all the plantations they could lay hands on, but they fell short of obtaining a monopoly. Sugar was too deeply rooted in the native economy to allow of that. Many old families recouped their war losses and got rich because of the central mills the newcomers erected to serve whole districts. Cuba was granted uniquely low tariff rates, and in a dozen ways her commercial system interlocked with that of the United States. Havana's stronger financial houses to this day are branches of New York banks.

Cuban patriots protested that their country had simply changed its colonial status to one that was semicolonial. This struck close to the truth; Cuba was, in fact, a protectorate. But the agreement was implicit that she would not always remain so, and in the meantime she prospered. The two peoples liked each other better than was the case in any other Latin-American country, and that counted for a great deal.

A summary of the administrations under the Republic will serve to show the drift of events, the pageant of men, the crystallizing of ideals that have at last produced a strong and progressive state. The first president was Tomás Estrada Palma, who had been one of the successors of Céspedes at the head of the shadow government during the Ten Years' War, had earned a frugal living teaching school at Central Valley, New York, and then had headed the junta in New York City founded by Martí. Don Tomás was a profoundly honest old man, and it has been said that he was a victim of his own excess of goodness. He proved to be naïve politically. After heading a sober, colorless regime for four years and accumulating a reserve in the treasury, he yielded to the persuasions of his followers and sought another term. He had been brought to believe that he was the only person who could prevent the looting of the public funds by eager grafters. But he was blind to the methods of those same followers, determined to hang on to their jobs through him, who conducted under his nose a thoroughly corrupt election.

Palma was inaugurated for the second time. His defeated opponent, the reckless, ebullient General José Miguel Gómez, took the field and blood ran again in Cuba. Disillusioned, the President resigned after a few weeks, and the United States stepped in under the terms of the Platt Amendment. Both the Cuban factions wanted this as a face-saving way of ending the civil strife and forcing a new vote, but they did not dream how long the intervention was to last.

William Howard Taft, then United States Secretary of War, administered the island for two weeks and was succeeded by Charles E. Magoon. The latter had been appointed governor by President Theodore Roosevelt, and governor he remained for two years and three months, increasingly disliked by the Cubans, who called him a plunderer and feared that his presence meant they had lost their independence. The truth was that, in his plodding, unimaginative way, Magoon was personally as honest as Palma. He built many roads and bridges. That rascals in his entourage hoodwinked him to their profit is highly probable.

When Washington felt that the time had come it ordered Magoon to hold elections. José Miguel Gómez won easily, and the government was turned over to him in 1909. He made a popular president because of his dramatic, free-and-easy manner, which was considered *simpático* and very Cuban, and his zestful canceling of ordinances that meddled with public morals. There can be no doubt that he was a grafter. They called him El Tiburón, or the shark, to denote his appetite for cash, but the sobriquet was used with a sort of affectionate tolerance. His party, however, denied him a renomination, and in revenge he fought it, helping to bring about the election of his younger comrade at arms General Mario García Menocal.

No finer gentleman and distinguished leader than Menocal ever attained the presidency. He was a cosmopolitan, having been educated in the United States as an engineer and employed for years on the abortive project to dig a canal across Nicaragua. He enlisted as a private when the last Cuban revolution broke out, but rose quickly to the rank of major general. His conduct of operations at Victoria de las Tunas was held to be the soundest in any pitched battle of the war. After the peace he managed the Chaparra sugar plantation and made it the largest of its kind in the world. He was very friendly to Americans, and the influential among them believed in him, from Woodrow Wilson to the latest Wall Street capitalist with an ax to grind. He had financial worries at first, owing in part to World War I, which cut off an important market for Cuban tobacco. When the war ended the situation was reversed. Sugar reached unheard-of prices and the island enjoyed a period of wealth run wild that is known as the "Dance of the Millions."

Menocal cannot be convicted of robbing the state. He appeared to take little interest in money for its own sake. But he allowed his supporters a good deal of license, and he had a failing that he indulged to a fantastic degree. He was a nepotist par excellence. Members of his family to the most distant connections were given posts, important or unimportant, and were protected if they misbehaved. There never was so large and ambitious a Cuban family, as the taxpayers learned to their cost. My friend Massaguer married a Menocal. I happen to know that he did not ask the General for a single favor. Which is one of the reasons why Massaguer can be taken seriously as a guide through the tangle of his country's politics.

Where his predecessors had failed in winning and holding a second term, Menocal succeeded, but not without irregularities at the polls and an armed revolt. He crushed his enemies by a display of military talent, and thus averted another American intervention. His last four years in office were less creditable than his first, yet he was able to retire as a national hero whose glory was but little diminished, and his courageous stand in a later crisis fully restored him to favor.

The fourth president was Alfredo Zayas, who had been striving to reach the palace since the first days of the Republic. He was called El Chino on account of his supposed Chinese patience, and presently earned the more defamatory nickname of "the peseta stealer," the idea being that while José Miguel Gómez and others had lined their pockets with pesos (dollars), he did not let even the small change elude him. He was accused of manipulating the national lottery to his advantage. In his four years, nevertheless, he accomplished a few good works, and he neither sought to overrule the Congress nor interfered with private liberties. His ludicrous egotism in raising a monument to himself has been mentioned.

There now ensued a regime that had the sad distinction of being one of the two or three most cruel despotisms in the history of Latin America. The Cuban system of partisanship and frenzied intrigue is not to be blamed for it. The fault lay with a monster whom it would have been hard to appraise correctly before he came to power, and who then rallied the support of parasites and paid thugs. A misfortune of that sort can happen to any land. General Gerardo Machado had fought bravely in the revolution against Spain, had been one of the founders of the Liberal party, had held minor offices acceptably, and had standing as a businessman in the city of Santa Clara. He had been out of politics for seven years when elected to the presidency in 1924.

For most of his first term he gave Cuba a fair administration, though he made excessive grants to foreign capitalists and profited by them. Then the man changed so violently for the worse that if he had lived in an age of mysticism it would have been believed that he was possessed by a devil. His financial dishonesty became gigantic. Those were the days of millions of dollars stolen in connection with the Capitolio and the new central highway from end to end of the island. Along with Machado's greed went megalomania, intolerance of opposition, and brutality carried to lengths that were scarcely human.

He jammed through a change in the constitution to extend his term for six years. The inevitable plots against him were met by loosing his notorious Porra, or secret police, against the people. There was an orgy of sadism that included the emasculation of youths and the ripping of women's breasts with gloves tipped with steel claws, as hundreds were put to the torture by Machado's orders. Massacres were a commonplace, notably in the Cabaña fortress, where Spaniards had once slain Cuban patriots, but where none could have anticipated that a president would ever murder his countrymen. It was widely believed that Machado had developed the symptoms of paresis, the result of a venereal infection in early life, and that he was rapidly going insane.

Former President Menocal threw down the gage in the only insurrection under the Republic that was fully justified. Although he failed and was captured, the people were with him. Even Machado did not dare to harm so eminent a man. The revolt continued undercover. Its most active center was Havana University. A secret society called the ABC was formed among its five thousand students. Three hundred professors met openly and pledged themselves to support the youngsters of both sexes in their fight for a free government. Machado countered by closing the university and launching a savage persecution of the teachers and students. Dozens were butchered, scores maimed and thrown into prison. But the movement hardened to one of almost unexampled self-abnegation, courage, and tenacity. Cuba actually was saved by these collegians, for if it had not been for their example the country must have sunk into chaos and been occupied by United States troops.

Natural leaders emerged, in some instances teen-age boys, in others favorite masters. Most prominent among the latter was Dr. Ramón Grau San Martín, a liberal idealist with a gift for winning the adoration of his pupils. He had done valuable research work on cancer and stomach ulcers, and was an authority on the secretions of the body. Young patriots flocked to his classes in anatomy. The government feared him, and he was imprisoned several times.

Machado's fall was hastened by a general strike in 1933. The United States then brought pressure to bear through Sumner Welles as its special envoy. The high command of the army turned on the despot. He was allowed to escape by plane, loaded down with gold, to die a dog's death of his maladies some five years later in Miami.

The provisional president agreed upon was Dr. Carlos Manuel de Céspedes, son of the first president in the Ten Years' War. But despite his glamorous name, it was not in him to impress the people. He was thought to be too conservative, and the rumor ran that he did not intend to get rid of those army officers who had been Machado's mainstay. A movement without parallel took form swiftly. The non-commissioned officers organized, threw out their superiors, and dominated the army. They were led by the sergeant-stenographer Fulgencio Batista, a man unknown until then to the politicians and to the country. He was in his thirties, of mixed blood with reputedly part Chinese ancestry, the son of a truck gardener. For some years he had been the court reporter at all important military trials, and this had given him valuable information.

In collaboration with the ABC, Batista asked for and obtained the resignation of Céspedes. A committee of five was appointed to take charge of affairs. This was composed of two professors, an editor, a lawyer, and a banker. Dr. Grau was one of the professors. Power is seldom exercised satisfactorily by a committee, and in a few days it was decided that Grau should be provisional president. Batista took the post of chief of staff of the army, with the rank of colonel. His first task was to conduct the famous siege of the Hotel Nacional and make captives of the officers who had once commanded him. Thereafter, he was to be for eleven years the real power in all administrations.

Grau lasted that time for four months. He had promised reforms, and he went about them radically. He seized a foreign-owned electric company and reduced the rates 45 per cent. He stopped payment of the interest on a huge American loan that Machado had obtained. By decree, he established votes for women, the eight-hour day, a social-security system, workmen's compensation, and maternity insurance. Ordinary politicians found it impossible to influence Grau. But he was in office by the consent of Batista, and when the latter concluded he was too radical and ousted him he had to go into exile.

Carlos Mendieta, an old-line liberal of great prestige, was now elevated by the president-maker. Batista seemed not to interfere much with him, the reason being that Mendieta could readily be induced to adopt suggestions and believe that he had originated them himself. Though honorable, he was slow-witted. The United States approved of him, and it was in June 1934, during his two-year incumbency, that Franklin D. Roosevelt made one of the salient gestures of his "good neighbor" policy and abrogated the Platt Amendment. American claims in the Isle of Pines had been relinquished several years before. Cuba was fully independent at last.

Batista could have made himself chief executive at any time. But he preferred to hold elections in 1936, at which he engineered the choice of Miguel Mariano Gómez, son of "El Tiburón," as president and Laredo Bru as vice-president. A pitiable experience lay in store for Gómez. He assumed that full power was being turned over to him, and he told his friends that if attempts were made to boss him he would resist. This was the course he attempted to follow, though none too vigorously. At the end of seven months, Batista got rid of him unconstitutionally by having the Congress vote him out of office. The crooked and servile Laredo Bru completed the term.

In 1940 Batista became head of the state in name as well as fact. He had allowed Grau to return to Cuba, and Grau was his opponent in an electoral contest he rigged to suit himself. Batista's rule, before and after he took the presidency, was a dictatorship in which some of the evils of the Machado regime reappeared. The opposition was grimly handled at times; killings occurred, as did graft and acts of cynical favoritism. But in other respects it was a beneficent dictatorship. Batista had a sense of patriotism, and in the fields of education, hygiene, and public works his record was progressive. A certain maleness in his character won him the admiration of many who condemned his politics.

It was Batista's preference to resume his old status of the power behind the throne. With an eye on public opinion in the democracies during the war, notably the United States, he took the remarkable step for a man of his type of holding an honest election in 1944. He must have felt convinced that his faction had become so strong that it could not be beaten. The government coalition nominated an estimable young senator, Carlos Saladrigas. The other ticket was again headed by Dr. Grau, who took a more moderate stand than in the old days. He promised to reduce and simplify the 125 different taxes then in effect. He stressed the rights of labor, both agricultural and urban. With fervid and telling passion, he preached the liberties that had been the ideological core of the revolution against Machado and that had ever since been thwarted.

Up to the last minute of election eve there was confident betting on the government candidates to win. But by noon of the following day it was clear that Grau had swept the country. Batista accepted the result and served out the remaining months of his term. Rumors of plots in his favor were frowned upon by him. On retiring he at once left the island for a prolonged tour of neighboring republics, including the United States. The victorious party, as well as his own, denied that pressure had been put on him to go, but he assuredly had the semblance of an exile for two years or so.

It was a vast gain in Cuban affairs, nevertheless, that power should have been peacefully transferred, that an administration pledged to reverse most of the policies of its predecessor should go ahead with its plans unhampered even by threats. Emancipation from Spain had been a half victory, after all. A further price, in the terms of internal warfare, had had to be paid before the processes of stable government could function.

Grau made a statement at this time that impresses me as being of vital significance. He said that "under no pretext" should men be deprived of liberty in order to foster the advance of social justice. Then he explained that, on the other hand, the "great and everlasting problem" is the creation of governments in which liberty does not destroy social justice through a struggle of interests. That realization and the willingness to affirm it gives me considerable respect for Grau. So many modern reformers find it easy to forget the value of liberty. Apparently he has tried to act according to his dictum, and in any event his rule has been the most humanitarian in the history of the island. He has forwarded the interests of labor by doing away with abuses, increasing wages, and shortening the hours of work. Conservatives hold that he has gone too far in this direction. Others say that he has grown enamored of office, listens to bad advisers, and is a weakling compared to the Grau of 1933. Still others—their number is large—worship him as one of the world's great liberals.

His personality is unique among Latin-American rulers, past and present. The medical research worker and the statesman are of equal stature within him. The two preoccupations go together, in his opinion. He once declared that politics is the business of such as he, for "in the true and full extension of the word it is the science and the art of regulating and directing the interests of the community." A nervous mannerism, said to be due to the fact that he suffers from tuberculosis of the bones, causes him to twist his hands one over the other as he talks. He is a bachelor, and his hostess in the palace is his widowed sister-in-law, Señora Paulina Alsina Grau. His devotion to her and her children has not escaped a scandalous interpretation by his detractors. There is a small and visionary, but noisy, movement to make her his successor in the presidency.

Dr. Grau favors an extension of the tourist traffic from the United States. He associates himself genially with receptions held for prominent visitors, and it is easy for any foreigner with good credentials to meet him. In this he is like Batista and other Cuban presidents, with the exception of the fear-ridden Machado.

Tourism is rated as Cuba's third most important industry, sugar being overwhelmingly the first, and tobacco the second at far remove. But sugar is a variable quantity. It is Cuba's worry as well as her blessing, for dependence on a single product is hazardous, especially when that product must meet stiff competition from other countries. The story has always been one of ups and downs. When war stops the manufacture of European beet sugar, not only is the price of the cane crystals boosted, but the demand exceeds the supply, and Cuba enjoys a bonanza. This was the case during the "Dance of the Millions" that followed World War I. The recent crisis was far wider in its scope. It cut off the cane sugar of the Philippines, the Netherlands East Indies, and other tropical lands, and strangled the European beet fields too. Cuba was left as the main reservoir, and she prospered accordingly.

But in ordinary times she faces an inexorable reduction of prices to the point where only the thinnest margin of profit remains. She depends upon the quota for which the United States is willing to contract, and we must remember that the United States also takes care of the planters of Puerto Rico, Hawaii, and the Philippines. Cuba would be better off in the long run if she diversified her agriculture more than she now does. Fruit and spring vegetables, for instance, could be grown in greater amounts for export.

Tobacco is a steady, valuable crop. By itself it could not come anywhere near supporting the island. Soil suitable for producing good tobacco is found only in a few limited areas. However, tourism can be expanded indefinitely, and this trend is so pronounced that I do not think anything can halt it. In the early summer of 1946 I was told that the average number of shuttle planes between Havana and Miami was twenty-five a day. Three months later there were as many as fifty on some days, most of the passengers being week-end or other short-term visitors.

Massaguer expressed the opinion to me that sugar will hold on its present basis for four or five years, and during that period there will be no collapse of the economic boom. Local manufactures may get to be a bigger factor and incidentally help to reduce the cost of living. The latter crushes the Cuban lower middle class, which has little share in sugar bonanzas. The ordinary clerk in a government job makes about seventy or eighty dollars a month, and according to Massaguer food for even the smallest family cannot be bought for less than fifty dollars a month. I noticed myself that the cost of ready-made clothing had skyrocketed. White suits, which before the war could have been bought for eighteen dollars at the most, were priced in the shop windows at forty-five dollars and up. Common handkerchiefs were one dollar apiece. Articles of this kind are imported, and somehow the middle class manages to buy them, pay its rent, and eat also.

After the boom does collapse, what? Maybe the tourists will be spending so much money that some of it will seep through to the little fellow on the ground. Massaguer quoted to me a saying that Cuba is *la isla de corcha* (the island of cork), which signifies that she is resilient, light but tough, and cannot sink.

CHAPTER 4

CUBA'S PICTURESQUE INTERIOR

MOST tourists see nothing of Cuba except Havana. I have had various figures quoted to me: "Three in a hundred go into the interior," "Five in a hundred," "Seven in a hundred"; only wishful thinkers ventured on the last estimate. Four in a hundred comes closest to it. The fact is deplorable, for while it proves the capital to be a place of entrancing pleasures, the visitor who goes no farther misses much beauty of another kind. The Cuban Tourist Commission is actively seeking to popularize the interior, and if what I write has an effect in this direction I feel that I shall have done the traveling public a service.

Only thirty-six miles from Havana, yet on the southern coast, is the little town of Batabanó, which as told in a previous chapter is the capital's original site. There are several busses a day, and it can also be reached by train. The trip by automobile is pleasant and educational, because the road passes the whole way between pineapple fields and sugar and tobacco plantations. Batabanó is famous for its sponge fisheries in the shallows that stretch for miles offshore, and as a starting point for deep-sea fishing. It is the port of departure for the Isle of Pines. Merely to go rowing in the harbor is an experience; you see a luxuriant marine life a few feet below the surface of singularly clear water. There is a picturesquely situated hotel, the Dos Hermanos, which serves good sea food. Those who want to devote a tropical holiday to sailing and fishing could not find a better headquarters than Batabanó.

You should by all means do as the crowd has not yet learned to do, and go on to the Isle of Pines. It is an overnight trip by boat. A plane direct from the Havana airfield makes it in just thirty-nine minutes. Columbus discovered Cuba's lesser island on his second voyage and called it Evangelista, but like so many of his choices this one did not stick. A variety of pine tree covered a large part of the thin soil, and when the Spaniards renamed it they meant to imply that it was wasteland. They took almost no interest in it. So the buccaneers and pirates used it as a rendezvous. Plunder was supposed to have been buried there, and it is credited with being the place Robert Louis Stevenson had in mind when he wrote *Treasure Island*. After the Spanish-American War a farming colony of two or three thousand Americans settled there, under the impression that it would be annexed. Many of these families remain, notably in and around the town of Nueva Gerona. They have specialized in the cultivation of grapefruit.

The Isle of Pines is on the outer edge of the shallow saucer of water off Batabanó. Identical marine conditions prevail on both shores, and again we find sponging and a rich field for the angler. Tarpon are plentiful. The climate is milder than that of Cuba in winter, and is cool in summer. There are several medicinal springs. Because of their radioactivity, which supposedly affects the general water supply, the remarkable claim is made that there has never been an original case of cancer in the Isle of Pines. The hotels at Nueva Gerona and Santa Fé are adequate.

Returning to Havana for a fresh start, you may go westward to the province of Pinar del Río or eastward through the main part of the island. The former journey, save in rare instances, has allured none but visiting tobacco men. More's the pity. For in addition to being the richest source of the celebrated Havana filler, it offers delightful scenery. I had been there on a previous occasion, and as I was pressed for time I did not go again. The first stop should be at Mariel, a port on a blue bay dominated by a hill on which stands the Naval Academy of Cuba. I recall a wonderful meal at a little inn at the water's edge, which I think was called the Villa Martín. The Organos Mountains run through the center of the province, and south of its main branch lies the Vuelta Abajo, the lowlands that produce the finest cigar tobacco in the world. The provincial seat, the city of Pinar del Río, is of no great interest, but fifteen miles north of it is Viñales Valley, the second loveliest valley in Cuba. We shall hear of the first in connection with the province of Matanzas. At Viñales, streams gush from the mountainsides, fall in cascades, and form lakes or else pass under natural bridges that they seem to have bored. The floor of the depression is lush with verdure.

I left Havana by train for the swing to the east, though if you have a car and leisure for the road I would recommend the Central Highway as the best artery for traversing Cuba. Even from a train window one soon notices that the congested motor traffic of the capital has been left behind. There are busses and trucks on the roads, but comparatively few private automobiles. The country people ride horses and mules or ride in carts. An occasional buggy is seen. Ox teams are used to drag many a heavy load. At the railroad way stations, the beasts hitched to posts or hobbled remind Americans of a way of life they will not see again in their own country.

My first stop was at Matanzas, where I put up at the Gran Hotel de Paris in the section that is nearest the station, but is not the really old part of the city. You continue down the Calzada Tirry and cross a bridge to get a view of the bay. For some reason, Cuban railroads have been built on the edges of most of the towns. The Paris is a provincial inn that maintains the best traditions. The rooms, located up one flight on a maze of galleries, are sparsely furnished save for the all-important matter of comfortable beds shrouded with mosquito netting. Downstairs in the patio and excellent dining room an air of quiet well-being prevails. The house has its specialties, not least of which is *langostino*, cooked in various ways but simply perfect as a cold salad. I have never eaten better crayfish than those there. With a combination of realism and the picturesque, typically Cuban, the Señor kept his supply of live langostinos in the basin of his patio fountain. I counted fifty or sixty of them, of all sizes, amusing myself by speculating which of the grandfathers I was going to have for lunch. The other guests found them too old a story to be worth a glance.

Matanzas is built in part on hills. Its charm is very Spanish, more consistently so than that of Havana. Here there are no foreign influences. At every turn of the winding streets you catch glimpses of courtyards, the more pretentious paved with tiles, and one and all glowing with brilliant flowers. There is the regulation central plaza, on which stand the Gran Hotel Velasco and the Casino Español, the latter a glorified club finished in marble and carved tropical woods. The new residential section is ambitiously called Versailles.

I carried a letter of introduction from Massaguer to a local doctor, and I hastened to present it. There ensued a harmless little comedy of errors. The pretty receptionist (Matanzas claims the Cuban championship in pretty women, by the way) took the letter, which was written in English, glanced at the signature, and said warmly that she would put me down for an appointment some time in the future. By misfortune, the doctor was out of town. I explained that my introduction was a social one, and that as I was traveling I regrettably could not keep an appointment. She answered that she knew I had come well recommended, for while she could not read English the signature was familiar to her as that of an esteemed friend of the doctor. The latter would be honored to give me an examination, and I must return whenever it was convenient. No doubt my Spanish was poor, for nothing that I added convinced her that I was not a sick man. She resolutely wrote my name in the appointment book and filed the letter.

Those were the circumstances in which I failed to have the good Dr. Dihigo as a mentor on Matanzas. But I explored the city and its environs on my own. The first permanent settlement on the bay was in 1693, which makes the port some 175 years younger than Havana. The Monserrate Church is interesting with its altar made of cork, and on a high hill is the Monserrate Hermitage, from the terrace of which is had a superb view of the valley of the Yumurí, one of the two rivers between which Matanzas is located. This is the valley that is held to surpass Viñales in beauty. The scene is not fantastic like the one in Pinar del Río. It is spacious, tranquil, and wondrously opulent, instead. The Yumurí flows down the middle of the vale, and on both its banks are seemingly endless columns of the royal palm, smooth-boled and symmetrically crowned with fronds, the tree so dominant in Cuban landscapes that it is a national symbol.

Close to the sea in the neighborhood of Matanzas are the Bellamar caves. Cuba is largely of limestone formation, and as a result is a country of caves, but these are among the most remarkable. Located beneath the surface of flat land, which is in itself unusual, the artificial roofed tunnel leading to them is surrounded by plantations of sisal hemp. The caves were discovered by chance in 1862, when a Chinese laborer working with a crowbar struck a void and heard the tool, which had slipped from his hands, fall to a great depth. The connecting chambers branch irregularly for miles and have not been fully explored. One of the caves has pillars from twenty to thirty feet high, which hold up the roof and apparently were formed by stalactites merging with stalagmites. A stalactite grows downward by accretions of lime carried by dripping water, while a stalagmite is the cone-shaped mass built up by the calcium with which the water was still charged when it reached the floor. Another Bellamar cave has a sink hole that has never been plumbed.

Almost fifty miles east of Matanzas is one of the prides of Cuban tourism, Varadero Beach. Another name for it is the Playa Azul (Blue Beach), not because the sands are tinted, but in honor of the glory of sea and sky so seldom clouded at that favored spot. Varadero is a development of the past quarter century, its first enthusiast having been the late Irénée Du Pont, the American munitions millionaire. When he saw the five miles of perfect white sand, at that time neglected save by casual bathers, he bought and lavishly improved an estate comprising part of the water front. Hotels and cottages were then erected by promoters, and the resort quickly became fashionable. The rhapsodies of those whose business it is to praise—and the Tourist Commission omits no adjectives in describing Varadero—are generally to be taken with a grain of salt. But in this instance the reality lives up to all that has been said about it. American warm-water beaches have nothing on Varadero, which is less crowded than Miami Beach and has a background of rolling tropical terrain that Florida cannot offer.

I decided that when I left Matanzas province I would go off the beaten track and see something of an aspect of Cuba familiar only to naturalists, but which other travelers would enjoy if they knew the road. The next province eastward is Las Villas (formerly Santa Clara), where the greatest concentration of sugar planting occurs, where the south-coast port of Cienfuegos is located, and where some of the smaller towns have preserved much of the charm of colonial days. The Ingenio Soledad (*ingenio* is Spanish for a sugar mill), a few miles from Cienfuegos, was founded before the Spanish-American War by Edwin F. Atkins, a Bostonian, whose catholic interest in botany led him to set aside eleven acres of his land as an experimental garden in 1901. He later enlarged the acreage to 221. The management of the whole was turned over to Harvard University and became full-fledged tropical botanical gardens and a bird refuge. Harvard House was built as a laboratory, with quarters for resident scientists and guests, and in time the dormitory called Casa Catalina was added.

The writings of Thomas Barbour (especially his *A Naturalist in*

Cuba) had stirred in me a romantic longing for the gardens at Soledad. I had heard that visitors were welcomed even if they were not scientists. So I had sent a letter from Havana asking permission, and had received a cordial wire from the director, Mr. Walsingham, inviting me to Harvard House. This was to be my first destination in Las Villas.

From Matanzas by train, I changed at Santo Domingo station and took a branch line to Cienfuegos, where I lingered briefly to get an impression of the city that is known as the "Pearl of the South." If one may take liberties with the simile, the harbor is the pearl, an admirable landlocked haven of deep anchorages, a natural center for yachting as well as commercial shipping. Cienfuegos itself is too modern to compete in charm with more aesthetically conceived Cuban towns. It was founded in 1819, destroyed seven years later by a hurricane, and rebuilt by stodgy merchants. But there is a fine plaza, heavily shaded by laurels and palms, and containing two marble lions given by Queen Isabella II of Spain. The name, which means "a hundred fires," is credited by legend to the exclamations of early voyagers astonished at the multitude of glowworms they saw in the underbrush surrounding the bay. But it is prosily true that Cienfuegos became Cienfuegos in honor of a governor of that name.

I proceeded the same afternoon to Soledad in a taxicab hired at an exorbitant rate. The chauffeur saw that I knew of no other way to get there, but if Walsingham is notified on what train a visitor is coming he makes arrangements to have him brought out for far less than I paid. It was mid-July, and a sugar plantation is deadest at that time of the year. The cane is young, requiring no attention except weeding; its green waves spreading for many hectares were fair in the golden sunlight. At intervals were pastures in which cattle grazed. I drove past some of the dwellings of Soledad employees, clean, attractive buildings with a common recreation center. Everything appeared to be on a model basis.

Harvard House, a one-story structure pleasingly designed for the climate yet evading the ordinary bungalow effect, was deserted for the moment. I left its broad, screened veranda and strolled on a lawn dotted with trees from the Orient. Behind the house were massed citrus and other Cuban fruit trees. I was at once struck by the numbers of birds of various species that flitted about the place, some probing the flowers, others pecking at the fruit, and all making the air joyous with their cries. This is not characteristic of West Indian gardens, particularly in the Latin countries, where even songbirds are trapped and frightened until they become chary of man. Their friendliness here was of course due to their having been protected for years, and I later found them to be equally plentiful and fearless in every part of the reservation.

Within twenty minutes I had noted mockingbirds, tyrant flycatchers, orioles, tinkling grackles, hummingbirds, and ground doves, as well as several redheaded woodpeckers darting across with their plunging flight. Invisible, but keeping up an incessant chorus, were dozens of mourning doves, and as twilight fell I heard the four-syllabled call of nightjars, the hoarse, hilarious challenge of limpkins, and the soft hooting of owls. In the morning I saw little green todies with gorgets like splashes of blood, rusty black anis to which the Cubans give the name of *Judío* (Jew) because of their high, curved beaks, and the tawny lizard cuckoos that tumble about so clumsily in underbrush and low branches of trees. The Soledad gardens are nothing short of a birdman's paradise.

This is incidental, however. The function of the gardens is to cultivate plants, whether utilitarian or decorative, from all parts of the tropical zone, and to promote the dissemination in Cuba of those that prove well suited to the island's soil and climatic conditions. This work is being steadily carried forward. There is a notable collection of palms, a botanical family of which there are many hundreds of varieties. The bamboos also are abundant. Sensational blossoming trees stand all about, such as the *mondora* from West Africa, which is literally covered at the proper season, the trunk as well as the branches, with flowers that resemble orchids; the triplaris from Panama, which has been compared to a huge candle dipped in blood; and the *flor de mico* from Guatemala, which first gets rid of its leaves and then puts out tightly packed blooms, burnt orange in color, on every twig. These are but samples cited on the authority of Barbour, who helped to create the gardens and whose joy in them was boundless.

Barbour tells how Robert M. Grey, an accomplished scientist, worked at Soledad for years under the auspices of Harvard University until he had developed two new types of sugar cane superior to the plant then being grown on the Cuban estates. They might have been adopted had not other canes that had been simultaneously perfected in Java suddenly convinced the world's sugar growers of their merit. Grey's labors had solved a difficult problem, nonetheless, and by similar methods crops of commercial value have been—and are being—improved in the gardens.

Though I am no horticulturist, I fell completely under the spell of the place. Its beauty and healthfulness have a relaxing quality. The men in charge are busy and do not pamper the visitor. You are given a plain cot and good, plain food, and you must make your own pleasures. I found it an excellent program during the three happy days I spent there. From the Casa Catalina dormitory, up the road from Harvard House, there is a sweeping view of the greater part of the land embraced by the gardens, of the continuation of the valley and the blue Trinidad Mountains beyond. A ramble down the slope and along any of the intersecting paths will furnish surprise after surprise.

There is plenty of space. So the groves and experimental plots do not crowd upon one another, as is necessary in the formal botanical gardens of cities. You can have the shelter of a banyan to yourself, that amazing Indian tree of the fig family, the branches of which send down aerial roots that form additional trunks until a circular wood results. Or a pool shaded by exotic bamboos and full of water fowl. The spot I liked best was a stretch of native woodland growing among limestone rocks, the underbrush light, and the trees adorned with orchids of many species that of course have been brought together by man. It was pleasant to linger on the rustic seats, feast the eyes on color, and watch the birds that flock there.

Harvard House makes a nominal charge per day. I know of no way of getting much for little that is better than this, unless the traveler is an incorrigible devotee of pleasure in the terms of night clubs and noise.

The city of Trinidad is a bare thirty miles down the coast from Cienfuegos as the crow flies, but no automobile road linking the two has yet been built. To reach Trinidad it is necessary to get back to the main railroad line, ride a short distance east, and change to another spur striking south. There is not even a decent driving road from the interior, though one is being planned to connect with the Central Highway. This isolation is irksome today, but it has saved a wonderful spot from being ruined by "modernization" during the brash decades of the early twentieth century.

I left Soledad early in the morning, and at Cienfuegos was seduced by the idea of taking the bus to Santa Clara and seeing the country roads at close range. It proved to be an experience not to be recommended to any but the most hardy. The bus was small and squat, with very narrow seats in which, once wedged, it was hard to change position, even to light a cigarette. Passengers came aboard with every sort of hand baggage, including vegetables and live fowls. But as all the places were not filled at the terminus, the chauffeur cruised about town looking for patrons and at last succeeded in crowding the vehicle to its limit. Then we were off at a terrific clip, which was not slowed after the good paved thoroughfares in and near the city had been passed.

We ran into long stretches of road that had once been hard-surfaced, but on which no repairs could have been made for years. Cracks had widened into depressions that rainstorms had scoured until nothing but a snarl of stones was left. Ridges had formed elsewhere, and so had deposits of dried mud. Over this hazardous course the bus sped, lurching, swaying, and bumping. Seatmates were thrown against each other, and tall passengers had to exercise care to avoid having their heads knocked against the roof. The dirt roads taken as short cuts were quite as bad in their way, for they were full of ruts and the whizzing tires stirred up clouds of reddish dust. The regulars aboard treated it as a huge joke, laughing and making mock bets on what the next obstacle would be like.

All Cuban busses are not so uncomfortable as was this one. Outside of the Central Highway and some of its branches, however, the roads of the interior are pretty poor. Nor are there as many roads of any kind, in areas of comparable size, as the Americans have built in Puerto Rico and the British in Jamaica.

Odd as it may seem, I was glad that I had made the trip. The glimpses of rural life that I got compensated for the jolting. We passed several of the biggest sugar estates and halted in colorful villages. I was again struck by the large amount of men I saw on horseback. This may be explained, in part, by the shortage of automobiles and gasoline caused by the war. It remains clear that many Cubans ride by preference and will continue to do so. They have handsome saddles and other accouterments in which they take pride. I found big and flourishing saddlery shops in all the provincial cities.

At Santa Clara I caught the train for Trinidad. The three-hour journey is one of the most rewarding that you can make on the Cuban railroad system. After traversing miles of fertile sugar country, the track rises and follows a snakelike course through those same Trinidad Mountains that bound the view from the Soledad gardens. The extreme elevation reached is not more than 2,000 feet, and this is an advantage, for the scenery remains tropical. Palms, flamboyants, and other vivid trees are not left below. The peaks and canyons, dense with greenery, are more rugged than one would expect in this comparatively low range. At the crossing of the Agabama River, the train passes over the highest viaduct (164 feet) in Cuba.

The Trinidad railroad station is an old Spanish fort that saw action as late as the war of independence, when it was stormed by patriots in 1898. It is a short ride to the main street where the only two hotels, La Ronda and the Canada, are situated. You have barely left the station when you perceive that this city is of the ancient past. The low stone houses, their walls flush with the narrow sidewalks, lean with the upward slope of the land; their roofs are tiled, for the most part in red. The streets are paved with big round cobblestones so irregular that an automobile navigates them with difficulty. Colonial mansions, deservedly called palaces, appear among the lesser structures that huddle close to them. Little squares dream under canopies of foliage and trailing garlands of flower-laden vines.

Trinidad is the third oldest town in Cuba, having been founded by Don Diego de Velásquez in 1514. Only Baracoa, built in 1511, and Santiago, also dating from 1514, came ahead of it. The original Baracoa is no more, and there is little of the Santiago of Velásquez except parts of its cathedral. Trinidad, too, cannot show much that is authentically of the first governor's day, but what remains is merged with building that was done a short while later and in the seventeenth century. The glories of the century after that were not erected at the expense of what had gone before. A beautiful harmony was maintained. Few additions and a minimum of destruction marked the nineteenth century. Unlike Santiago, Trinidad was not treated as a port that must show profits.

Yet for three hundred years it was one of the island's busiest and historically most significant points of entry and exit. Hernando Cortés rushed to Trinidad when the settlement was only four years old, to elude Velásquez on the eve of the great Mexican adventure.

The ceiba tree to which he moored his ship is pointed out a short distance within the mouth of the Guarabo River. For fear of marauders, the city was not placed on the shore, but three miles inland, and was served by the little port of Casilda, as is the case to this day. When Jamaica was captured by the English in 1655, those of its Spanish residents who escaped made their way to Cuba, some landing at Santiago and perhaps a larger number at Trinidad. This fact was a surprise to me, for I had supposed all the fugitives went to Santiago. I was inclined to question it until Don Francisco Marín Villafuerte, the historian of Trinidad, brought out documents in which descendants of the refugees cited the hardships the families had suffered in fleeing Jamaica.

The near-by lowlands are ideally suited to sugar cane, and the district was one of the first in which the crop was produced on a large scale. The fortunes of the leading colonial residents—the Iznagas, Canteros, Borrells, Brunets, and others—came from sugar in the 150 years that may be said roughly to have run from 1710 to 1860. They were thus enabled to build their palaces, the luxury of which reinforces the contention that, for its size, Trinidad was once the richest place in Cuba.

The Iznagas have a connection with the United States. An Iznaga heiress married into the Vanderbilt family, and it was her daughter, Consuelo Vanderbilt, who became the Duchess of Manchester in one of the most publicized international weddings early in the present century. The Iznaga palace is still well preserved. Outside the city, the Iznaga plantation is being operated, and a handsome tower erected there is a landmark of the neighborhood.

Some of the fine palaces are unoccupied, and several of these are in need of repairs. The Cantero and Borrell structures are among the best. Private houses containing antiques and works of art include those of resident families such as the Torredos, Frias, and Palacios, which can be seen by permission. I have left the palace of the Conde de Brunet till the last, for it has become the local headquarters of the Cuban Tourist Commission and houses the beginnings of a museum. The representative of the commission is Manuel J. Béquer, a native of Trinidad and a genuine enthusiast about the preservation of his city's treasures. He is the secretary and one of the founders of the Pro-Trinidad Society, which was organized in 1942. Two years later the government of Cuba passed a law declaring the old section of Trinidad to be a national monument. This statute is similar to the one adopted in Louisiana for the saving of the Vieux Carré, New Orleans. It prevents the demolition of historic buildings or the marring of them by changes that clash with their period. The government assumes the right to compel the owner of a given building to restore it at his own expense, by taking out a mortgage if he cannot afford to do it otherwise.

Señor Béquer was one of the five men who helped me to form an idea of the artistic glory of the city. The others were Señor Marín Villafuerte, author of the *Historia de Trinidad* (1945); Dr. Rafael Rodríguez Altunaga, former Cuban diplomat and Undersecretary of the Treasury; the genial Dr. Manuel Rabasa, to whom Massaguer had given me a letter; and Mr. James S. Trench, a Jamaican who had served in the United States Army in the Spanish-American War, had been discharged in Trinidad at his own request, and had lived there ever since.

The Brunet palace is a shell stripped of its gorgeous furnishings. Architecturally it is unspoiled. The high-ceilinged rooms, the balconies, the curving stone stairways, the patio, all are in a noble tradition. Fairly high on the slope of La Vigia hill it commands a view in every direction. The tourist will probably go there first to seek the guidance of the commission, and luckily there could be no better starting point. Close by is Serrano Plaza, laid out on the spot where Cortés recruited soldiers for Mexico. Fray Bartolomé de las Casas, champion of the Indians, held services on a triangle of ground preserved oddly among dwellings as though it were somebody's garden. A tablet marks the house where Alexander von Humboldt stayed on his visit to Cuba in 1804.

I was too late for Trinidad's curious summer equivalent of Carnival, a religious fiesta in honor of Saints John and Peter. This takes place from the twenty-fourth to the thirtieth of June. Holy images are paraded. There is also dancing in the streets to secular music, and many of the participants wear costumes. The *parrandas*, a strictly local feature, consist of groups of young men who appear at night and conduct mass serenades beneath the grilled windows of favored beauties.

But I culled memories of Trinidad at its quietest that will always be ineffaceable. The central plaza, downtown, has a bandstand covered with a huge arbor that is in doubtful taste. A crumbling stone platform would have been more suited to the seventeenth-century square. Unchanged, provincial society eddies through the flower-banked walks in the early hours of the evening. The custom observed in some Spanish-American cities of having the young men and girls take different paths, so that they cross each other in a sort of figure-of-eight effect, is not followed here. The sexes promenade naturally together, and as everyone knows his neighbor constant greetings are exchanged. I sat on a bench with Rabasa and Marín Villafuerte, fascinated to hear them cry, "*Adiós*" as a salutation, for the word in modern Spanish is commonly used only in the sense of "good-by." They gave it the archaic meaning of God's care evoked for a friend at sight or parting. Back came the word with a singing intonation, the "s" dropped after the Cuban fashion and the "o" heavily accented: "*A-dió . . . a-dió*." The musical voices and the soft winds lulled me. When the crowd broke up, long before midnight, I roamed the darkened streets, and it was in keeping with the medieval scene that an old man with a lantern came by and offered to light me home for a *real*.

The next day I called on Marín Villafuerte at his home, where I found him in a book-lined study, his desk covered with old manuscripts he had brought out to show me, and surrounded by fourteen cats. I also went to see Rodríguez Altunaga at the house that has been in his family for over 150 years. These courteous gentlemen and scholars would have dropped all else to spread the whole history of Trinidad before me, if I had been able to linger for that purpose. As it was, they told me much lore that stressed the individualism of their city. Marín Villafuerte, for instance, called my attention to Trinidad's coat of arms, which has British red ensigns on either side. These, it appeared, were adopted as trophies to make the point that following the capture of Havana in 1763 the invaders sent a force to take Trinidad, and were stingingly repulsed. The Jamaican origin of some of the old families is said to have been an additional reason for using the flags, the inference being that Jamaica would eventually be reconquered.

My last bit of exploration was a drive with Trench through the environs and into the mountains to the Topes de Collantes. The slopes become steep a short distance to the north of the city. Thereafter, the ascent is abrupt, the culminating peak being the Potrerillo, 2,920 feet above sea level. A *tope* is a summit, but not necessarily an apex. Those of Collantes, twenty-one kilometers from Trinidad, are closely massed. I had been informed that I would see a remarkable unfinished building that it was hoped to turn into a hotel and gambling casino. This proved to be a mild preparation for the surprise that awaited me. The car spun around a shoulder of the mountains, and I found myself looking up at an edifice that is a modern rival in setting, immensity, and—I do not hesitate to add—folly of King Christophe's citadel in Haiti. It stretched for a good fifth of a mile along the top of the most prominent bluff, was several stories tall, broad in proportion, and solidly built, as far as it had gone, of stone and cement.

What was the purpose of this gigantic structure that could be reached only by the narrow, imperfect road I had taken from the isolated city of Trinidad? It had been designed by the Batista administration as a tuberculosis sanitarium, to comprise 1,100 rooms and suites, with elaborate hospital and other medical services, and provision for entertainment that included club rooms and a private theater. The project was so lavish and would have cost so much to maintain that prices equivalent to those of a de luxe hotel would have had to be charged. Few, if any, charity patients could have been admitted. Batista appears to have conceived it as a monument to his ego, without stopping to ask himself whether a steady clientele of 1,100 rich invalids could have been attracted.

When President Grau took office, $7,000,000 had already been spent on the building and accessories. It would have taken $3,000,-000 more to complete it. The cost of running the place was estimated at $3,000,000 a year. Meanwhile, doctors had pronounced that the climate at Collantes was not a good one for tuberculosis sufferers! So Grau canceled the plan at a stroke. It has been pointed out, and it is true, that Cuban presidents in the past have not cared to finish large works started by a predecessor, but have chosen rather to launch ideas of their own. This petty motive cannot be ascribed to Grau. He is a physician, and a practicable sanitarium unquestionably would have had his support. It can possibly be held against him that, for reasons that may have been chauvinistic, he is said to have rejected an offer by the United States government to lease the white elephant as a home for World War II incurables.

I looked over the interior of the building. The ground floor and the first floor are practically ready, but there is considerable work still to be done on the upper stories. The outer walls and roof of the theater, which connects at the rear as an annex, are in place; the pit is a junk heap. Stacked in the corridors for literally hundreds of feet are unopened crates containing huge metal pots for the kitchens, crockery and glassware, lavatory fixtures and other equipment, bought for the most part in the United States at the high prices that prevailed during the war. The figure of $500,000 was mentioned to me as the cost of this material. I quote it without verification.

Checking on the local talk I had heard, I asked the Tourist Commission, Havana, about the future of the building, and was told in writing that "in all probability the sanatorium at Collantes will be converted into a tourist hotel in the future." But this strikes me as being both an expensive and a dubious venture. Admittedly there would have to be a driving road to Collantes from the north, as well as a landing field for airplanes close to the hotel. The "future" suggested is likely to be a far future. I favor any effort that will bring visitors to the beautiful region. There is more immediate promise in the effort being made by Cuban intellectuals to get the government to form a national academy of art in Trinidad. It would attract painters from all over the world, for the old city has the authentic flavor of Hispanic genius in the tropics.

Other towns in Las Villas Province that have kept a colonial atmosphere are Sancti Spíritus, San Juan de Remedios, and the village of Isabela de Sagua. Sancti Spíritus is important. With its narrow streets and graceful buildings, including a sixteenth-century church, it is not unlike Trinidad. I did not have the time to stop there, but went on by train to Camaguey.

Both the province and the city of Camaguey were first called Puerto Principe by the Spaniards. This was because Velásquez founded a port on the north coast where Nuevitas now stands, and for years it was the most significant feature of the territory. Sea marauders attacked it so often, however, that it was shifted inland while continuing to be known as Puerto Principe. The name was changed under the Republic to one of Siboney Indian origin.

Camaguey is the center of the cattle business and of agriculture less exclusively devoted to sugar cane and tobacco than the rest of Cuba. Fruits and vegetables thrive in the rich, well-watered soil. It is also the junction point of the western and eastern railroad systems. Sir William Van Horne, builder of the Canadian Pacific

Railway, decided to give the eastern provinces rail transportation while Leonard Wood was still military governor. Van Horne made Camaguey his headquarters and took a great liking to the place. It was he who converted a Spanish cavalry and infantry barracks, extending over nearly five acres and designed to house two thousand troops, into the celebrated Hotel Camaguey. The building was modernized without any sacrifice of the picturesque. There were bars and lounges beguilingly located, and a series of large patios filled with palms, decorative shrubs, and flowers. It came close to being the preferred hotel of Americans who really knew Cuba, and tourists who stumbled upon it by accident were enchanted. Alas, it was a casualty of the recent war. A school is installed in the wonderful old barracks.

The existing hotels are adequate. Visitors from the north usually go to the Plaza, opposite the railroad station, or to the Gran, a dozen blocks away. My favorite is the Colón, very Spanish in atmosphere and offering a native cuisine of the first order.

A rapid growth of population has made Camaguey the third city of Cuba. This tends to obscure the charm of a community that likes to call itself the "city of churches," "the aristocrat of the cities," and the "cradle of patriots." Yet the core of the original town is little altered. Churches assuredly abound, including La Merced and San Francisco, in both of which Henry Morgan, the master buccaneer, locked his prisoners after he had stormed Puerto Principe on Holy Thursday, 1668. John Esquemeling, who was there, wrote in his *History of the Bucaniers* that, after the usual pillage, the victors "set to making great cheer," without sending food to their captives, "whom they left to starve in the churches; though they tormented them daily and inhumanely, to cause them to confess wherein they had hid their treasure; though of a fact little or nothing was left to them . . . and whereby the greater part miserably perished."

I cannot feel that Camaguey ever had the dignity of Havana or Trinidad. It is a good example of a provincial capital. You feel this not only in the relics of the distant past that have survived, but in the buildings and monuments of today and the intense character of local pride. The province's outstanding hero of the struggle for independence was General Agramonte, to whom a square containing a handsome statue of him is dedicated. The city supported Agramonte with such ardor and furnished so many lesser officers that it has every right to boast about its patriotism. Camaguey also has been meticulous in paying tribute to foreigners who have helped the *patria*. A large number of streets are named for Americans whose pro-Cuban sentiments may have been forgotten elsewhere, but not in Camaguey. There is one for Charles A. Dana, editor of the New York *Sun*, who engaged Martí to write for his paper and used his own pen to back Martí's cause. In the small square at the crossing of Charles A. Dana and Estrada Palma is what must surely be the first bust of Franklin D. Roosevelt erected in a foreign country after the President's death. It was paid for by public subscription and unveiled on July 4, 1945.

Houses on the old streets were sometimes built with their ground-floor living quarters a little above the level of the sidewalk. I noted traces of exterior steps to right or left of the doorway, and clearly intended to bring passing gossipers even with the persons within. The smaller shops have an easy, neighborly air reminiscent of stores in a Mediterranean town. When they try to be American, they are funny. I saw a bargain sale announced in one of them as an "elephant sale" —meaning jumbo—with the silhouette of a pink elephant hung in the doorway and others pasted on the windows.

The native bars do as big a business in coffee and soft beverages as in liquor, if not bigger. It was good in the early morning to see green coconuts piled on every bar. The attendant would chop away the husk at one end and serve the coconut milk with a piece of ice in it for a dime. As a before-breakfast fruit drink, this could not be beaten.

The largest province of all is Oriente, its capital Santiago de Cuba. Observe that at Camaguey you are 354 miles from Havana, and that to reach Santiago you travel 247 miles more. The island is much broader, too, at its eastern than its western end, and Oriente is where by far the highest mountains are located. Though it is the part of Cuba that was first seized by the Spaniards, the nature of the terrain has caused wide areas to remain uncultivated. The eternal sugar cane is the chief source of wealth, but the province also grows coffee at elevations above 1,500 feet, and on the north coast around Nipe Bay the United Fruit Company has old and important banana plantations. Directly opposite is Guantánamo Bay, on the south coast, the major American naval base in the West Indies.

Tourists seldom see any other place in Oriente but Santiago, which used to be a port of call for some ships that did not touch at Havana, and will be again. I had visited it before, and now my feeling was reaffirmed that this, the second city of the Republic, is surpassed only by Havana in interest. Always excepting Trinidad, which is *sui generis, hors de concours*, or what you will.

The harbor is one of the best in the Caribbean, with a bottleneck entrance that expands into a great lagoon dotted with cays, its branches feeling their way into depressions formed by the encircling mountains. A *morro* resembling the one at Havana, though not so elaborate, stands on the easterly bluff of the harbor mouth. The port's water front is a comparatively narrow strip of flat ground amply developed with deep-water piers. The city crowds back from it, up steep inclines to a second level. All addresses in Santiago are given as *alta* or *baja*, to indicate whether they are on upper or lower streets. There is a park and a drive, the Alameda, along the foreshore. But the ancient plaza and center of things, now called the Parque Céspedes, is on the higher level.

Here you find the cathedral, which has had many vicissitudes since Diego de Velásquez completed the original structure in 1522 just in time to be buried there. It was destroyed by fire four years later, rebuilt, and again burned by corsairs in 1602. An earthquake wrecked it in 1666, but it was patched up. The present edifice was begun in 1810 and completed in 1818. Materials from the former cathedrals were employed wherever possible, and on this fact rests its claim to being one of the oldest churches in the New World. The ground floor, approached by steps, is some twenty feet above the plaza. On two sides extensions from the substructure have been divided into cubicles that are rented as shops, a compromise with business more often seen in Europe than America. The tomb of Velásquez is pointed out, unviolated through the turmoil of the centuries.

Also on the square is the Casa Grande Hotel, formerly a mansion on a palatial scale, the rooms enormous, the decorations ornate. This is easily the place at which to stay. The Venus Hotel opposite was once its rival, but suffered damage in an earthquake several years ago and had not been repaired when I last saw it. There are, of course, many smaller hotels. Santiago does not offer Havana's varied choice in restaurants. The dining room at the Casa Grande is excellent. Of the strictly Cuban places, La Higuera (The Fig Tree) is perhaps the best. There is a pleasure garden at the distillery of the Bacardi rum concern, where drinks are on the house.

The climate of Oriente province is warmer than that of the rest of the island, and Santiago consequently is a more tropical city than Havana. Flowers and greenery are luxuriant in proportion, and gardens of any size contain towering trees that are both lovely and useful, such as the breadfruit, the mango, and the avocado pear. This and the quaintness of the hillside streets, where you often find yourself on a sidewalk bordered by the roofs of houses on the next street below, make a stroll about Santiago fascinating.

For Americans no less than Cubans, the historical associations are poignant. Here the control of Spain was broken forever in 1898. Admiral Pascual Cervera's squadron took refuge in Santiago Harbor and was blockaded there by the fleet under Admiral W. T. Sampson and Commodore W. S. Schley. On July 3, Cervera's ships steamed out in single file, passing the half-submerged *Merrimac*, which Lieutenant Hobson had sunk in a gallant failure to block the channel, and attempted to burst through the American line. He was overwhelmed by gunnery and forced to flee westward along the coast, where his ships were beached in succession to a point nearly a third of the distance to Cape Cruz.

Meanwhile an army under General W. R. Shafter had been landed between Santiago and Guantánamo, centering at the Playa de Siboney, near Daiquiri. Its high officers included Colonel Theodore Roosevelt, Colonel Leonard Wood, and the former Confederate general "Fighting Joe" Wheeler, who at the Las Guásimas action climbed a tree to reconnoiter and was so carried away by excitement at finding the Spaniards in retreat that he shouted, "See them damned Yanks run!"

The destruction of Cervera would not have sufficed to reduce Santiago. The army had made the city untenable by the smart fights at El Caney, Kettle Hill, and San Juan Hill. Roosevelt led his Rough Riders at the storming of Kettle, not San Juan as is still often stated, but he witnessed the other operation and supported it with rifle fire. Which of the two hills he stormed was of small import. The exploit and his verve throughout the war were what caught the popular imagination and headed him toward the presidency.

The Spanish commander, General Toral, signed the preliminaries for his surrender following a conference with Shafter under a ceiba tree about four hundred yards from San Juan Hill. Carefully preserved and a stopping point for tourists, this ceiba is called the Peace Tree. Above, a Spanish blockhouse has been restored as a memorial. It bears tablets honoring the American and Cuban armies and, if I recall correctly, the valiant behavior of certain Spaniards. There is a list in bronze of the Americans who fell. Other monuments are projected.

This hilltop is a park from which one gets an impressive view of the country round about, with glimpses of the city and harbor. I can conceive of no better spot than San Juan Hill at which to say a romantic farewell to Cuba.

CHAPTER 5

JAMAICA: THE ISLE OF SPRINGS

BACK at Camaguey, I took to the air. That city is where a service of Pan American Airways branches off to Jamaica, Colombian ports, and Panama. It was my plan from then on to make all major jumps by plane, for though a few of the steamship lines had resumed limited schedules and it was possible at several places to catch small interisland boats, I needed to hoard my transportation time. The new mode of travel would be a trail-breaking experience for me. I had been up in planes as far back as the middle 1920's, but oddly enough I had never made a passenger flight. Above all, I had never seen my native Caribbean from the air. It is my thought to record impressions as if flying were a novel thing, which undoubtedly it still is to some persons who have been prevented by the troubled conditions since 1939 from going on voyages of any kind.

The Camaguey airport is a long distance from the city, a drive of about half an hour by car. The practice has been to lay out most fields at such locations, and this constitutes one of the annoyances of air travel. The difficulty of getting sufficiently large sites in a metropolitan area, as well as the cost of the land, are mentioned as controlling factors. The argument is countered by some excellent and convenient fields in the West Indies. From time to time I shall have a good deal to say about the airport problem. The companies are, at least, unfailingly courteous in the way they handle passengers, and they do their utmost to provide prompt bus and taxicab connections.

I left my hotel at six A.M. to catch a seven-thirty plane. It is necessary to allow from three quarters of an hour to an hour at an airport, because of a certain ritual that must be observed. Passport and other information was noted when you bought your ticket. This is now rechecked. Your baggage is examined, presumably to guard against material it would be dangerous to permit aboard a plane, and to satisfy special customs regulations. It is weighed, and you are given a free allowance of twenty-five kilograms (about fifty-five pounds), with a high charge for any excess. Sometimes the passenger and everything he is carrying—overcoat, brief case, camera, lady's handbag, etc.—are placed on the scales along with his baggage. This is only done when all, or nearly all, of the seats on the plane are to be occupied, when also there is much excess baggage, and it becomes important to know the total weight of the load. A fat man or two might push the figure too close to the limit allowed by law.

The formalities having been completed at last, my fellow passengers and I walked part way across the wide field and climbed aboard the waiting clipper. It had accommodations for thirty-two persons, but barely a dozen were leaving that morning. There began the noisy spinning of the propeller, the testing of the two engines one after the other, the circling about the field with which everyone who has so much as seen a take-off in the movies is familiar. Then we drove down the runway at swiftly increasing speed and left the ground. It is impossible to tell the moment that this last occurs, so smooth is the violent motion of the soaring plane. Peering down through a tightly closed glass window, you observe that the earth is a little farther away than it was, that is all. But in the next few minutes the change becomes radical. Houses, fields, and trees are pushed far, far back and take on the appearance of a map in low relief. The map may appear to rotate on an axle and tilt a bit as the plane alters its course.

An altitude of from five to eight thousand feet is usual when the weather conditions are perfect, as they were that day. An ardent absorption in the scene possessed me. The checkerboard pattern of the cane fields was expected. Treetops of a forest seen from above as an undulating meadow did not surprise. But I had not stopped to think that the royal palms would keep their unique silhouettes, though reduced by distance to the size of matchsticks, or that symmetrical, densely foliaged trees, on the other hand, such as the mango, would look like sponges emerging from the ground. In the brilliant sunlight, the shadow of our plane could be distinguished, racing across the landscape. The rapidity with which it ate up the stretch from one fenced field to the next gave a true understanding of our speed, which was about 165 miles an hour.

We passed over the rather flat country to the south of Camaguey, and in half an hour had reached the coast with its outlying cays. Beauty in astonishing aspects greeted me. My preconceived notion— if I had one—was that the colors of the water, the sand, and coral reefs would fade to a single neutral tone when viewed from a great height. But the precise opposite was true. They were pulled together, as it were, and intensified. A broad band of shallow water that would have been pale green at sea level was now a narrow strip of a brilliant emerald. The sandy shores were golden. The surface of the cays showed a wondrous mottling of green, purple, and orange, the latter hue predominating. The effect was of semiprecious stones, jade or malachite. Nothing could surpass the loveliness of these islets, the ones that were just emerging from the ocean being more pictorially striking than the older cays already clothed with vegetation. Farther out the water was a pellucid azure, the scarcely perceptible wavelets and white caps causing the illusion of a ripple such as satin has. Depths where no motion at all could be perceived were like the sky on a glorious morning, but the actual sky through which we were rushing had paled to a grayish blue. There were almost no clouds; the often superb massing of these around a plane will be described in connection with later flights.

We sighted Jamaica at its western end, where the mountains were not so high as in the east. Soon we crossed the island at a neck where it was less than twenty miles wide and skirted the southern coast toward Kingston. Jamaica had virtually the physical appearance of Cuba, save in two respects: More houses were seen, because of the denser population; the road system was plainly a much more elaborate one. The first fact does not always lead to the second in the West Indies. Road building has been a virtue of British colonial administration. You look down at macadamized highways twisting and looping, scaling and descending the hills of Jamaica like an armful of ribbon flung there by a titan, making Cuba seem needy in comparison.

I had left Kingston and returned to it many times by ship. The approach from the air thrilled me, especially when old, familiar landmarks surged into view. The harbor has been rated among the half dozen grandest in the Americas, being mentioned in the same breath with Rio and San Francisco. It is seven miles long and about half as wide. The Blue Mountains tower in the near background to an elevation of over 7,000 feet. Extending from east to west like a curving finger is a narrow peninsula called the Palisadoes, low and flat but sufficient as a breakwater, which comes to within a mile of the opposite shore and thus creates the harbor. At the tip of the Palisadoes is what is left of fabled Port Royal, headquarters of the buccaneers and of Sir Henry Morgan in particular, the town to which the looted treasure of the Spaniards was brought, and which at its heyday in the middle 1660's was larger and richer than New York then was. Subsequently they hanged pirates by scores at Gallows Point on the outskirts, and close by there is an islet called Rackham's Cay because the corpse of "Calico Jack" Rackham, the celebrated freebooter, swung there for months as a warning to other marauders.

We swooped over Port Royal and landed at the airport completed three or four years ago midway of the Palisadoes, at the latter's broadest point. Contact with the ground frequently involves heavy bumping of the plane on its tires, but this time the operation was as smooth as the take-off had been. The Jamaican customs, health, and immigration rules are not irksome, but tourists are somewhat more closely quizzed than in Cuba. At the time American citizens had to show passports, the formality of a British visa being waived. The rules have since been liberalized, and proof of nationality is all that is required. I nevertheless counsel visitors to carry passports, if convenient, for the same reasons that I gave when dealing with travel in Cuba.

The currency restrictions are a nuisance in Jamaica, as in most countries ruled by England. You must declare the amount of American money in your possession and are not allowed to take out more than you brought. Traveler's checks are unrestricted, but if you cash a larger amount than you want to spend you will be unable to use your surplus local money to buy dollars, except on the black market. The local currency would be no good to you elsewhere, so you have the choice of purchasing things you do not need or leaving it in a bank against some future visit. This may serve the purposes of Empire trade and the famous British sterling bloc, but it irritates foreigners and does not benefit the colonial peoples. The latter, too, are forbidden to buy dollars unless the control authority approves, with the result that American goods cannot be imported freely to take the place of exorbitantly priced or nonexistent British articles. The tourist should provide himself with checks in small denominations, so that he may cash them prudently to meet current expenses.

Palisadoes Airport is seven miles from Kingston by the road that doubles around the closed end of the harbor. The sandspit itself offers no scenic attractions. The coconut palms that once lined it were blown down by a hurricane in the recent past, and for some reason have not been replaced in any numbers. Mangroves and sea grapes choke the foreshore. An uninteresting thorny scrub binds the thin soil. But there are exquisite views of the shallow, opaline water on the harbor side, and the mountains are a majestic, shifting panorama of peaks wreathed in mist, valleys shading from lavender to dark blue, nearer slopes green to their tops, and sunshine and shadows playing across the whole. How well I knew it all! But I must put myself in the position of the person who is seeing Jamaica with a fresh viewpoint. The name, incidentally, is derived from the Arawak "Xaymaca," which may be freely translated as "Land of Woods and Waters." Modern Jamaicans call their country "The Isle of Springs."

On the mainland you drive along the Rockfort Road and the Windward Road into the city from the east. Ramshackle shops and the dilapidated houses of the poor will be the first encountered and may make a bad impression. But the picture changes rapidly from one thing to the other and then back again. Kingston is not at all like a Spanish-American city. It is to a much greater extent embowered in trees, among which the finer dwellings stand back, and there are ample gardens enclosed sometimes by street-front walls but never hidden away in patios. James Anthony Froude, the historian, remarked in 1887 that there was nothing "specially characteristic of England or the English mind" in the architecture of Kingston, and I agree with him. It is an adapted plantation style, resembling the building done in Charleston and elsewhere in the American South, with deep verandas on the first and second floors, open corridors running from front to rear, and other devices for letting the air circulate and shutting out heat and light. I refer, of course, to the older houses. In the suburbs there has been the usual trend toward bungalows and villas, and lately a rash of modernistic freaks.

Kingston has only one first-class international hotel, the celebrated Myrtle Bank, which has received travelers at the same stand for longer than fifty years, though rebuilt after the earthquake of 1907.

There are also the South Camp Road Hotel, well run, a nice tropical sort of place; and a number of guest houses, some of which are excellent. I planned to stay at Myrtle Bank for a week and then move to a guest house. A similar course is recommended to those visitors who have the time for it. International hotels have undoubted merit, but you will not get to know the life of a country if you confine yourself to them.

Myrtle Bank is one of the most seductive, beautiful hotel sites in the West Indies, adjacent though it be to slums. Located in downtown Kingston, a little removed from the business section, it is a large square directly on the harbor. The main building, which stands back from the street behind shrubbery and a curved driveway, pretends to no imposing appearance. But the verandas are spacious and cool beyond the average; behind there is a great sweep of lawn shaded by palms, extending to the shore, where you find a swimming pool and a private pier. The view across to the Palisadoes is uninterrupted. Twice a day the trade wind blows, rattling the coconut fronds crisply as if they were blades of silver. Mockingbirds warble on the boughs of blossoming shrubs. The charm by daylight is languorous. Soft music and Chinese lanterns turn the lawn into another kind of Elysium when dances are held there at night.

Rates run to about ten dollars a day, American plan. The rooms are comfortably furnished, though not up to the minute. The entire interior of the hotel above the ground floor could stand a little renovation. In my opinion, the cuisine aims too much at making the Englishman and American feel at home, for commonplace items like braised beef with potatoes and lamb with green peas dominate the menu. The best native dishes are sometimes offered; there should be more of them. I do not know how it may be with English tourists, but Americans have often told me that they regard the chance to sample exotic foods as one of the pleasures of travel. The Myrtle Bank bar leaves nothing to be desired. In addition to all the standard concoctions, it serves Jamaica rum punch—a time-honored island drink—to perfection. Here is the traditional recipe:

> One of sour,
> Two of sweet,
> Three of strong,
> Four of weak.

Which, being translated, means:

One measure of lime juice,
Two measures of syrup, or the equivalent in bar sugar,
Three measure of Jamaica rum,
Four measures of water, or the equivalent in ice.

Add a dash of Angostura bitters, if you like. Shake well before serving. Remember, this punch was invented in the days when ice was rarely obtainable in the tropics. It used to be made with water cooled in earthen jars. So in mixing it for yourself, judge the cracked ice carefully or the result will be too weak.

The guest house to which I transferred afforded an example of how to live pleasantly and cheaply in the British West Indies, even in these days of high prices. It was Warden Court, Mr. Harry Fulford proprietor. For a pound ($4) a day, I had a neat single room and three meals. The room was at an upstairs corner of one of those old houses I have mentioned, cooled by the breezes blowing in cross-currents, surrounded by the green of palms and mangoes and the bright blazonry of flowers. The food was simple but good, about equally balanced between native and northern dishes. Jamaican cookery, it may be said, bears a general resemblance to Cuban, while less inventive. Curried goat kid is a *pièce de résistance*.

Sight-seeing, dining out, and night-clubbing in Kingston do not offer much variety. There are a few spots, however, that should on no account be overlooked. The Institute of Jamaica on East Street is a combined national library and museum of great interest. Its collection of reference books on the history of the West Indies is the best in the region, for though smaller than the one in Havana, it clearly surpasses it in organization and in non-Hispanic items. This library is the work of a scholarly enthusiast, the late Frank Cundall, a Londoner who served as its head for forty-six years and handed on his creation to able successors. The museum is rather ordinary.

But if you care anything about sociological trends, go across the street and visit the Junior Institute. The latter, founded less than ten years ago for children, has been supported by the youth of Jamaica with a spontaneity seldom seen. It is half cultural school, half library, and the members enrolled are obligated to study hard. Many more applied than could be admitted, and the present waiting list is long. The artwork produced by the youngsters seems consciously Jamaican; this, stemming from the original eagerness to learn, should probably be ascribed to the nationalist awakening in the island during the past decade. Swung by the same tide, a native theater has been making rapid progress.

A West Indian university, to be located in or near Kingston, has been approved by Great Britain and by the colonies concerned. The task of organizing it was begun in 1947.

The Anglican parish church and the Roman Catholic cathedral are the only ecclesiastical buildings worth attention. Both postdate the earthquake of 1907, the cathedral being new, and the parish church a reconstruction on an ancient site. The city's statues, with the exception of the one to Edward Jordon, a popular leader, are mere expressions of nineteenth-century colonial sentiment. The same Queen Victoria statue, imperceptibly modified if at all, is to be found in almost every center of government in the Empire. Headquarters House, where the legislature meets, is a converted mansion of minor architectural merit. King's House on the outskirts, the governor's residence, makes an agreeable impression in its broad grounds, but it may not be inspected without a permit difficult to obtain.

Port Royal, over which we flew, is worth a side trip, which should be broadened to include a sail around the western end of the harbor. The buccaneers' port of orgies has dwindled to a poverty-stricken village of about eleven hundred inhabitants, mostly fishermen. But an aura of romance still dwells about it. A terrific earthquake in 1692 rent the tip of the peninsula and hurled the better part of the original town into the sea. Hence the myth that the submerged buildings can still be seen in clear weather, and that during storms the waves set the bells of the sunken church to ringing. More credible is the belief that a considerable treasure foundered with the city, and that it would be practicable for divers to cut through the incrustations of coral and recover it. There were later disasters by fire and hurricane, yet Port Royal remained important for longer than two hundred years as the station of England's West India Squadron. Nelson commanded there in 1779. An exterior platform in seventeenth-century Fort Charles is called Nelson's Quarterdeck, because the future victor of Trafalgar was in the habit of pacing it as he watched

for a French fleet that never came. On a wall below is a tablet that
reads:

IN THIS PLACE
DWELT
HORATIO NELSON
YOU WHO TREAD HIS FOOTPRINTS
REMEMBER HIS GLORY

St. Peter's Church, built in 1725, contains a noteworthy organ
loft carved at the time with a palm motive by local craftsmen. The
wall memorials bewail death after death of yellow fever. Port Royal
was once a pesthole for unacclimatized English sailors and soldiers,
but never quite so bad as was Fort Augusta on the aptly named
Mosquito Point diagonally opposite. Tradition has it that entire companies perished at Fort Augusta, and that of one regiment only a
quartermaster and a corporal survived—an exaggeration, no doubt,
reflecting the dread the services had of the place. Fort Augusta, now
in ruins, was a huge works built to accommodate three regiments.
Its magazine, with three hundred barrels of powder, blew up in
1782, and the damage was never repaired. A little down the coast
southwest of Port Royal are the remains of the Apostles' Battery,
where each of the guns was named after one of the twelve who rallied about Christ. This ironic jest in nomenclature was paralleled by
a twelve-gun battery at the Cabaña Fortress, Havana.

Hope Botanical Gardens, five and a half miles inland from the
center of town, is the most beautiful show place of the Kingston area.
Its two hundred acres under cultivation make it a bit smaller than
Soledad, but there can be no comparison between the two gardens.
Hope has been under development much longer and has lost the
semiwild aspect of my Cuban retreat. Instead, it is a closely knit
series of experimental nurseries. Thousands of tropical trees from
all over the world are on display there. The collection of orchids is
exceptionally fine. Attached is a government stock farm. Midget zoos
containing Jamaican birds, reptiles, and small quadrupeds are maintained at Hope and on the grounds of the Institute of Jamaica.

Outside of the hotels, there is only one large public restaurant,
the Esquire, that caters along the lines the ordinary tourist would
demand. Personally I enjoy some of the unpretentious eating places,
where the food is wholly tropical, beginning, say, with *callalu* soup

made from a green that somewhat resembles spinach, salted fish
cooked with the yellow pulp of the akee as an entree, breadfruit and
fried plantains for vegetables, and preserved guavas for dessert. The
night-club possibilities comprise the Colony, the Glass Bucket, and
Springfield in the city, as well as a few roadhouses. I give first place
to the Colony Club because it features Jamaican music, songs, and
dances more consistently than its rivals. The Glass Bucket is older
and better known to tourists. Brand-new and flashy is the Henry
Morgan roadhouse on the Spanish Town Road.

In the season there is excellent horse racing at Knutsford Park on
Halfway Tree Road. The government conducts a sweepstake, but
gambling in any other form is illegal. Good tennis and golf clubs
exist. Swimming may be had at several pools and "beaches," the latter being enclosed areas on the harbor where it is necessary to take
precautions against sharks.

Jamaica, in days gone by England's most profitable and jealously
guarded colony, is no longer what is called a "white man's country."
Instead, it is a state where a preponderantly Negroid population,
collaborating with a small white minority and Hindu and Chinese
elements, is creating a new nation. The process is a current phenomenon throughout the British Empire, but nowhere is it so swift and
intense as in Jamaica. The nationalism of Ceylon, for instance, or of
Burma is not comparable, for there old civilizations are trying to
reassert themselves without regard to members of other races who
happened to be born in the land. Nor is there any similarity with
the self-governing dominions, which are straight offshoots of the
British stock. Jamaica is the outstanding example of the plantation
colony neglected by its owner when it became unremunerative as
an estate, and now suddenly coming of age.

To be at ease in a place, you must comprehend what makes it tick.
This is especially true of Jamaica today, where signs of popular fer-
ment and the antics of certain politicians might cause the tourist to
fear, quite unjustifiably, that it was not a safe country to visit. So
let us take a brief glance at the march of history.

The Lord Protector Cromwell, deciding to challenge Spain in the
Caribbean with what he called his Western Design, sent out an expedition in 1655 under Admiral William Penn, father of the founder
of Pennsylvania, and General Robert Venables. They attacked the

city of Santo Domingo in April, bungled the affair disastrously, and were forced to retire. But they had heard rumors that the near-by island of Jamaica was feebly held by the Spaniards. It had been until a few years previously a private fief of the Columbus family, which had neglected it, and the number of white males there, including soldiers, was estimated at only fifteen hundred. The ranking descendant of the Admiral of the Ocean Sea, by the way, styles himself to this day Duke of Veragua and Marquis of Jamaica.

Penn and Venables entered Kingston Harbor unopposed, marched a force ten miles inland to the old capital, Villa de la Vega, now called Spanish Town, and easily took possession of the island. Thereafter the English held it continuously, though at first all reasonable chances seemed against their being able to do so. The Crown was helped in maintaining the conquest by the buccaneers of English nationality, who moved to Port Royal from Tortuga Island off the coast of Hispaniola, and outstandingly by the genius of Henry Morgan. This Welsh adventurer was a ruthless buccaneer, but his military gifts soon exalted him. He struck telling blows at the Spaniards by sacking Puerto Principe, Porto Bello, and Maracaibo. Finally he performed the notable feat for those times of crossing the Isthmus of Panama at the head of twelve hundred men, routing the enemy in a pitched battle, and seizing the city of Panama, which was already in flames. He returned to Jamaica with enormous plunder.

Spain and England being formally at peace, the court of Madrid was successful in persuading Charles II to summon Morgan to London and try him for high misdemeanors. But the freebooter was coolly acquitted by the king, knighted, and sent back as lieutenant governor of Jamaica. It was Morgan's duty some years later to repress a practice that had served its purpose, and he went about it with zest. Those buccaneers who declined his offer to set them up as landholders were hounded by him and hanged when caught.

Meanwhile, gentlemen and former soldiers had poured into Jamaica and engaged in the planting of sugar cane and other crops. A few Negro slaves had been taken from the Spaniards. Cromwell sent out large numbers of Irish, as well as some English, Scotch, and Welsh royalists, to work on the soil as seven-year bondsmen. Many survivors among these last ended up as planters themselves. Under Charles II, the importation of Negroes from Africa began, and continued for longer than 125 years. In the early eighteenth century the island bought an average of five thousand slaves a year.

The whites established their own form of government, based closely on the systems that had been followed in Virginia and Massachusetts. There was an elected assembly with the power of the purse, and a council appointed by the governor. The latter exercised a first veto and the Crown a final one. A written constitution was finally approved, and under it the planters and merchants ran things to suit themselves. They more than once successfully defied London on minor issues.

In 1694 a French expedition from St.-Domingue, commanded by Jean-Baptiste du Casse, raided Jamaica, fought one severe skirmish ashore, and departed with plunder. Strange to say, this was the only foreign invasion that ever occurred. But there were many serious threats, and in return the Jamaicans shared in several of England's Caribbean forays. Local troops accompanied Admiral Vernon in his assaults on Porto Bello and Cartagena, 1739–41; they went with the Duke of Albemarle and Admiral Pocock to the siege of Havana in 1763. At the outset of the American Revolution, the Jamaican Assembly memorialized the Throne in favor of the thirteen colonies. It has been said by historians that only the isolation of the English sugar islands prevented them, and Jamaica in particular, from throwing in their lot with the Americans. Sympathy turned to fear when France and Spain entered the war, for it was rightly felt that both those countries wanted to annex Jamaica. Bernardo de Gálvez, the Spanish governor of Louisiana, planned the conquest of the island in 1781, after he had driven the English from Florida, and gave up the idea for the sole reason that he could not get Madrid to send reinforcements fast enough to suit him.

The gigantic fleet concentrated by France at Martinique in 1782, under Admiral the Comte de Grasse, had as its first objective the seizing of Jamaica. There were six thousand soldiers with him as a prospective garrison. When Admiral Rodney defeated De Grasse in the Battle of the Saintes, he preserved not Jamaica alone but all the British possessions in the West Indies. Without that victory, England would have been forced to agree to a far more calamitous treaty of peace than the one she signed the following year. A decade afterward the governor of Jamaica intervened in St.-Domingue (now

Haiti) in behalf of the white planters engaged in a death struggle with the slave revolution led by Toussaint l'Ouverture. The troops sent held their ground in various localities for several years, but were at last expelled.

With the coming of the nineteenth century, Jamaica's sugar bonanza started to decline. Factors beyond the control of the planters brought this about. A process for extracting sugar from the European white beetroot was perfected during the Napoleonic Wars. Cane was cultivated in vast new areas in the Orient. The slave trade was abolished by both England and the United States. Then in the 1830's England emancipated the slaves in all her dominions, and in the 1840's adopted free trade. It became impossible to produce sugar on the old profitable scale in such small territorial units as composed the British West Indies. The loss of tariff protection did the most serious harm to a business that had been slipping into a false commercial position anyway. Yet sugar has stayed alive, somehow, as one of Jamaica's chief exports, along with rum, the spice called pimento, which grows nowhere else, and in the comparatively recent past bananas.

The most radical social changes were brought about by emancipation plus the collapse of the great plantations. Many of the influential families sold out for what they could get and moved to England. Others practiced absentee landlordism, which nearly always ends in bankruptcy, the loss of the land to venal managers, or its sale piecemeal. Nothing had been done to help the freed Negroes solve their economic problems, and discontent spread among them. At the same time men of color emerged as political leaders, and some of them who had acquired estates succeeded in winning election to the Assembly. The franchise and officeholding, needless to say, were strictly limited on a property basis.

In 1865, shortly after the close of America's War between the States, there occurred the so-called Morant Bay Rebellion. This started as no more than a riot by ignorant, restless Negroes without a plan and following impromptu leaders. Militia guarding a courthouse where a parochial board was sitting fired injudiciously on the mob, which overran the building and killed eighteen persons, mostly whites. This was avenged by the governor with extreme severity. Nearly 100 Negroes were hanged or shot without trial, 354 put to death after court-martial, 600 sentenced to flogging, and some 1,000 cottages were burned. George William Gordon, a member of the Assembly, a light-colored man who had been agitating for reforms, was accused on slender proof of having instigated the outbreak. He was brought into the district, tried for treason, and hanged. Thereby a martyr was created.

The Jamaican legislature, professing to fear a wave of anarchy that only the armed might of Britain could check, voted itself out of existence and the island became a crown colony governed without the participation of its inhabitants, white, brown, or black. This was distasteful to everyone concerned, except the few rich planters and merchants who had wanted the step taken. The majority of the other colonies followed suit. Froude writes that "the Crown was impatient of the addition to its obligations." He adds that, at a certain moment, to his knowledge, "a decision had been irrevocably taken. The troops were to be withdrawn from the islands, and Jamaica, Trinidad, and the English Antilles were to be masters of their own destiny, either to form into free communities like the Spanish-American republics, or join the United States, or to do what they pleased."

Some historians do not share Froude's categorical certainty on this point. But it is a fact that a clique among the whites openly favored annexation by the United States, whereas the colored people feared such an event because of American race prejudice. If informal negotiations ever took place, Washington rejected the idea. Then public opinion changed in England. Halfway representative government was granted in installments until at last there was a legislature partly appointed by the governor and partly elected, which could initiate nothing, but which voted on the projects of law submitted to it. A general apathy possessed the people, and the British ruled happily.

This state of affairs lasted for about seventy years after the Morant Bay disturbances, a long time for a Caribbean country to be disinterested in politics. It could not go on forever. A generation ready to react against it had grown up. The launching of a self-government and of a labor movement overlapped between 1936 and 1938. The Jamaica Progressive League advocated a party to fight for autonomy, and one took form as the Peoples' National party under the leadership of Norman Washington Manley. There was a wave of strikes by unorganized workmen; Alexander Bustamante, who had had no adequate experience with trade unionism, marshaled fifty thousand of the unskilled into unions that he named after himself and ruled as a boss. Toward the end of the war England gave Jamaica a constitution that provided for universal suffrage without a literacy test, a popular house of representatives, an upper nominated house, and an embryo cabinet. The elections that followed were won by the so-called Labor party, and Bustamante became the equivalent of a prime minister and the most powerful man in the administration next to the governor. Manley continued his work of political education with a view to the future.

In the meantime, the United States had acquired a naval and air base in Jamaica as part of the deal whereby fifty destroyers were exchanged for defense sites on British territory in the New World, from Newfoundland to British Guiana. The Jamaica base was rushed to completion and heavily garrisoned. It is being maintained less elaborately on a peace footing.

Manley and Bustamante offer a salient contrast. The former is a brilliant intellectual and sincere democrat, a Rhodes scholar, the most prominent lawyer in the island, and a king's counsel. The latter is a demagogue, a man whose confused ideas of government will not bear analysis. Both are light-colored. Their respective parties take the political issues with fervor. But nearly all Jamaicans, whether party members or not, have been stirred to a sense of responsibility by the new nationalism. In a country where ten years ago public affairs were scarcely discussed by the ordinary man, every group you encounter on the streets or on country roads is likely to be doing it now, and doing it seriously. Clashes between the factions occur, and there are frequent strikes incomprehensible to an outsider. Tourists, however, need have no fears on their own account. Jamaicans of all classes unite in welcoming them.

CHAPTER **6.**

THE FAIR JAMAICAN
COUNTRYSIDE

KINGSTON is not all of Jamaica to the holiday tripper in the sense that Havana is Cuba. Unless he is addicted to international hotels and prefers to spend his time at Myrtle Bank, he exhausts the possibilities of Kingston in a few days. Perhaps he has read enthusiastic comments by writers on the beauty of the Jamaican countryside, and even if that is not the case the mountains stand there, visible and close, to tempt him. Every travel agency features scenic drives. The tourist center, anyway, for those with a little leisure, is admittedly not Kingston but the north-coast town of Montego Bay, which has superb sea bathing and where a multiplicity of small hotels and guest houses cater to all tastes. There are some lesser resorts, as well as one or two wholly rural hotels, all with a reputation rivaling that of Montego Bay. The Jamaica Tourist Commission has less trouble than its Cuban counterpart in getting visitors to look at the interior.

I found it a very progressive, helpful body, owing to the intelligent interest in his subject and real passion for Jamaica shown by its chairman, Mr. F. H. Robertson, a Britisher who has spent many years on the island. The correct name is the Jamaica Tourist Trade Development Board, just as in Cuba it is the Corporación Nacional del Turismo. Other countries indulge in other variations. To avoid confusion, I shall use the one standard term. "Tourist Commission" is what both residents and strangers commonly say. When in Jamaica, go for information on almost any local subject to the commission's attractive building on Harbour Street a couple of blocks down from Myrtle Bank Hotel.

One of the easiest short trips to make from Kingston is the nine-

83

teen-mile drive by car to Castleton Botanical Gardens, a companion establishment to the one at Hope. It was founded in 1861. Castleton is in a valley some 2,000 feet above sea level, on the banks of a river called the Wag Water. This is a curious example of how Spanish names were corrupted in Jamaica by the English. Originally it was Agua Alta, meaning high water. Agua (water) was twisted into Wag, and Alta (high) into Water. After the first six miles, the drive is over a spectacular road that ascends abruptly yet with smooth grades and turns, and gives a characteristic view of the Jamaican mountains. The volcanic formation is manifest. Precipitous slopes and abysses are jumbled together, creating a fluid, noble picture. Everywhere there is vivid greenery. The lesser peaks are forested to their summits, except where cultivators have laid out fields of yams and taro, often terraced and at angles exceeding forty degrees. Anthony Trollope, writing in 1859, held that the grandeur of the ravines had no parallel anywhere, "either in colour or grouping."

A pleasant thing to do at Castleton is to bathe in the Wag Water, which up here, near its source, flows over huge polished boulders, among which pools have formed with a bottom of pebbles ground so fine that they are like a coarse sand. The authorities charge a derisory fee for dressing rooms in cabins. Fresh from shadowed gorges, the surface of the water is warmed by the direct rays of the sun. You plunge, exult in the cool of the depths, let the current carry you along, and then come to rest on some rock or shoal. The air is loud with the gurgling of the stream, and if you are lucky you will hear the flutelike call of the solitaire, a species related to the thrushes, which has been described as "the sweetest, the most solemn and the most unearthly of all the woodland singing" to be heard in the tropics.

Another good one-day trip is to Bog Walk, farther to the west. This name is meaningless in English, since there is nothing resembling a bog to be found, but instead a beautiful canyon through which the river Cobre has graven its course. The corruption is from the Spanish Boca de Agua (mouth of the water, or water exit). The idea of a "walk" is probably drawn from the road that runs along one bank of the river; part of the way it is cut from the sheer side of the mountain, and at all points the vegetation is exuberant. Bog Walk is at a considerably lower elevation than Castleton, and so is more tropical.

A railroad system traverses the center of Jamaica from Kingston to Montego Bay, 113 miles, with a main branch line to Port Antonio on the northeast coast, 75 miles, and two short spurs. It is not to be recommended for speed, or its cars for comfort. Automobile roads take you over the same territory and to every other part of the island as well. Two important driving routes from Kingston are the one that scales Mount Diablo beyond Bog Walk, crosses the grazing parish of St. Ann, and then follows the north shore to Montego Bay; and the one south of the railroad, which runs to Savanna-la-Mar.

A visit to the original capital, first under the Spanish domination and then under the English for longer than two hundred years, is imperative. The town stands on the alluvial plain thirteen miles east of Kingston and six miles from the sea. Though it is in an extremely run-down condition today, its central square and some of the adjoining streets have colonial architectural relics of interest, and its few monuments are remarkable. The Spaniards called the place Villa de la Vega, dedicating it in due course to Santiago, their patron saint. The English adopted this as St. Jago de la Vega, but in time changed to the homely name of Spanish Town. The Anglican cathedral, on the site of a Catholic chapel of the Red Cross, is the oldest cathedral in the British colonies and still the episcopal see of Jamaica. In its aisles, on its walls, and in its churchyard are memorials in the grand manner. A tablet over an entrance door of the tower tells that the building was "thrown down by ye dreadfull Hurricane" of 1712, but was "by ye Divine Assistance, through ye Piety and at ye expence of ye Parishioners" restored on a more substantial scale.

The finest monument inside the cathedral is by John Bacon, a celebrated eighteenth-century sculptor, erected to the Earl and Countess of Effingham, both of whom lie below the communion table, the Earl having died while serving as governor. But the favorite with the public is the romantic portrait in marble, by Sir John Steell, of the Countess of Elgin, wife of another noble governor. The outdoors tomb of Sir Thomas Modyford, the chief executive who gave Henry Morgan his letters of marque and shared his profits, declares him to have been "the soul and life of all Jamaica who first made it what it now is . . . the best and longest Governour . . . the ablest and most upright judge." And across the way Sir Thomas Lynch, the successor and bitter enemy of both Morgan and Modyford, proclaims from his slab of black marble weighing a ton that he lies "in Peace, at Ease, and Blest. Would you know more, the World will speak ye Rest."

What was the plaza and remains a very Spanish-looking square has the burned ruins of the old King's House on one side, the parliament building now turned to baser uses on another, and on a third the grandiloquent monument to Rodney. The last-mentioned is a marble statue by Bacon, which portrays the admiral in the toga of a Roman emperor, his left hand on a sword hilt and his right outstretched with a baton. There are bas-reliefs on the pedestal. The whole stands within a low-roofed classic temple, which makes it difficult to get a good view of the hero. Near by the walls of crumbling houses show the unmended fissures caused by the earthquake that wrecked Kingston and spread damage through the region in 1907. Parasitic growths are sprouting in the cracks, and in time will split asunder the stoutest masonry. Ragged children and goats play in the thick white dust of the streets. For the rest, heat and torpor brood over the departed glories. That is Spanish Town for you. A brief stay there will suffice.

Mandeville, sixty miles from Kingston, on a plateau averaging 2,000 feet above sea level, is an utterly different locale. Scarcely more than a village with its population under 2,500, it is a place of handsome country homes, some of which have been occupied for generations and some built by English and American *rentiers*, who seem to prefer it to any other part of Jamaica. The surrounding district is rolling, fertile, not the deep tropics in appearance, a land largely planted in grass for stock raising, and ideally suited to the growing of citrus fruit. Mandeville impressed Froude as being "an exact reproduction of a Warwickshire hamlet before the days of railways and brick chimneys," with its green, or common, its parish church, market house, "modest inn" as he calls it, and a shop or two. He was an observer given to carping, but for Mandeville he had nothing but eulogies, inspired maybe by homesickness and a longing to find *something* in the island that recalled familiar scenes. "It was as if a branch of the old tree had been carried over and planted there ages ago, and as if it had taken root and become an exact resemblance of the parent stock."

The town does look rather English, but not so English as all that. The verandas are too deep, the mantling vines too vivid, and the

perfume of jasmine and orange blossoms too languorous to suggest
Warwickshire. The common has been turned into a park with decorative shrubs and pathways. There are two hotels, both attractive,
and a country club with a golf course that extends privileges to tourists without requiring an introduction. Agreeable drives may be had
in all directions, and if you like horseback riding it will be easy to
indulge yourself; the parish breeds excellent mounts as well as cattle.
From certain spots you get the feeling of being on an island within
the larger island, for to the west you look down steep slopes across
an immense savanna to a new range of hills; to the east is the plain
you crossed to reach the plateau; while southward gleams the blue
of the Caribbean Sea.

Beyond the savanna is Malvern at a slightly higher elevation than
Mandeville, a tiny place blessed with a singularly healthy, dry atmosphere. Farther still are rich sugar-cane lowlands. Bluefields, a
fine plantation house in this section, has been converted into a hotel;
it was the headquarters from which the naturalist Philip Henry Gosse
studied the birds of Jamaica a hundred years ago.

On the north coast, Montego Bay claims first attention. It is not a
city, for the population as shown by the last census was only 11,500.
A settlement existed there, however, since early times. The Spaniards
used it as a port for intercourse with Cuba, and under the English
the township grew slowly along the curve of the azure bight. The
near-by beach to the east has always been considered the best in
Jamaica, and decidedly is the most attractive that has yet been developed. At one spot the rocks form a sort of cave where the water
is bewitchingly clear and bracing. This is called Doctor's Cave after
Sir Herbert Barker, a distinguished local surgeon, who loved and
praised it until he, more than anyone else, created Montego Bay as
a boom resort after World War I.

The approach to the town by train is exceptionally picturesque.
The railroad tracks wind through a mountain barrier, and abruptly
the whole sweep of coast becomes visible several hundred feet below. The low-lying Bogue Islands pass in review. Then the train
dips down, runs between sugar-cane fields for a short distance, and
pulls up at its terminus, a station that looks as if it dated from the
year one of railroading. The driving road via Mandeville reaches
the shore west of the Bogue Islands, and it does not furnish the same
startling first view of Montego Bay. The most traveled route is

the broad coastal road that comes in from the east. A small airplane makes the journey daily from Kingston in one hour.

Here there is everything that one could demand in the way of hotel accommodations and amusements. Prices are a bit high in the winter season, sufficiently reduced in summer to make a real difference. The Casa Blanca and its cottages constitute the luxury choice, but there are many other satisfactory hotels, including the Chatham, the Beach View, and a few miles westward the Hotel Tryall, which faces a good secondary beach. The Doctor's Cave Bathing Club admits all visitors to temporary membership for a small fee. Riding, tennis, and golf are to be had, and there is deep-sea fishing, including tarpon, a short distance offshore. Boating aplenty, but first-class yachting is yet to come. Horse racing is held from January to March.

The parish church has little claim to distinction as a building, but it contains a monument about which legends have grown. This is a memorial by Bacon to a Mrs. Palmer, of Rose Hall, a plantation about ten miles distant. The female figure in marble is of a delicate, almost saintlike beauty, a fact that made the godly of the last century shiver; for the Mrs. Palmer they recalled had been monstrously cruel to her slaves and had been suspected of murdering several husbands in succession. She was supposed to have arranged for the monument and left money to defray the cost, in order to whitewash her reputation. Much has been written about her, including a novel, *The White Witch of Rose Hall*, by the late Herbert George de Lisser, a noted Jamaican author. Research has shown that the figure is no portrait, but emblematical, while the Mrs. Palmer honored was of the generation preceding that of the sadistic mistress.

Montego Bay used to be patronized—local people apart—almost entirely by visitors who could stay for a number of weeks or for the season. Many such continue to favor it. With improved means of transportation, however, there is no difficulty in getting there for week ends, or even for an overnight stop. Increasingly it is the fashionable thing to flit up from Kingston as often as possible, an argument that appeals to the moneyed tourist. Before the war, cruise ships had made experimental calls at the bay, and there appears to be ample reason for some of the lines to start doing this regularly. Pan American Airways has lately made it a point of call.

When the visitor has had his fill of Montego Bay, he almost always doubles on his tracks. It does not occur to him to explore the possibilities of the thirty-mile stretch of coast westward to the tip of the island. The district in that direction is the parish of Hanover. Precisely because it has never been tapped by the railroad, and because in so many ways Montego Bay has been accepted as a travel terminus, Hanover has retained an archaic charm It is psychologically a good twenty-five years behind the rest of Jamaica. Along with this its climate is delicious and its scenery, both rural and marine, is of great beauty. I have now thoroughly explored Hanover, which I had not had a chance to do before, and I regard it as one of the prime discoveries of my trip.

The parish seat is Lucea, and the drive there from Montego Bay skirts the sea the whole way. You come to one inlet after another with a narrow entrance leading to an approximately circular bay, the margins cultivated or wooded, but with scarcely a house on them. It seems incredible that these wonderful little havens should not be utilized as ports; some of them have been in the days of sail, and with a little dredging they could be made serviceable for modern craft. That they are more lovely as they are is not to be denied. Anyone who has dreamed of a South Sea Islands paradise can find one here within a few hours by plane from New York or New Orleans.

Until a few years ago the coast was bordered uninterruptedly by coconut palms leaning into the trade wind, and at intervals there were extensive coconut plantations. A disease has killed the palms over part of the area, but it will pass like other tropical scourges and a new growth rise swiftly. Other trees on roadside and foothills provide an undiminished pageant: scarlet poincianas, lignum vitae with emerald-green foliage and sky-blue flowers, bamboos like stands of giant plumes.

The town of Lucea is on one side of a bay larger than those passed, but of the same general character. It was once a flourishing little sugar port. Banana boats and some coastwise shipping still come there. Behind the water front the site is hilly, and from some houses a magnificent view is had of the Caribbean Sea on one side and the harbor on the other. The point overlooking the channel has a fort that never accomplished anything in history, and doubtless for that reason stands unharmed as an example of the works on which eighteenth-century colonists depended for protection. It is a corner of Morro Castle in miniature. Wide open to the sky, it would be a sitting duck for airplanes, while the sea-washed escarpments that mocked the pirates could be blown to rubble by a single high-explosive shell. There is pathos in the scene that makes Fort Charlotte, the barracks, and the wide parade ground, all turned now to peaceful uses, a park touched by the glamour of the past and the romance of isolation.

No hotel of any kind exists in Lucea, a need that it will be profitable for someone to fill. But the best opportunity of all, Negril Bay, is waiting untouched at the extreme western end of Jamaica. I knew about its historical associations, but I had not been there. Robertson of the Tourist Commission told me that he thought it potentially the finest beach in the West Indies, and refused to back down when I mentioned Varadero, Cuba. I decided to go and see for myself, and as it turned out, friends in Hanover arranged a picnic for me at Negril.

The beach is five and a half miles of clean white sand fringed solidly by coconut trees, the blight having not reached this district. The long indentation of the bay is open to the surf, and all that is required to make it a perfect swimming spot is the erection of bath houses. It could be more than that. It could be a permanent resort on the scale of Varadero, with hotels and amusement clubs. But before that can even be thought of, transportation to Negril will have to be improved. The need is for twenty-five miles of modern automobile highway connecting the beach with the main roads of both the north and south coasts, the draining of a morass situated behind the beach, and the building of an air landing strip on the reclaimed land.

Negril Bay has had its share of excitement in days of uproar. Here "Calico Jack" Rackham was seized, defending his barque to the last with the doughty assistance of Anne Bonney and Mary Read, best known of female pirates. Here late in 1814 a British fleet of fifty warships and transports carrying the army of Sir Edward Pakenham assembled secretly for the invasion of the United States from the south. The blow was launched a few weeks later, and it met with utter defeat at the Battle of New Orleans. Negril needs only a promoter to become now, by contrast, a celebrated name in the world of pleasure seeking.

Returning to Montego Bay and traveling east, you find a consistently pleasing shore. St. Ann's Bay is the Santa Gloria of the Spaniards, where Columbus was wrecked on his fourth voyage and remained for a year. Near Ocho Rios are falls with bathing pools, a gorge noted for its extraordinary growth of ferns large and small, and a superb plantation-house type of hotel, the Shaw Park.

Port Antonio has had a curious record. During the height of the banana boom in Jamaica, 1905 to 1925, this town was the tourist capital, while Montego Bay was a poor second. The shipping company built and ran a fine hotel on the peninsula that forms the harbor. Subsidiary amusement places sprang up, and visitors trooped to the town. But with the decline of bananas in that part of the island as a result of soil exhaustion and blights, the port and the hotel were neglected and the latter finally closed down. It seems ridiculous that this resort should virtually have been abandoned by the tourist trade. The harbor has been praised by many writers as being very lovely. Seven miles away is the Blue Hole, or Blue Lagoon, an inlet of the sea with an entrance so narrow that from some angles it cannot be perceived. The round cove, its shores richly clothed with palms, breadfruit, and other tropical trees, is of a blue so intense that it appears magical. It is, of course, reputed to be bottomless. The narrow encircling beach is an ideal setting for picnics.

There are two hot springs in Jamaica, one at the east end near a town called Bath, and the other at Milk River in the south center. The baths at both places are primitive, but the more fascinating for that. They are due to be modernized into spas where, I suppose, we shall no longer be able to see the steaming water spurt from fissures linked directly with the heart of a buried volcano; or, as at Bath, to loll in a stone pool crowded close by vegetation so lush, because of the humid heat, that it suggests prehistoric plants in a museum piece. All this stands to be regulated with hygienic cells and metered taps.

For persons of the adventurous sort two expeditions are possible: the first to the country of the semi-independent Maroons, and the second to the summit of Blue Mountain Peak. Advance arrangements have to be made with the Maroon chief, who bears the courtesy title of colonel, and the material aspects of the trip are fairly arduous. The Peak is a long but not difficult effort of mountain climbing on muleback.

As in all the other islands of the Greater Antilles, the Spaniards destroyed the Arawak people by plain butchery or by forcing them into a servitude they could not survive. But a few of these gentle Indians escaped into the woods of Jamaica, where they were joined by runaway Negro slaves. At the time of the English conquest a considerable number of the blacks owned by the Spaniards fled en masse, not caring to exchange one kind of bondage for another. The fugitives in the interior became an important factor. They had been called *cimarrones* (wild men) in the Spanish, hence the corruption Maroons. The Arawak blood was pretty well swamped by interbreeding with the much more numerous Negroes, but Indian physical characteristics are to be noted even today among these people.

The English had clashes with them from the beginning and found it prudent to win over their leader, Juan de Bolas, by making him colonel of a free black regiment. From then on the Maroons regarded their holdings as a protectorate rather than a possession of the invaders. Sometimes they were content to be allies, and sometimes they took the field against the whites. Two or three "wars" with the Maroons occurred, and amazing to say, the advantage rested with the wild men, in that the English found it too costly to extirpate them and preferred to make treaties recognizing their right to manage their own affairs. Five separate areas were recognized as self-governing. In 1795 there was a final flare-up when one of the Maroon townships, located in an inaccessible mountain terrain, rebelled against the government. Eight officers, including a colonel, and thirty redcoats were killed in ambuscades before the Maroons were beaten, and then they surrendered only in fear of one hundred Cuban bloodhounds that had been imported to track them down. Most of their land was annexed to the near-by township of Accompong, which had not joined the revolt, and the rest confiscated. The remaining three were small, isolated settlements.

Accompong is the center of interest, about which myths are told, but which few outsiders have the hardihood to visit. It lies on the edge of what is called the Cockpit Country, one of the strangest limestone formations in the Americas. Fifty years ago this was described as follows in a report to the Institute of Jamaica:

"Tall cliffs and broken rocks are honeycombed with openings and pit-marks, presenting a rough, jagged surface which is sometimes almost impassable. The Cockpits . . . comprise an area some ten by fifteen miles in extent, and for the greater part one vast labyrinth of glades among rough cliffs, with here and there patches of smoother ground, and at other places, coming one after the other, a general collection of impassable sink-holes."

Only the Maroons know the trails through this wilderness. They hunt wild hogs and shoot pigeons there. They utilize scattered pockets of earth for the cultivation of bananas and vegetables. Their town, however, is surrounded by several hundred acres of fertile soil from which they derive a good living as farmers. The place looks like any other Negro village. The fact remains that the "colonel" who comes forward to greet you is a magistrate with special powers, and on occasions he and the governor of Jamaica exchange traditional courtesies.

The Maroons used to have a patois of their own, which Bryan Edwards calls "a barbarous dissonance of African dialects with a mixture of Spanish and broken English." In conversation with whites, their speech is undistinguishable now from that of other backwoods Jamaicans, though they claim to remember an "old language" about which they are secretive.

The ascent of Blue Mountain Peak (7,388 feet) involves a thirty-mile journey from Kingston. A main road enables you to reach the hill village of Mavis Bank, seventeen miles distant, by automobile. At this point mounts and pack animals can be hired. Sturdy walkers have often completed the climb on foot. On clear days Cuba is visible from the summit, and otherwise the view is magnificent.

It is my unprejudiced opinion that, apart from the city of Havana, Jamaica has greater existing attractions to offer the majority of tourists and is susceptible of a broader development than any other place in the West Indies. Scenery is not the decisive factor. All the islands, and the Guianas too, are beautiful. Though the Jamaica mountains are grand beyond the average in the tropics, they are equaled in eastern Cuba, Haiti, and the little island of Dominica, of which more anon. The beaches of the north coast have several worthy rivals. But the following points swing the balance in Jamaica's favor:

It is the largest of the English-speaking units, with the exception of the hinterland of British Guiana, which is still clothed by the primeval forest. Americans and Britishers will constitute, in any predictable future, the mass of pleasure seekers in the Caribbean. Not many of them will have a ready command of Spanish or French, and except for the briefest of stays they are going to give the preference to resorts where their own language will get them around.

Jamaica's size means varied resources as against those of its rivals among the Britannic islands. It means comparative sophistication, because of numerous foreign contacts and a more complicated development of native culture. The choice of locales, hotels, and sports must inevitably be wider.

Jamaica is tropical, but not so deep in the tropics as to scare off those who are timid about equatorial heat. Its mountains are high, and at different levels you can find almost every sort of climate. Some countries in the region are less fortunate in these respects.

Finally, Jamaica is closer to the United States than any big island except Cuba. This will make no difference to passengers with unlimited time and money at their disposal, but it will appeal to the many who want to finance a trip on an economical basis. Even if a long stay is planned, saving on the fare will count.

I foresee rosy prospects for the Isle of Springs in Caribbean air and surface travel during the years to come.

Jamaica has two dependencies: the Cayman Islands about midway of the distance to the Isle of Pines, and the Turks and Caicos Islands at the eastern end of the Bahamas. The former group consists of Grand Cayman, Cayman Brac, and Little Cayman, with a total area of 104 square miles and a population of about 6,500. There is no way of getting there except on a motor boat that runs fortnightly from Kingston. The casual traveler never goes, which is a pity, for life is lived in Arcadian fashion on these singularly healthy, low-lying islets with magnificent beaches. No hotels exist, of course, but it is possible to board cheaply in private houses. The people are expert boatbuilders and fishermen; their specialty is the great green Carribbean turtle, which they sell to the world through Kingston and Tampa. They also catch the hawksbill turtle for shell. A minimum of farming is done to supply local needs. One of the chief sources of revenue is the sale of postage stamps to collectors, for although a dependency, the Cayman Islands have their own issue. The annual amount realized has been known to exceed that of import duties.

I shall reserve comment on the Turks and Caicos Islands for my chapter on the Bahamas.

CHAPTER 7

PUERTO RICO:
EXOTIC STEPCHILD

THERE is no direct plane service between Jamaica and Puerto Rico, and as I had decided to visit the latter country next, the best plan was to return to the Pan American Airways junction at Camaguey. I caught a northbound clipper at the Palisadoes Airport shortly after midday and flew back over the short course of a few weeks earlier. Again the weather was perfect, and I rejoiced in the impressions of sea and sky, coral islets and woodlands already described. There was a short wait at Camaguey. Then I transferred to a plane bound for San Juan by way of Port-au-Prince. The afternoon had clouded over, and in a short time I was experiencing some new sensations.

We flew at a greater elevation than had been the case before, for the mountains of eastern Cuba are high. The earth assumed a more contracted pattern of fields that looked like the squares on a checkerboard, rivers that were metallic threads, towns all of a piece as they are on a map, and alternating peaks and valleys reduced to the proportions of a rock garden viewed from a housetop. Broken clouds swirled past, long streamers of mist or shapeless masses that resembled puffs of fog. The plane began to buck, dropping an indeterminable number of feet and recovering its old level with a jerk. This is what the layman knows as "getting into air pockets." But if you ask one of the officers aboard, he will assure you that there is no such thing as an air pocket. The real explanation is that when the atmosphere is disturbed it moves in waves similar to the waves of the ocean, and as a result the plane is tossed more or less roughly, according to the force of the commotion. It is not in itself dangerous, and ordinarily it is not even disagreeable. But it can be alarming to the green passenger.

By cutting a beeline through the center of Oriente province, we passed directly over Guantánamo, the United States naval base. The harbor, masked by Nature, strongly fortified, and at the time filled with warcraft, was impressive from the air. We were past it in a flash and flying over that semienclosed reach of the Caribbean which has been called the Jamaican Sea. This is bounded by the coast of Cuba's broad eastern end, Haiti's two outstretched peninsulas, and the north coast of Jamaica. Its northerly outlet, the famed Windward Passage beween Cape Maisi, Cuba, and the Mole St. Nicolas, Haiti, is quite narrow; the one between Cape Dammarie, Haiti, and Morant Point, Jamaica, is broader but spotted midway by little Navasa Island, which the United States controls; and the one between North Negril Point, Jamaica, and Cape Cruz, Cuba, is wide open. A sea within a sea it nevertheless is, just as the Tyrrhenian Sea and the Ionian Sea are given that status in the Mediterranean.

The course lay along the shore of the southern peninsula of Haiti. Now we were flying rather low and the air was very bumpy. I caught on to the fact that whenever we pierced a torn cloud the plane was sure to undulate. The vapor could not affect our powerful machine, of course, but the same unseen agency that had blown the cloud apart caused us to dip and rise on its waves. The overcast sky of that afternoon and the ensuing short, murky twilight made the first view of Haiti unattractive. We grounded smoothly at Bowen Field, Port-au-Prince, after dark, and there the few passengers got out with the exception of one man and myself. We were asked by the second officer and the hostess to join them in the two tail seats for the take-off. When a plane had so light a load, they explained, it was well to do that for ballasting. The hostess added with a smile that this was only the second time she had known it to be necessary. It wasn't that travel was falling off, but our plane was an extra making a special flight no farther than San Juan.

Night travel by air, especially on a pitch-dark night such as this one was and over country known to be rugged and wild, is something that gives the beginner a curious feeling of detachment. Much more than in daylight, you are conscious of having entrusted yourself to a supernormal force, the machine. You might as well be inside a rocket bound for the moon, as far as having any control over your own fate is concerned until the end of the journey. The first travelers who ventured on a boat that sailed out of sight of land must have had the same feeling, though keyed to a slower tempo.

I peered down into the void and occasionally saw the glint of lights in some village or isolated house. Haiti is densely populated and the Dominican Republic beyond is by no means a desert, but electricity is plainly not used much in the interior. I lost count of time and thought I was still over Hispaniola when I next looked down. To my astonishment, I saw not merely a small town blazing with lamps but rows of lights stretching in all directions, connecting one settlement with another and radiating into the hills. The hostess set me straight. We were flying along the coast of Puerto Rico. It was a meaningful approach to the problem land of the West Indies, on which the United States has lavished modern improvements without being able to cure its most serious ills.

We landed at about ten P.M. The airport had a tranquil appearance, which the arrival of two passengers did nothing to disturb. What a deceptive state that proved to be! The San Juan field is one of the most crowded bottlenecks of air traffic in the hemisphere, as was to be brought home to me on several occasions. I went that night to a near-by expensive, pretentious hotel standing in attractive grounds and with an outlook on the ocean. But a noisy orchestra held forth there for merrymakers until the small hours of the morning, and the well of the building carried the sounds to every floor. My unscreened room swarmed with mosquitoes, and irrationally the bed was not protected by netting. The next day I moved to the Spanish-style Hotel Palace in the center of town.

This is as good a point as any for a digression on the subject of mosquitoes. Since the discovery in India by Surgeon Major Ross of the British Army, in 1897, that a variety of anopheles transmitted malaria, and above all since the stegomyia was found guilty of conveying yellow fever by Drs. Reed, Carroll, Agramonte, and Lazear of the United States occupational forces in Havana, in 1901, mosquito control has been practiced throughout the American tropics. Yellow fever has been eliminated and malaria greatly reduced, because of concentration upon the breeding places of their insect carriers. But there are many other species of mosquitoes, and only in localities where the most intensive campaign is waged are all of them destroyed. The harmless kinds are none the less annoying stingers, and it is a perfectionist's dream to suppose that these will ever be driven from all pleasure resorts, or even from the majority of them. The communities lack the necessary funds, or the authorities are slack. One way or the other, human frailty is going to fall short of the ideal.

Now, in the old days, every bed in a well-to-do home or a hotel was provided as a matter of course with mosquito netting, which hung from a canopy of various designs, was rolled up or thrown over the back of the bedstead during the daytime, and tucked in around the edges of the mattress at night. In Dixie it was called a "mosquito bar," a corruption of the Creole word *baire*. It completely served its purpose. In every West Indian country it remains in general use. Some of the swank hotels, however, have discarded it, apparently on the theory that it gives the rooms an old-fashioned air obnoxious to the ultramodern traveler. Where there are mosquitoproof screens in the windows, I have no objection. But if these are lacking, I regard it as downright stupid not to furnish netting, and I shall not have a good word to say for any hotel where I found that condition prevailing.

The harbor of San Juan is a smaller edition of the one at Kingston, with the location of the city reversed. There is a similar narrow peninsula acting as breakwater, but at San Juan it is rocky, has an average elevation of fifty-seven feet, and terminates in a bluff. On the latter the Spaniards built a morro castle, behind which the ancient town huddled, its streets picturesquely laid out on the slopes. There has never been anything larger than a village on the mainland side of the harbor. But San Juan has spread down the whole length of the peninsula, absorbing the suburb of Santurce and establishing contact with Río Piedras. The name given by Columbus to the island when he discovered it on his second voyage was San Juan Batista, while Ponce de León, who colonized it, called the city then founded Puerto Rico (Rich Port). Through the years these names were inexplicably shuffled, the island becoming Puerto Rico and the city San Juan.

Of all Spanish colonies in the New World, this one probably had the least eventful history. It also had minimum trouble over African slavery. Farmers from the home country were attracted to the fertile, peaceful island, and a surprisingly large number of them cultivated their own land. The bigger planters did import Negroes, particularly when sugar became the major crop, but the racial balance was not tip-tilted. Puerto Rico today is easily the "whitest" of the West Indian islands.

The French corsairs of the early sixteenth century pillaged and burned several coastal towns, but failed in an attempt to seize the colony. They never attacked San Juan. Sir Francis Drake and Sir John Hawkins did so in 1595 and were driven off with heavy losses. Enraged, the English returned three years later under George Clifford, Earl of Cumberland. They landed at the head of the peninsula, stormed their way into San Juan, and held it for five months. The Dutch under Bowdoin Hendricks seized the city in 1625, but were almost immediately forced to abandon it and flee the island. Subsequent forays by the French and English were widely spaced, and in each instance were repulsed.

The great revolutionary movement under Simón Bolívar and others that freed the continental colonies of Spain had but faint repercussions in the little island of Puerto Rico. As was the case with Cuba, physical isolation postponed the issue. The one really serious attempt at armed revolt occurred at the little town of Lares in 1868, seemingly encouraged by plans for the Ten Years' War, which was about to start in Cuba. It was suppressed mercilessly. But the Spaniards tried to win over the people by giving them representation in the Cortes in Madrid, and afterward by offering a limited form of autonomy. The latter was on the point of going into effect when the Spanish-American War broke out. The morro at San Juan was bombarded uselessly by Admiral Sampson. General Nelson A. Miles landed a small expedition on the south coast, and at the end of two weeks the island surrendered. By the terms of the peace treaty in 1899 it was ceded to the United States. The present regime is the one under which Puerto Rican nationalism has reached its fullest development. But before we go into that, let us take a look at the country.

San Juan is no Havana on the score of the beauty and splendor of its monuments. For its size, however, it has some interesting buildings. La Fortaleza, now used as the governor's residence, was the first fort to be erected, 1533 to 1540. The placing of it well down the harbor curve of the tip of the peninsula aroused the scorn of Gonzalo Fernandez de Oviedo, the early historian, who was also somewhat of a military engineer. He declared that "if it had been constructed by blind men it could not have been located in a worse spot," since it could be enveloped by troops landed on the Atlantic side. Odd to relate, his advice was followed promptly in that age of procrastination, and the Morro was started.

The entrance tower and dome of La Fortaleza strike a decidedly Moorish architectural note, which is repeated in several other exterior details. The spacious rooms, remodeled after the original role of a fort was abandoned, are luxurious in design and decoration. Mahogany and other native woods employed for the stairway, doors, and paneling have a velvety gleam due to age and incessant polishing. The gardens are charming, and the terrace facing the sea is assuredly one of the loveliest spots in the West Indies where official entertaining is done. The roster of those who have ruled from La Fortaleza contains the name of many a Spanish grandee, for though the charge was relatively unimportant in the imperial scheme it was coveted for its elegance and its lordly leisure.

A short distance away, at a higher elevation, is Casa Blanca, a palatial mansion built for Juan Ponce de León in 1523. He had died meanwhile from wounds received in Florida, but his descendants occupied the house for close on 250 years. The Spanish authorities then requisitioned it as a public building, and after the American conquest it was made the residence of the commanding officer of United States troops in Puerto Rico. The generals and colonels who have fallen heir to it have been lucky men.

The foundations of the cathedral date from the same period as La Fortaleza and Casa Blanca. A succession of structures was ruined by hurricanes, earthquakes, and fires, and the final rebuilding was done in the early days of the nineteenth century. A rather ordinary church in the Spanish Renaissance manner, it is visited by tourists chiefly for the sake of Ponce de León's tomb with its epitaph attesting that he "achieved great name by his deeds." The near-by church of San José, founded in 1523, claims to be the oldest church in the Americas that has been in continuous use.

Two castles guarded San Juan in the old days: the Morro on the rocky headland at the harbor mouth, dating from the sixteenth century, and San Cristóbal, built a hundred years later at the eastern or land end to prevent a repetition of the coup by which the English privateer Clifford had taken the city. These elaborate fortresses resemble the morros of Havana and Santiago, Cuba, and according to the standards of their day they were impregnable. An interesting feature was the system of tunnels (now closed) that radiated under the city and connected the Morro, San Cristóbal, La Fortaleza, and some minor strong points.

Modern buildings of importance are all located in the newer city on the neck of land toward Santurce. The Casa de España is one of the handsomest Spanish club buildings in the Caribbean region; smaller than its Cuban counterparts, it is the equal of the best of them in other respects. The Puerto Rico Casino, the Insular Library, and the School of Tropical Medicine should be mentioned. Predominant, the capitol rears its Renaissance silhouette, not outrageously large like the structure in Havana, planned as a gem of shining white marble. But although started in 1925 it is far from being completed, and you pick your way through rubble to reach some of the public chambers. This is typical of Puerto Rico, where the tendency is to embark on reckless expenditures difficult to meet from the national revenue.

Wealth, culture, and power exist in San Juan side by side with the most dire poverty. Limited geographically, it is an overcrowded city. The sugar-cane planters, who own a disproportionate amount of the island's arable land and who are themselves controlled in the main by American corporations, have their headquarters here. There is more commercial activity of all sorts than one would look for in the metropolis of a country a good deal smaller than the state of Connecticut. The housing grades down from rich homes and well-appointed apartment blocks to back-street tenements gorged with humanity, and finally to the squatters' slums ironically called La Perla below the grounds of the Morro and the still worse jumble of shacks on stilts in the mud of Puerta de Tierra on the harbor. The desperately poor can get by on little or nothing for shelter and clothes. But the prices of food, including native products, are extremely high; the slum dwellers hover on the border line of starvation, even though they have benefited by relief measures ever since the early 1930's.

What does it mean? Just this: Puerto Rico is notoriously overpopulated, and its economic system is unsound. The first census held under American rule showed that there were 953,243 inhabitants in 1899. Recognizing that the land could barely feed that many, Congress wisely passed an act limiting corporations or individuals to five hundred acres. But enforcement of this provision was evaded until the Popular party, headed by Luis Muñoz Marín, came to power seven years ago and made a serious issue of it. Meanwhile, the census of 1940 revealed the almost incredible rise of population to 1,869,255, or double the figure of forty years before. It is estimated that there are now well over 2,000,000 inhabitants. The breaking up of estates into small farms has helped. But if sugar were abandoned and every acre were planted to food crops, it is doubtful whether enough could be grown to satisfy the needs of all. One effect certainly would be to reduce Puerto Rico to a subsistence-farming basis with little or no purchasing power for foreign goods.

A community of the kind should be free to import necessities from the cheapest markets. The United States from the beginning has made this impossible by applying the same tariffs as on the mainland and by including Puerto Rico in the framework of the Coastwise Shipping Act. The latter prevents American goods from being carried to the island in foreign bottoms. It adds high American freight rates to the original cost of imports, and in practice it has allowed one or two steamship lines to enjoy a monopoly and to charge exorbitant rates. As a result, Puerto Rico to a very considerable extent eats out of cans from New York and New Orleans and pays more for the stuff than mainlanders do. Order soup, hash, and vegetables on the side in an ordinary San Juan restaurant, and five chances to one you'll be served standard American tinned brands. Worse still, in the tropics where fruit ought to be plentiful, ask for orange juice with your breakfast, and you're likely to see the waiter pry open a can from California and pour the contents over a piece of ice in a glass. There just aren't enough Puerto Rican foodstuffs to go around.

The United States government has been generous to the island in some respects. For example, the local rum is not only admitted to free competition with the mainland's distilled liquors, but the excise tax collected is turned back in full. During the recent war, when the distilling of grain was suspended, an immense demand for rum sprang up and the insular government enjoyed a revenue such as it had never dreamed of. The American policy is in marked contrast to that of England. The latter heavily taxes rum from her West Indian colonies.

In the depression years Puerto Rico benefited by so many WPA projects that it was jestingly said that the whole population managed to get on the pay roll. The overstatement bears testimony to the widespread nature of the help given. Then, with the coming of war, the United States embarked on defense works of such magnitude in the island that it was equivalent to the launching of large-scale industries. The surface prosperity that one notes in San Juan today is due to these activities, plus the boom in rum. Unhappily, they were temporary fountains that have stopped spouting, and the luxuriance to which they gave birth is due to dry up.

The optimistic Yankee thought that financial considerations, business and social contacts, and especially the new regime in the schools would induce the Puerto Rican people without much trouble to become Americanized. This proved by no means to be a fact. Ever since the annexation, they have clung to their own customs and to the Spanish language. English has been taught to all children, but in the majority of cases they discard it the moment they leave the classroom. Those who do use English make no secret of their preference for Spanish; they are bilingual for reasons of interest, that is all.

At first it was taken for granted that American sovereignty would be permanent. The party that had been for independence from Spain reorganized with the object of winning a greater degree of self-government under the Stars and Stripes. Later, several factions crystallized, including a Socialist party. The most rosy hope was to become a full-fledged state of the Union someday. But Washington always was cool to that idea, withholding the territorial status that would normally have preceded statehood, and refusing even to grant collective American citizenship to the Puerto Ricans until 1917. That year, limited home rule along colonial lines was also conferred, with an elected legislature and an appointed governor. The island has never been called a colony; in effect, that is what it is. The younger generation intensely resented the condition. As early as 1922 Pedro Albizu Campos, an extremist with fascist tendencies, founded the Nationalist party, which demanded independence. From talk the Nationalists passed to violence in the 1930's. The American chief of the Insular Police was assassinated, and an attempt was made on the life of a governor. Albizu was tried for treasonable conspiracy, and he and other leaders were imprisoned. The movement, which had commanded only limited support, died down.

Now arose the star of Luis Muñoz Marín, a natural chief and the one man who has succeeded in welding majority opinion in his country. He was the son of Luis Muñoz Rivera, a famous liberal and autonomist under the Spaniards and early in the American regime. He received his education in New York and was known first as a poet. In 1938 he broke with the survivors of his father's following, who had grown ultraconservative, and formed the Popular party. The professionals gave this no chance of immediate success, but Muñoz personally carried his views to the remotest corners of the island in a long campaign, and in 1940 he won a majority of one in the Senate and obtained an even break with the opposition in the House of Representatives. He was elected president of the Senate, and ever since has been the most powerful figure in Puerto Rico. His Popular party made an almost clean sweep of both houses in 1944.

Muñoz is a sincere nationalist. An advocate of independence, he is realistic about it, knows that Puerto Rico could not at present stand upon its own feet economically, and wants a gradual loosening of the ties similar to the procedure followed by the United States with the Philippines, but with a much longer period during which island products would be admitted to the American market duty-free. He is a reformer with a social program too long and complicated to be detailed here. It stresses education, public works, and, above all, the distribution among small farmers of excess land held by the sugar-cane and other corporate interests. Though no socialist, Muñoz is by temperament unfriendly to the claims of capital as against those of labor. He is a New Dealer, with variations, Caribbean style.

Largely through his influence in Washington, it is said, Rexford Guy Tugwell, one of the earliest and most uncompromising of the Roosevelt New Dealers, was appointed governor of Puerto Rico. The two worked closely together, and of course both incurred the hostility of the moneyed class and of big business generally. When the time came for Tugwell to retire, Muñoz could probably have become governor himself. Instead, he obtained the designation of Jesús T. Piñero, one of his original lieutenants in the launching of the Popular party, as the first native-born chief executive. This was in 1946. The following year the U. S. Congress enacted a law giving Puerto Rico the right to choose its own governor, beginning with the elections of 1948.

To my mind it is indisputable that the policies of Muñoz have benefited the little fellow, particularly the *jíbaro*, or peasant, who for centuries has been making a bare living from the land while owning almost none of it. Co-operative agrarian plans, which have been extended even into the monopolistic sugar industry, have given new hope to that type of citizen. But until the problem of overcrowding is solved, by emigration or in some other manner, I cannot see how the standard of living can be raised to the proper level for all concerned.

It is only fair to add that his enemies charge Muñoz with extravagance and dictatorial methods. They assert, convincingly enough, that if his course is not modified it will ruin the country financially. Celestino Iriarte, president of the Unión Republicana and one of the few opposition members of the legislature, pointed out to me that the budget, which in the comparatively recent past had been $16,-000,000, was now around $100,000,000. He denied that any of the new schools promised had been built. He said that government funds to the tune of many millions had been used without an accounting to ensure the re-election of the Populares in 1944. When I suggested that he must mean this in the sense that Roosevelt was accused of buying his first re-election by huge disbursements for WPA projects, I was told that it had been more serious than that in Puerto Rico, where agents had gone about the land placing cash in the hands of jíbaros and laborers with the statement that it was a personal gift from Muñoz.

I asked Iriarte whether he was not at least gratified that Piñero, a native, had been made governor. "Well, he is better than the good Tugwell!" he replied, laughing sarcastically. "We call him Don Piña —he-he—remember, in the war there was a little grenade known as a pineapple! He, too, may cause an explosion."

All of which goes to show that Puerto Rico has the same political foibles as its cousins in the region. Washington has indicated that it is willing to hold a plebiscite and give its stepchild independence if the voters so decide. Should that occur Puerto Rico cannot count, any more than Cuba and other Caribbean countries, on establishing a stable form of self-government without an intermediary period of bitter factional struggle.

The Condado Hotel, which faces the ocean in the Santurce section, is one of the older first-class tourist hostelries in the West Indies.

It is beautifully landscaped and offers many forms of outdoor entertainment. The newer Hotel Normandie stands not far distant. These, with the Palace in the old town, constitute the list of San Juan's hotels, except for a few places of the second order. The Escambrón Beach Club, however, can take care of a few guests. Primarily it is an amusement center with a casino, a restaurant and bar, and an excellent dance hall. Its swimming pool is a twelve-acre cove with a sandy beach, protected from sharks and the even more dangerous barracudas by an iron screen. At least two additional hotels are badly needed. The Puerto Rico Development Company, a government-backed organization, is building one at a cost of about $3,000,-000 and has signed a contract for its management with Conrad Hilton of the Mayflower in Washington, D. C., and other famous caravansaries.

Río Piedras, a few miles southeast of the capital, is best known as the location of the University of Puerto Rico. A pretty little town founded in 1714 under the name of El Roble (The Oak) to serve an agricultural district, it has grown steadily since the university was placed there in 1903. It may be the youngest of Latin-American institutions of learning, but it is among the most interesting. It has an enrollment of some five thousand students of both sexes, and the scope of its curriculum is extremely wide. It aspires laudably to be the chief meeting ground of Hispanic and Anglo-Saxon culture in the Americas.

The second city of Puerto Rico is Ponce on the southern coastal plain, three and a half miles from the sea. Like so many of the old towns of the Caribbean region, it was built inland as a precaution against pirates, but it has always been a busy port through its shore-front projection at Ponce Playa. Heavy shipments of sugar and coffee go from here direct to the United States. The fertile region of which it is the center makes it the best Puerto Rican market for tropical fruit.

Ponce is more colorful in a Spanish-American sense than San Juan, and has a more leisurely atmosphere. There was little space in the older parts of the capital for gracious patios and balconies, but here they are to be seen at every turn. The central plaza is oddly divided by a broad avenue that leads to the cathedral, so the city takes pride in having two plazas attractively shaded with palms and laurels and decked with monuments. The cathedral dates back only a century, but is on the site of previous churches. It is dedicated to the Virgin of Guadalupe and features a painting of her, above the altar, as she appeared in a vision to a Mexican Indian. The building is a pleasing combination of Renaissance and Gothic.

Rather more than the average number of smaller Catholic places of worship and convents stand in quiet Ponce. But historically speaking, the post of honor belongs to the ordinary, mission-style, new-looking Anglican, or Episcopalian, Church of the Holy Trinity. This is the first Protestant church ever authorized in the Spanish dominions in America. The short-lived republican regime of the early 1870's in Spain gave its permission, and Queen Victoria sent an iron and frame building in sections to Ponce as a gift. With the return of the monarchy, the closing of the church was ordered. The British queen then intervened on the basis of asking a personal favor, and Holy Trinity was allowed to hold services so long as it did not ring its bells. The present structure was erected in 1926.

Mayaguez is the third largest city and the only other that is an important port. It is Spanish in character, but with no buildings of outstanding merit, and it is swiftly being modernized to a level of commercial drabness. The embroidery and needlework industry for which Puerto Rico is celebrated is largely a Mayaguez enterprise. Thousands of women and even young children used to toil in their homes turning out articles de luxe, for which they received scandalously small pay on a piecework arrangement. New York wholesalers found it profitable to ship out raw material and pay the return freight on completed orders, so wide was the margin of gain on this sweatshop labor. The Federal Wage and Hours Law, backed up by local social legislation, has improved conditions in recent years. I was told, however, that one result had been a falling off of the number of those employed, a serious matter in a country where general unemployment is chronic.

On the outskirts of Mayaguez the United States government conducts an agricultural experimental station that is said to have the largest collection of tropical plants in the New World, the emphasis being upon marketable crops and timbers. Over sixty varieties of mango have been introduced, and over thirty kinds of bamboo. Adjoining this station is the College of Agriculture and Mechanic Arts, a branch of the University of Puerto Rico.

Among the little towns, San Germán in the southwest is the most striking. It is less colonial than ancient Spanish, being reminiscent of any one of a dozen mellowed villages along the Mediterranean coast. The original site was a port, but this was destroyed so often by French corsairs in the early sixteenth century that the inhabitants moved to a valley seven miles inland in 1570. Coamo, north of Ponce, is prettily situated on the first slope of the foothills, and near by are hot sulphur springs that have been used since the days of Ponce de León. Aibonito, some ten miles farther up the old Spanish military road that crosses the island, has a correspondingly more impressive mountain site. Here the opposing forces were about to give battle when news came of the Spanish surrender in 1898.

The best of Puerto Rico is rural, and as the roads surpass those of any other West Indian country, with the possible exception of Jamaica, a complete survey can be made by car or bus. The local variety of guagua, by the way, is just as small and crowded as the Cuban species and is driven with even more frenzied speed. It may be safe on hairpin turns and the edges of chasms, but it does not give that impression and so is bad for the nerves. Use a car if you can. The scenery is bewilderingly lovely, as in all the Greater Antilles. Unfortunately the mountains have been to a large extent denuded of trees, partly in an attempt to place even poor, rocky land under cultivation, and partly in an ever urgent quest for fuel. This has a bad effect upon the water supply, and some of the streams are in danger of drying up. These are scarred areas that fairly cry out for reforestation, but there are not enough of them to spoil the visual pleasure of even half a day's trip in any direction.

Near Cidra is a unique upland resort called the Treasure Island Camps. It is a large plantation on rolling ground especially well suited to the cultivation of pineapples, other tropical fruits, and vegetables of every description, including some from the Temperate Zone. Cabins, with all modern conveniences, yet thoroughly Puerto Rican in appearance, have been placed within easy reach of the central building, where meals are served. Some of these cabins are picturesquely masked by shrubbery or secluded in groves of trees. I know of no more delightful atmosphere of privacy in connection with a country guest-house project anywhere in the West Indies. Should the visitor want company, on the other hand, he can get plenty of it. Tennis and other sports, horseback riding and swimming are featured. Many island residents patronize it for week ends and longer stays. I was told by a former manager that Luis Muñoz Marín, Jesús T. Piñero, and other founders of the Popular party did the first planning of their movement at Treasure Island.

Puerto Rico has a magnificent public domain in the form of the two units of the Caribbean National Forest, with a total area of 65,-000 acres pre-empted and some 35,000 acres already in the hands of the government. The island owes this to the foresight of that great lover of the outdoors and friend of conservation, President Theodore Roosevelt, who in 1903 set aside lands in the Luquillo Range, which had formerly belonged to the Spanish crown, and provided for the purchase of adjoining territory. The site was at the eastern end, and at first was called the Luquillo National Forest. Franklin D. Roosevelt carried forward the project when in 1935, by presidential proclamation, he established a second section in the Cordillera Central, or main mountain range. The general name of Caribbean National Forest was then made official, Luquillo being retained for the old unit and Toro Negro adopted for the new one.

The economic importance of the forest may be judged by the fact that it contains three fourths of all the virgin timber remaining in Puerto Rico today; and only within its boundaries is it possible to cultivate fresh stands on a large scale. It has been estimated that, with careful management, these restored woodlands will eventually supply half of the lumber now being imported by Puerto Rico at a cost of nearly $6,000,000, and produce as well an appreciable quantity of tropical hardwoods, such as mahogany and lignum vitae, for sale abroad. In the Toro Negro unit, a nursery has been established for the growing of foreign trees suited to the local soil.

Recreational facilities exist in both units and are being steadily developed. At Toro Negro there are picnic grounds and a natural swimming pool at the headwaters of the Doña Juana River, the altitude being about 3,000 feet. Five or six miles to the west soars Los Picachos, 4,398 feet, the highest peak in the island. But Luquillo, longer established as a park and on the whole more favored by Nature, may be described without exaggeration as a wonderland. Its culminating point is El Yunque (The Anvil), 3,496 feet, from the summit of which it is possible on a clear day to see one third of Puerto Rico, the near-by islands of Vieques and Culebra, and the American Virgin Islands, forty miles distant. I never tire of visiting this forest, combining as it does all the charms of West Indian mountain landscapes and affording a chance to study the flora and fauna in comfort.

The Puerto Rican mountains do not attain the heights reached in eastern Cuba, Jamaica, and Hispaniola. There is a certain pictorial loss, compensated for by the fact that it is more practicable to roam all over them. Above four thousand feet, peaks are chiefly interesting to the man who likes mountain climbing for its own sake; the temperature becomes chilly up there and the manifestations of life sparse. At Luquillo the slopes are consistently rewarding. They are clothed for the major part of the way with rain forest, the foliage dense, the trunks and larger branches of the trees covered with parasitic growths. Orchids abound, as do many species of vines bearing brilliant flowers. When you arrive in the upper zone where the trees are all dwarfed and hung with gray moss instead of the colorful air plants, there are fewer blossoms and a less varied underbrush. At every altitude the ferns and mosses are singularly beautiful.

Birds find a refuge here, and if for no other reason it is lucky that the Caribbean National Forest was created when it was. The enormous increase of human population militates against wild life. Except for a few sorts that thrive near the dwellings of men and seem half domesticated, birds are becoming uncommon in the rest of Puerto Rico. At Luquillo and Toro Negro you see several varieties of hummingbirds and in great numbers tropical finches, orioles, cuckoos, tyrant flycatchers, mockingbirds, todies, doves, and even parrots. The latter are now scarce in the Greater Antilles, and the Puerto Rican species assuredly would have been extinct by this time if it had not been for the forest reservations. Lizards fairly swarm. The snakes are all harmless, as in the entire Antillean chain north of Martinique. Butterflies by day and fireflies by night dot the woods with numberless shifting points of color.

La Mina, at the foot of El Yunque, is the center of the amusement area of the Luquillo unit. The community building has a tiled floor for dancing. There are picnic shelters with open-air fireplaces, a swimming pool, and a bathhouse. Sites for the erection of holiday cabins may be leased in this vicinity. Trails from La Mina lead up the mountain and deep into the forest. At intervals rest huts have been provided, in each case with a well-constructed outdoor fireplace. Comparatively few make the excursion as yet, but this is obviously the future playground of the Puerto Rican people. A model has been established that should be imitated elsewhere, particularly in the Sierra Maestra Mountains of Cuba and the Blue Mountains of Jamaica.

Before the war there used to be an active tourist commission in San Juan that put out much appealing literature, ran an information bureau for visitors, and organized tours. It also waged a promotion campaign by means of advertisements in the American press. I understand that the insular government felt that the money spent had not paid big enough dividends in the form of new tourists attracted to the island. It was natural that the commission should suspend its activities during the war, when there was no pleasure travel, but I fear it is an error of judgment that it should not have been reinstated since. Puerto Rico has plenty to offer in the way of beauty, climate, and recreation. More than any of its immediate neighbors, however, it needs to "sell" itself to the prospective traveler. Reasons for this are the high cost of living in Puerto Rico and its lack of enticement as a shopping center. The tariff prevents foreign luxuries, such as perfumes, from competing successfully. Almost nothing save rum is cheaper than in the United States, and many things are far more expensive. Local taxation has boosted cigarettes, for instance, to twenty-two cents a package, and locally brewed beer to twenty and twenty-five cents for a small bottle. A tourist commission might be able to convince the government that revenue thus obtained makes for a sick goose that declines to lay golden eggs. Nuisance taxes on the pleasures of everyday are the worst thing possible for the tourist trade. Cuba knows this, does not impose them, and profits enormously, as I have shown, from an army of contented visitors.

When I prepared to leave the island I learned how mistaken I had been, on my arrival, in thinking the airport a quiet spot. It is the principal transfer point in the Caribbean region of Pan American Airways and a number of other lines. Large though the field is, it can scarcely accommodate the planes that land and take off there at most hours of the twenty-four. The traffic has outgrown the capacity of the administration building to handle passengers smoothly. The waiting rooms have only a few seats, and during the rush periods of the day travelers and the friends who have come to see them off stand packed like cattle in a corral. My first impulse was to find this outrageous, but I soon perceived that if benches had been furnished for all, the people would have taken up twice as much room and half of them would have been forced outdoors into the sun or rain.

Plane schedules cannot be guaranteed with the accuracy to which land travel has accustomed us. Too many factors cause legitimate delays and postponements. Yet the passenger must be on time or risk missing his connection. I have waited in that jammed San Juan airport for hours with no place to sit, and with a soft-drinks bar at which one has to struggle to be served as the only means of diversion. This state of affairs is not Puerto Rico's fault. It is not the fault of anybody, really. Air travel resembles a boy who is springing up so fast that his parents are driven to distraction to supply him with clothes that fit. Plans are afoot to provide adequate facilities at San Juan, and by the time my book appears in print the conditions I found there may have been wholly rectified.

CHAPTER 8

ELEVEN THOUSAND VIRGINS, MORE OR LESS

BEATING west by north on his second voyage, as he felt his way toward Hispaniola in 1493, Columbus passed through a group of small islands, cays, and rocks so numerous that they reminded him of St. Ursula and her eleven thousand virgins who had been martyred by the heathen. He named them accordingly, and they have since been known in all languages as the Virgin Islands. Actually, counting every outcropping, there are some 150 of them, only 6 being relatively large, and their total area is about 200 square miles. For so tiny an aggregation, they have made a deal of noise in the world. France, England, and Denmark disputed their ownership with Spain, divided them, and later fought one another for certain units. The buccaneers and pirates meanwhile had had lairs among the multitudinous coves. The share lastingly acquired by the Danes was bought by the Woodrow Wilson administration in 1917 and became the Virgin Islands of the United States. England had long since established her claim to the rest. Collectively they have possibilities as an Eden, but the English colony is poor and neglected, and the American possession is pretty nearly as poor while serving as an incubator for social experiments and exercising a special lure as a tourist resort.

The one name in the group that has international currency is St. Thomas, the chief American island, where Charlotte Amalie, the capital, is located. This has been a free port for two centuries, and as such has had a remarkable history. I had never visited the place. It was next on my list after Puerto Rico. Everything connected with the transfer combined to make it a sojourn of amazing contrasts.

Until recently the only way of getting from San Juan to St. Thomas was by taking a little boat that covered the distance in eight or ten hours. Before the war a semiweekly plane service was established, mainly for the purpose of carrying the mail. When the German submarine campaign decimated shipping in the Caribbean and the surviving craft were assigned to the transport of materials vitally needed by the Allies, the planes became the sole contact that St. Thomas had with the outside world. More of them were put on, and still more after hostilities ended. There are now two clippers a day in each direction. The flight takes twenty-five minutes. That means that in point of time St. Thomas has been brought closer for a resident of San Juan than any of the important country resorts in Puerto Rico itself. The latter's leisured class have discovered the Virgin Islands and taken the place of the tourists that the cruise ships used to bring. It is the vogue to fly from San Juan for week ends, or even for overnight trips.

I obtained a seat with some difficulty. We soared above the bay, saw the city turn below us as on an axle, and darted in the contrary direction along the course that Columbus had followed from his Virgins of St. Ursula to his one Puerto Rican landfall. It seemed that we were hardly out of sight of land when the first islets of our destination emerged like details of a map viewed through a stereoscope: Cockroach Cay, Salt Cay, Savana Island. Then came the indented coast of St. Thomas and hills that looked unexpectedly brown and bare. We lost altitude and in a few minutes were rolling to a halt on the airfield a couple of miles from the town. A single glance around was enough to show that this was indeed no opulent, fertile land such as the word Antilles conjures up in the imagination. The fields and slopes were dry, with patches denuded of all vegetation. Here and there a hillside had been coated with cement to provide what is locally called a catchment for rain water, a device used where there are no streams or wells. The cement diverts the rain by means of gutters into a series of cisterns, which are the farmers' inadequate reliance for water in times of drought.

The road into Charlotte Amalie skirts the foot of a ridge and is shaded most of the way by palms and tall trees. It runs by the settlement of the Chachas, descendants of French fishermen, passes an ancient Danish cemetery, then merges with the main street of the town, the only long street that is at sea level. The rest of Charlotte Amalie is built on a series of terraces up the mountainside, and it dominates one of the really fine harbors of the West Indies. A Danish note is struck in the architecture, but not to the extent that the Spaniards and the Dutch have adapted their styles under Caribbean skies. The older stone houses here are solid and without much decoration. The mansions are roomy structures of the plantation type seen also in the English and French islands, their deep verandas embowered in bougainvillea and other glowing creepers. On the water front are great warehouses, low and with thick walls, reaching back like tunnels from the elaborate system of wharves that once were among the busiest in the New World.

Visitors who have not informed themselves about the Virgin Islands are astonished to find the whole population speaking English. They ask how a Danish colony could have been so quickly transformed. The fact is that the language always was English. The Danes realized that they could not do an international business in a tongue not spoken outside one of the smallest of European countries. The talk used in the countinghouses spread to the homes and was picked up by the slaves. The lingo of the modern St. Thomas Negroes has its oddities, but is by no means a patois. The American ear has no trouble with it. A few families of pure Danish blood still live on the island, and a considerable proportion of the inhabitants of all shades of complexion have Danish names. But the language of the Norse colonizers has been preserved only on the name plates of the streets and the inscriptions on some monuments.

The two principal hotels are Bluebeard's Castle on a high hill at the far edge of town, and the 1829 atop a long flight of steps at the center of things. There is also the Grand facing a little park by the harbor, a hotel that had seen much better days under the Danish regime; I liked its location and got out of the cab there. At once I discovered that the housing situation in St. Thomas was serious. Two or three persons were already standing disconsolately at the desk, where the Puerto Rican proprietress was announcing that she had no rooms but would telephone around to see if any were available. After good-humoredly adding my name to her list, she called both the big hotels and a list of guest houses. The reply everywhere was monotonous, "All filled up." My companions drifted away. Luckily for me, I lingered. When we were alone, the woman said that she did have one room, but that it was reserved for an old patron who was to arrive on the plane the next day to stay a week. I could have it until he arrived. I gladly accepted, and as it turned out the patron canceled by radio in the morning. The room was mine by right of possession as long as I needed it.

The dining room of the Grand is an enormous veranda with a stone floor, and protected against hurricanes (many have raged harmlessly against it) by a waist-high bulwark and sturdy pillars. The view over the blue haven is charming. To the left is a red fort built in 1671, to the right old warehouses, and immediately below a respectable-looking bust of King Frederik VIII of Denmark in the middle of a square of greenery. I sat there and dreamed of the days when the hotel had been a resort of fashion. No fitter setting for men in uniform and women in hoop skirts, dining to the strains of soft music, could be conceived; but the veranda is all that remains unspoiled. The ballroom behind it is dismantled, shabby, with a bar in one corner, a wheezy piano on a platform, and a blaring radio. The bedrooms are comfortable enough, save for the drawback of an uncertain water supply to which the whole of St. Thomas is subject. While I was there, water was regularly cut off part of the day, which caused deplorable results in the lavatories. Nothing but seawater was furnished for the shower baths, and on one occasion this was turned for several hours into the pipes serving the washbasins.

The 1829 Hotel was originally a mansion built in that year by a Spanish family. Bluebeard's Castle also was a private palace, said to have been erected by an eighteenth-century pirate who kept a harem of thirteen women there. This half-mythical individual is often confused with Edward Teach, whose *nom de guerre* was Blackbeard and who unquestionably was one of the region's master pirates. A round tower in Charlotte Amalie is known without much justification as Blackbeard's Castle. But the castle that has been turned into a luxury hotel is the one on the hill accredited to Bluebeard. It had been virtually a ruin for years when the United States government renovated it in the early 1930's at a cost reputed to have been $100,-000, as part of a campaign to save the Virgin Islands economically. The place commands a sweeping view, and its adjuncts include picturesque touches such as a terrace composed of gravestones, which serves as an outdoor cocktail lounge. Prices range from $6 a day at the Grand for room and meals to $8 and up at the two smarter hotels. Living comes high in modern St. Thomas, yet a few short years ago it was one of the cheapest spots in the West Indies. I shall return to this angle presently.

After I had lunched that first afternoon, I went strolling in the town. Following closely one after the other on the main street were shops that could not fail to rejoice a traveler, and that have been delighting the tourists on cruise ships for many a year. Here were shops selling silverware from Denmark, from Mexico, from Peru, at prices as low as and in some cases lower than those prevailing in the country of origin; perfumers where the products of the best French makers were offered at similar rates; liquor and tobacco stores where the charges were derisory from the standpoint of a resident of the United States. A bottle of prewar Benedictine cost $4, of champagne $3, of genuine Scotch whisky $2.25, of various good West Indian rums from $.75 to $1. The standard brands of American cigarettes cost eight cents a package, or seventy cents a carton. That is what it means to go shopping in a free port. The goods are obtained direct from the manufacturers, and not only pay no customs duties, if of United States origin, but are exempt from excise charges. If the goods are from foreign countries a flat 6 per cent is paid.

Remember, however, that these articles and others I have not mentioned that fall into the same class are all luxuries. Precisely because they are heavily taxed elsewhere, they seem cheap as dirt in St. Thomas. Necessities are a different story. The margin of advantage in importing clothing and food from this market or that is not great, and because of shipping difficulties there has been no choice, anyway, for the past several years. The necessities mostly come from the United States or Puerto Rico, often from the former by way of the latter, which causes freight rates to pile up. The Virgin Islands manufacture little or nothing except sugar and its by-products, and bay rum; they do not begin to be self-sustaining in the matter of food. So the moment you turn aside from the luxury shops, you note cloth goods, shoes, canned products, etc., at prices a shade higher than those in Puerto Rico, and the few local eggs, vegetables, fruits, etc., offered at relatively fantastic figures. I saw a dozen eggs change hands at ninety cents and one water coconut at a dime. How could the ordinary citizen of Charlotte Amalie maintain such a scale of living? I wondered.

That ordinary citizen is black or of mixed ancestry, for the total number of whites is under 10 per cent. As far as I could judge, there were not enough jobs to go around. The harbor was empty of shipping. The West Indian Co., Ltd., which I had been told furnished most of the steady employment for the community at its deep-water dock, warehouses, and machine shops, must have been functioning with a skeleton force. There was an air of loaferism in the streets. Carpenter, tailor, and stationery shops, retail stores and other individual businesses appeared to be marking time. But the bars were crowded. Gangs of boys roamed about, ostensibly competing for the rare opportunity to shine shoes and killing the empty hours with games and fights.

My only means of getting at the significance of things was to talk to those I knew. The next morning I climbed the hill to Government House, the handsome administration building and official residence inherited from the Danes, and had a chat with Governor William Henry Hastie, the first colored man to receive a federal appointment as chief executive of a territorial possession. I had met Hastie in Washington in connection with the work of the Anglo-American Caribbean Commission, on which he had served. He had previously been judge of the federal court in the Virgin Islands for two years. He is an able lawyer, a liberal intellectual, a polished gentleman. His light complexion could easily lead him to be taken for a European of Mediterranean origin. Only under the social system of the United States would it be a point that he has an admixture of Negro blood. But it was as a Negro that he was sent to Charlotte Amalie to rule a preponderantly African people. He would make a distinguished governor anywhere.

Hastie and I discussed tourism and the political setup in the islands. There was no time for other subjects. He was hopeful that an influx of visitors might do much toward solving the economic troubles of the inhabitants. The turnover in the luxury shops would be a small factor, because it was not taxed. But those shops were a proven attraction, and the outsiders who came for silver and perfumes would buy a certain amount of the stuff produced by the handcraft co-operatives that exist and can be expanded. More and more persons should be interested in making long stays, and if the holiday population rose to important numbers the furnishing of services would give employment to many residents. The Governor said that several new hotels and dozens of villas for tourists were needed in St. Thomas and St. Croix, and that St. John, the third and last big island, was a field for unlimited development from scratch. He pointed out, however, that there was a paralyzing lack of building materials, and no immediate prospect of importing the quantities required. I had seen for myself how difficult it was to get a room. A private house, he could assure me, was almost unobtainable. The tourist trade in which he had faith was for the future.

He declared that he had been forced to underplay the advertising of natural beauty, climate, and restful surroundings that the Virgins have to offer. It was unfair to encourage any sort of visitor *now*, except the cruise passengers who sail away on the same boat that brought them. Smiling, he remarked that a well-known columnist on a New York newspaper had done his readers a disservice by bringing out one allurement that might be good or bad, but assuredly was potent. The Virgin Islands have a six weeks' divorce law, and the judgment is handed down by a federal court. A few lines to that effect published in the column had caused thousands to dream of Charlotte Amalie as a superior tropical version of Reno. A flood of letters of inquiry had been received at Government House, and while efforts had been made to discourage the hopeful, it was to be feared that some had arrived and others were planning to come in the belief that they could rent cottages while awaiting their decrees.

We talked about the free-port system. The Governor said that the financing of the administration would be helped, naturally, if customs duties were increased beyond their present nominal figure, but the local legislature would not hear of it. The people, too, were attached to the *status quo,* believing that on the whole it benefited them.

This led to a review of the form of government. Under the Danes, the Virgin Islands had been a colonial estate pure and simple, run by officials from Europe aided by the counsel of white planters and merchants. After the purchase by the United States, it continued to be ruled arbitrarily as a possession for some fifteen years, all the early American governors having been naval officers. Control of the islands was then vested in the Department of the Interior and the first civilian governor appointed. In 1936 an organic act was passed giving the franchise to citizens twenty-one years of age or over and providing for two elected municipal councils, one to represent the island of St. Croix and the other the islands of St. Thomas and St.

John. Joint sessions of the two councils, to be called by the governor at least once a year, or whenever both councils passed resolutions to hold such a session, constituted a parliament with broad legislative powers. Its acts, however, were subject to annulment by the United States Congress.

The populace welcomed this measure of self-government. Parties were formed, and save in a few instances the victors at the polls have ever since been colored, with the spokesmen of labor predominating. The change from the paternalism of the Danes and the United States Navy has been striking. The older elements, particularly among the whites, are ruffled by it. Hastie thinks it a worthy experiment in democracy, and feels sure it is going to work out all right. That is the way it looks to me. But I heard many divergent views, even among sympathizers.

It is at all events debatable (I am no longer citing the Governor) that the Virgin Islanders can scarcely hope to gain full control of their political destiny while their economic situation remains so bad that the federal government has to meet frequent deficits. The territory is too small and resourceless to launch a workable plan. That problem, admittedly, must be solved by the United States, and the wisdom of the latter's methods is open to question. The vicious circle again.

Herbert Hoover visited the islands as President and caused great offense by dubbing them "an effective poorhouse." At the time, wages were far below the scale prevailing in the United States—but living was very, very cheap and nobody starved. Then came the Roosevelt administration with a generous rehabilitation scheme for the sugar and rum industry, the Federal Wage and Hours law, vast WPA projects and home relief for those who could not be aided otherwise. Money was placed in circulation. Incomes were boosted to figures the proletariat had never known before. Along with this, inevitably, the prices of everything went up. The people were conditioned to a new standard of comfort on the easy-come, easy-go basis. But the war knocked it galley-west, and the peace has not so far created a prosperity that justifies fat pay checks. Unless Washington is to treat the Virgin Islanders as pampered dependents in perpetuity, subsistence farming may be the only solution for the many; that and emigration, which has already reduced the population, despite a high birth rate, from 26,051 in 1917 to 24,889 in 1940.

The few should do well out of the tourist business and an improved export trade.

The above summarizes the opinion of two or three intelligent persons with whom I talked. I give it for what it is worth.

Governor Hastie introduced me to a man, Frederick Dorsch, executive secretary of the Chamber of Commerce, whose attitude was sympathetic, optimistic, and founded upon a thorough knowledge of local affairs. Dorsch is an American who came to the islands about twenty years ago and decided to make them his home. He has been identified longest with St. Croix, but now has his headquarters in St. Thomas. He believes that agriculture can be made profitable, despite the drawbacks of a thin soil and lack of water. The answer, he thinks, lies in setting up evaporators for the turning of sea water into fresh. Five evaporators are needed to serve the two main islands, and they could be built at a cost of $500,000. When running at full capacity they could produce water for all purposes at a little over one cent a gallon. I find that during one year of the war federal aid to the Virgin Islands took the form of $480,186 spent on a variety of lesser projects. It does seem that evaporators would have been a better buy.

Dorsch holds that the public schools have erred in not emphasizing the dignity of manual labor, and have given too many islanders the notion that the only job worth having is a white-collar job. It was noteworthy that in registering for employment not a single returned veteran put himself down as a day laborer. But Dorsch felt that this complex could be and would be corrected. He favors the stimulating of minor industries, such as the manufacture of mats from banana leaves, the bottling of fruit extracts, and the preserving of tropical delicacies. The largest hope lies in an adjusted economy for the whole West Indies through some sort of customs union.

Enough of economics. It is the scene that counts most from the standpoint of this book. Roaming about little Charlotte Amalie will be enjoyed by the pedestrian if he has strong legs and no distaste for climbing. Down by the water front there are some interesting alleys and courtyards that do not suggest the Spanish patio, but are paved and sparsely adorned with potted plants. For the rest, it is a matter of mounting endless flights of steps, some straight and some zigzag, that lead up the slopes. There is one famous ascent that has ninety-nine steps. Landings occur at intervals, and from most of these the harbor may be seen to new advantage. The terrace in front of Government House is particularly well placed. As you gaze at that blue expanse chiseled out of the bases of the hills, remember a few of the extraordinary things that have happened and it will gain in meaning.

The slave trade had its greatest West Indian depot here for a hundred years. Always the free port, Charlotte Amalie sold black ivory to all comers as willingly as it sold cloth or wines. Yet when sentiment against the traffic began to stir in Europe, conscientious Denmark was the first country to abolish it. What is more, she did this in 1792 at the height of the French Revolution and while the black insurrection was raging in St.-Domingue. The English descended on the port during the Napoleonic Wars, overwhelmed Danish resistance, and ruled the group of islands for several years. In the War between the States, blockade running to the Confederacy was an important activity.

In November 1867 an earthquake shook the group with extreme violence. Seismic disturbances had been felt before, but this one behaved in a unique manner. It sucked the water out of Charlotte Amalie Harbor, leaving the bottom bare, then hurled it back as a tidal wave, causing great damage at sea level and for some distance up the heights. The Virgins are located on the edge of the Brownson Deep, which goes down 30,000 feet at some spots and is the most profound depth yet located in the Atlantic Ocean. Science is short on evidence that would enable it to predict what may happen when earthquakes start, as this one did, so far below the surface of the sea. A convulsion originating in the same area struck Hispaniola in 1946, and I shall have more to say about it.

If you want to explore St. Thomas outside of Charlotte Amalie, it can be done by car in a day. The roads are good. Trips on horseback are recommended. For my part, I got my lasting impressions from walks I took in the environs and into the interior. The cemetery I mentioned at the beginning of the chapter has quaint aspects. Very many of the tombs are built of conch shells with the voluted side outward; in some cases, just the shells tightly packed are used, in others they are locked together with cement, and in still others there is a ridge of shells atop a cement base. The local fancy is to paint the shells some bright color: sky blue, or rose, and in one instance a crimson the hue of blood. I found a tomb decorated with a row of stone pineapples. Several bore sculptured portraits of the deceased in high relief. One of these last was unforgettable in its naïve realism. It showed the face and shoulders of "Ann E. Lindeman—born Lind—1799–1874," a severe old matriarch with tight lips and bushy eyebrows, most accurately garbed in a high-necked blouse and bonnet fringed with lace.

In the countryside you see more cattle than you would expect. The tendency of late has been to convert the unproductive farming land to grazing; an advantage is that in periods of drought the beasts can be brought to the cisterns and troughs, whereas it would be impossible to water wide fields not served by an irrigation system. There are beautiful coves all around the coast of St. Thomas, and at some points the swimming is excellent. My most amusing encounter was at a village called Pollyburg just outside Charlotte Amalie. An enormously stout black matron came up to me, said I looked lonely, and offered her company on my walk. "I'm not busy," she explained politely, "and a woman has to live somehow." I gave her a quarter, but excused her from risking heart failure on the rugged hills.

The prime discovery for me was the island of St. John. Not that I hadn't heard that although few people went there it was captivating and something special in the West Indies. But a judgment of the kind has little weight until you have seen for yourself. St. John is nearly as large as St. Thomas—twenty-one square miles as against twenty-seven—and is only three miles from the latter's eastern tip. It is about thirteen miles long by three wide. Two hundred years ago it was almost solidly planted in cane and cotton and rated as a rich colony. The unit was too small, however, to compete under changing conditions, and it was gradually abandoned. The population dispersed, sinking rapidly after 1850, when it was 2,228, to a mere 750 today. Yet it is more fertile than St. Thomas, and the climate is singularly healthy. Through some freak of nature, the common cold is unknown there. Its wild bay trees yield the best oil for the manufacture of bay rum.

This much I had been told. I asked Governor Hastie about getting to St. John. He said that a doctor made the trip twice a week to care for patients at a clinic, there being no resident physician on the island, and that he would instruct him to take me the next time. Early one morning Dr. Smith, a young black Virgin Islander who had studied in New York on a scholarship and had come back to serve his people, called for me at the hotel. We drove to a landing at Red

Hook on Pillsbury Sound and there boarded a small motor launch, the *G. W. Watts*, which maintains the sole regular service between St. Thomas and St. John, and which the government charters on certain days. It had a cockpit with a seat running around it, on which ten passengers could be squeezed at a pinch, and a dark, evil-smelling cabin that none would willingly patronize. The skipper took the wheel, and his helpers—you could scarcely call them a crew—sprawled on the roof of the cabin until they should be needed. The chance passengers were colored housewives who had been shopping in Charlotte Amalie, some nondescript ancients of both sexes, and a clutter of children. Their baggage, consisting of native baskets and burlap sacks, was piled about our feet.

I had made voyages of this kind before in the West Indies and had always found them amusing. We chugged into the sound and steered a straight course for Cruz Bay, St. John. Headlands, cays, and rocks were on all sides of us. It was difficult to tell which formed part of St. Thomas, of St. John, or of the British Virgin Islands, so rapidly did the panorama shift. We were not much closer to the water than Columbus had been on his caravel, and I could well see how he had been deluded into thinking that he had come upon thousands of islets.

St. John, at Cruz Bay, looks the half-savage tropical island in every respect. Hills covered with trees rise fairly steeply. The foreground is a narrow strip of level ground with a coconut-shaded beach. A single house of some pretensions stands on a rise to the left; it is occupied by the administrator, the only man on the island who has a car. A few smaller dwellings appear here and there amidst the greenery. A wooden wharf reaches for a short distance into the opalescent water. Most of the passengers got out there. I stepped ashore with the doctor, but no one required his attention and we made the briefest of stays. The launch, with plenty of elbow room aboard now, went cruising along the south coast of the island bound for Coral Bay.

The silhouette of St. John is bold and extraordinarily varied. Mountains extend down the center. They attain an elevation of only a little above 1,000 feet, but their conformation is that of a complete chain with peaks, ridges, and valleys. Cliffs rise sheer from the sea at many points. Elsewhere, broad savannas open and merge in the distance with forested foothills. Suddenly it came home to me that this was a prototype in miniature of the greater West Indian islands.

All the topographical features to be found in the chain were here. The fact that it had been allowed to relapse to the primitive, that it was mostly covered with jungle, strengthened the impression. It looked exactly as it must have looked to the first Spaniards.

It was clear weather, but with a light breeze and occasional rain squalls that were over in a few minutes. This made for a choppy sea. Wherever the shore was rocky the surf pounded against it, sending up clouds of spray. Riding just behind the breakers, the launch deliriously pitched and rolled. The motion was particularly exuberant as we rounded Ram's Head, a promontory that from a certain point offshore really does flaunt the profile of a gigantic billy goat. It was not a voyage that sufferers from *mal de mer* would have appreciated. A couple of hours later we entered Coral Bay, a deep, broad haven where it was once thought that a flourishing port would be built. In the middle of the eighteenth century a city was planned, and the site surveyed and divided into town lots. But it never came to anything. The bay glitters in pristine beauty, and apart from fishing craft the *G. W. Watts* is about the only boat that ever enters it.

On the west shore is a landing called Calabash Hole, which is where the clinic is located. I accompanied Dr. Smith to the neat, whitewashed building furnished with all modern appliances and in permanent charge of a graduate nurse. A few cases had been held for observation and other patients had arrived on foot to see the doctor. He told me that there is comparatively little sickness on the island, serious or contagious diseases being actually rare. Neither T.B. nor V.D. are much of a problem, whereas they are the twin curses of the Negro population in most West Indian islands. He hesitated to confirm the popular belief that the common cold never occurs in St. John, but agreed that there was virtual immunity.

His duties being light that day, we were soon back on the boat and crossed over to the wharf and scattering of houses called Coral Harbor. A short distance inland there was a large dwelling with outbuildings, fields of cane, bananas, and other crops. Dr. Smith said that this was Carolina plantation, one of the two or three that had survived from the old days, but run now as a self-sustaining enterprise with almost no sales for export. First let us take a walk over the hills, and then we would visit Carolina.

I have seldom had an experience so interesting as that excursion into the St. John bush. The roads have deteriorated to trails along which an automobile, or even a horse-drawn carriage, would be able to force its way only on a few stretches of flat land. Cottages stand at long intervals, haphazard, among fruit trees. The thatched huts of the poorer Negroes are hidden more deeply in the underbrush. You get the feeling of being in an equatorial wilderness, but a beneficent one since there are no signs of dangerous wild beasts or snakes. The single roadside store we encountered was a quaint mixture of the civilized and the rude. It had a refrigerator run by kerosene, and this was the wonder of the whole district; yet its shelves held nothing except fresh meat and some bottles of soda pop. Sardines, crackers, and American tinned preserves were on sale, as well as a variety of cheap household articles. The stock of native rum had been exhausted, but the cosmopolitanism of the Virgin Islands as a free port provided a quart of South African brandy as substitute.

While we lunched at this store, several poker-faced, jet-black young Negroes came in. They knew the doctor, which I am sure accounted for their earnest acceptance of me as a visitor who intended to write about their island. One of the men declared that he had read books by me, which I found hard to take literally and interpreted as a polite attempt to make me feel among friends. The doctor said he wished me to know that the people of St. John had a brotherly spirit rarely found in cities, and that when trouble came they helped out one another to the limit of their resources. The other's eyes glowed at this; he answered that he liked to think St. John could be an example to the Negro race. Any way you look at it, that was a remarkable statement to hear made in so small and isolated a community.

We roved on through lovely glades and across ridges from which the sea was always visible. Obviously this island could be cultivated to better advantage than St. Thomas. Wherever the moisture comes from, it gets enough to keep it green; no doubt natural reforestation accounts for this. I noticed that the usual tropical birds were plentiful, in contrast with depleted St. Thomas. Oranges, guavas, and other fruit grew wild in spots where the woods were not too dense.

Circling back, the doctor and I arrived at the Carolina plantation and were warmly received by the Marsh family, which has lived there for generations. Everything conceivable is raised on Carolina: cattle, pigs, poultry; coconuts and all the vegetable staples required to keep a clan in luxury. The Marshes boil their own sugar, distill their own liquors. They keep a little shop in which they sell their surplus to neighbors, and they have built a guest house with three rooms for the accommodation of occasional boarders from the outside. This is the ideal retreat for a honeymoon couple with a flair for the tropics, for a naturalist, or for a painter. Hurry up and take advantage of it before some travel agency starts running excursions to Coral Bay.

The motor launch made the return trip in the late afternoon, and we called again briefly at Cruz Bay. A short distance from the bay, on the north coast, is the only tourist development that has so far got started on St. John. It is known as the Caneel Bay Plantation resort and comprises seven cottages somewhat after the order of those at Treasure Island in Puerto Rico. The charges are high, running from $45 a week or $175 a month for a cottage accommodating one person to $100 a week or $340 a month for a cottage with space for six. There is paradox for you: artificially priced escapism on the edge of the wilderness; but it is characteristic of the Virgin Islands. The government, incidentally, will sell you land for $19 an acre. There is a genuine beachcomber at Cruz Bay who squatted on his site and built a hut with his own hands, at an outlay of nothing an acre and nothing for materials. He seems contented with his lot, though he is a surly-looking individual who never speaks to anyone if he can help it. I got a glimpse of him as he strode under the palms, dressed in shorts and a sun tan. There are said to be only seven white men on St. John, and he is one of them.

St. Croix, the largest of the Virgin Islands of the United States, is not visited by tourists as much as St. Thomas. This is a pity, for it has much to offer. The island lies forty miles to the south of the rest of the group. It depended upon the sugar cane for centuries, but the low yield per acre because of soil conditions and shortage of water put it out of the running in modern times. Though there has been a revival of the industry through government aid, cattle raising has the edge. Homesteading by small farmers is on the increase. Horseback riding, boating, and swimming are the chief amusements; hunting is confined to the shooting of birds and an occasional chance at a Virgin Islands white-tailed deer.

Christiansted, the capital, and Frederiksted, the only other town, have three or four hotels of the pension type between them. Paul J. Gilles, an American, who formerly managed the Treasure Island Camps in Puerto Rico, is planning to build a hotel on Protestant

Cay, an attractive site off Christiansted. St. Croix shows a good deal more Spanish influence in its architecture than St. Thomas does; it also seems more tropical, though the prevailing aridity touches the vegetation with notes of burnt ochre and grayish green.

There are many associations with American history. Alexander Hamilton, who was born in near-by Nevis under the British flag, spent his boyhood years in St. Croix. Cruger's store, where he first worked, was in Christiansted, but at the age of thirteen he was sent to Frederiksted to manage a branch of the business, and his stay there had the greater effect in shaping his precocious genuis. Philip Freneau, earliest of American poets, lived on the island in 1775–76 and wrote "The Jamaican Funeral" there. Judah P. Benjamin, Secretary of State of the Confederacy, was born in St. Croix.

The British Virgin Islands consist of Tortola, Virgin Gorda, Jost van Dyke, Anegada, and numerous islets with a total area of some sixty square miles. Their population is around five thousand and living conditions are only slightly less primitive than those I found on St. John. Few travelers go there, and certainly no tourists. The adventurous can catch a motor launch that leaves twice a week from Charlotte Amalie for Roadtown, Tortola. Between Tortola and Virgin Gorda runs a passage known as Sir Francis Drake's Channel, through which the great Elizabethan privateer took his ships on his way to attack Puerto Rico in 1595.

CHAPTER 9

BOUNTEOUS TRINIDAD AND TOBAGO

PORT-OF-SPAIN, Trinidad, was my next objective. St. Thomas is off on a siding, so to speak, for Pan American planes. I had to go back to San Juan to make connections. In the days of dependence on surface shipping, the thing would have been to catch one of the small passenger boats that called at Charlotte Amalie, followed the curve of the Lesser Antillles with stops at many ports, and took about two weeks to reach Trinidad. There was no other way. Now you had yourself whisked to San Juan in twenty-five minutes and transferred to a plane that drew a beeline on Port-of-Spain and set you down there in three hours. What a fantasy from the court of Scheherazade!

This time I boarded a regular thunderbird, bigger than any I had ever seen except at a distance. It was one of the new four-motored clippers on the run down the east coast of South America to Rio and Buenos Aires, and it seated three score passengers, five in a row. The interior of the type of plane on which I had previously traveled had given me the feeling that some sort of motor bus had soared into the air. The present monster suggested a flying railroad car. It took off with impressive nonchalance and roared southward above the Caribbean, undulating now and then when it got among air waves, but manifesting a formidable efficiency that appeared superior to anything the elements could do. You could not get away from the individualism of this unit of power to which you had confided yourself.

Here is a suggestion that I have since had in mind to urge upon the airlines. The planes should be given names, in place of the confusing jumble of initial letters and figures by which the vast majority of them are now designated. Both practical and romantic reasons for the change exist. Passengers have to fill in official documents of one kind and another, which contain a line for the craft on which they arrived. The forms were drawn up for steamship travel, and it was easy to set down "S.S. *Amazon*," or whatever she was called. But ninety-nine persons out of a hundred simply cannot remember a statistical jargon like "K.Q.Z. 69006." They put down that they came on a plane and let it stand. I have looked over many shoulders, and I know it to be the case. Sometimes a flying officer completes the information. At other times no one does, and that cannot be satisfactory to meticulous immigration and customs departments.

As important, if not more so, is the fact that travelers like to personalize a craft. They like to tell their friends that they went to Havana or World's End on such and such a boat, and to recall details that made it different from other boats. This sentiment would apply just as strongly to planes, which are not so identical as they may seem superficially to be. Again, some planes could become celebrated—if they had names—because of outstanding incidents, such as an accident averted by the cleverness of the pilot, or the rescue of refugees after an earthquake. It is tourist psychology to make much of exciting associations, and the companies miss a bet when they ignore the point. I have been told that it would be a hopeless task to find suitable names for thousands of planes. Nonsense. With less excuse, all the Pullman cars in the United States are labeled easily enough.

We made a night landing at the Piarco Airport, which is twenty miles from Port-of-Spain, another of those unfortunate locations, but explained in this instance by the opportunity of developing a first-class field in connection with the United States naval and air forces. Pan American has arranged for a good, low-priced taxi service to the city, and has also found it necessary to build a hostel at the airport. The idea was to provide accommodation for employees, chiefly flying personnel taking a lay-off between trips. Quite a number of passengers who were there to make connections and who did not want to go into Port-of-Spain, however, jumped at the chance to use the hostel. The latter was expanded and became an institution that is being copied at other airports remote from cities. I foresee a time in the near future when a chain of ever more elaborate hostels will be maintained at strategic points.

Passport and immigration formalities like those in Jamaica were quickly settled. The drive to town by moonlight, between rows of coconut palms at first and then under the canopy of wide-branched, towering trees, was one of memorable felicity. The air was languorous, heavy, scented; even a person who had never been in Trinidad before would have realized he had come to deeper tropics than the climate of the Antilles. This was South America. Trinidad is an island merely by the accident of having been detached from the mainland in prehistoric times. Its very night sounds—the croaking of frogs and the notes of birds and insects—are continental in character.

I went to the Queen's Park Hotel on the Savannah, a grass-covered open space of 130 acres that is the city's center for racing and games rather than a park. The hotel has been for many a day the only one of the international type in Port-of-Spain. The original building was of plantation architecture with wide verandas and galleries overlooking flower gardens. Some years before the recent war, the central part was torn out and replaced by a semimodernistic structure of several stories, but the old wings have been preserved. The effect is a little incongruous; it succeeds in being not displeasing because rains and intense sunshine have worked together to mellow the newer façade. Charges at the Queen's Park begin at $8 a day, American plan, for a single room. While the cuisine is good, it would be more interesting if native dishes were given a larger place on the menu. The bar serves admirable rum drinks.

Other hostelries are the Hotel de Paris and the Parisian Hotel, facing each other on Abercromby Street downtown and under the same management; the Hotel Sand and the Saddle House uptown. There are a number of guest houses similar to those of Kingston, Jamaica; one of these, Dundonald Hall, is just around the corner from the Queen's Park. The lack of superior restaurants, apart from the hotels, strikes every visitor. The business is mainly in the hands of the Chinese, and even they have failed to develop the good catering for which they are noted elsewhere in the world. I looked in at one of their places that advertised in the window "Good Food and Polite Waitresses," and found it to be a slipshod canteen without benefit of napery; others were of a rather higher order. The crying need for one or two first-rate Creole restaurants is admitted locally.

A sense of strangeness permeates the life of Port-of-Spain, owing no doubt to the many racial crosscurrents that meet there. Superficially the English colonial spirit is strong. The whites, who as else-where in the British West Indies are in a very small minority, continuously use such phrases as "this colony" and "colonial interests," which are seldom heard any longer in Jamaica. Yet those same whites are of a more mixed ancestry than the upper-class Jamaicans, French and Spanish strains being important in Trinidad. Negroes constitute a majority of the population, but not overwhelmingly so. About a third of the inhabitants are Hindus, a phenomenon that I shall explain shortly. The Chinese are numerous, and there is a strong infiltration of American Indian blood from near-by Venezuela. No other British-ruled territory in the Caribbean matches it as a pot-pourri. And Trinidad is not the contented imperial preserve that the whites would have you believe it to be. A self-government movement second only in strength to that of Jamaica is under way there, ably led by the Honorable Albert Gomes and others.

As you wander about Port-of-Spain, you observe the Latin note and the Oriental note almost as frequently as you do the African. Save for a few English-style shops on Frederick Street, the stores resemble those in a Spanish-American city, and the lodging houses that cluster about Marine Square have an olive-skinned clientele (Venezuelan political refugees, as likely as not) that spills out on to the sidewalks for purposes of sociability. "Coolie" women wrapped in saris, their forearms loaded with bangles, their nostrils often adorned with gold, peddle exotic novelties. Not far from the center of town there is a district that is entirely Hindu. It has its temples, its bazaars, its metalworkers' shops, like a quarter in Madras. Near the water front, many holes-in-the-wall sell Indian curries, sweet-meats, and beverages.

One of Port-of-Spain's institutions is the plant where the famous Angostura bitters is manufactured. Dr. J. G. B. Siegert & Sons, the proprietors, maintain a cozy bar where tourists are received, presented with a drink and a sample of the firm's specialty, and encouraged to try the rums of the island. The story behind the bitters is curious. It has often been told, but is worth repeating. The original J. G. B. Siegert was a surgeon of a Prussian regiment who emigrated to Venezuela during the earliest days of the Republic. He settled at the city of Angostura, where he became chief surgeon of a military hospital. He invented the bitters in 1824 as a digestive, and prescribed it also as a preventive against certain tropical maladies. But it quickly became the rage as an addition to alcoholic drinks of one sort and another. The recipe was kept a secret, and it made the fortune of the Siegert family.

Angostura was for a long time the revolutionary capital of the Liberator, Simón Bolívar, who may be said to have perfected there his plans for the freedom of six Spanish-American countries. Its name was eventually changed to Ciudad Bolívar in his honor. After he had passed from the scene, conditions became more and more chaotic politically. The Siegerts tired of the perils of revolution and moved the business to Port-of-Spain, where the bitters has been manufactured since without interruption. Before World War II, the firm figured that it served 1,500 persons free at its cocktail bar each year, at a cost of thirty-eight cents a head, but felt that it was well worth doing. Like the Bacardi Company at Santiago de Cuba, it had discovered that hospitality was the cheapest way of obtaining good will.

The Red House, where the legislature meets and most of the administrative departments have their offices, is on Brunswick Square in the middle of the city. An old structure on the site was destroyed during a riot in 1903, and the present one was erected with a lavishness not displayed elsewhere in the British West Indies. It occupies an entire side of the square. The principal halls are well proportioned and handsomely decorated by local craftsmen. Government House, the residence of the governor, is on the inland side of the Savannah; it is reminiscent of the large official mansions reared by the British in Hindustan.

Modern homes of the rich and bungalows favored by the middle class abound in the suburbs, especially on the slopes of the hilly district called St. Ann. Many of the older houses in town have a puzzling appearance, their roofs steeply pitched and with dormer windows in attics that are unsuited to the climate. Commonly the building is topped by a wooden spike like a spearhead, and lesser spikes are seen above doorways at the front and rear. This is neither a Spanish nor an English style. The only other capital in the West Indies where it is favored is Port-au-Prince, Haiti, so I must suppose that it was a nineteenth-century French fad for the tropics. All the Port-of-Spain dwellings, however, are provided with shady verandas, while the yard space that usually encircles the building is planted thickly with flowering shrubs and is pretty sure to have a few tall trees that overshadow the roof. "Embowered in verdure" is no catch phrase here. What with the lush South American flora and the warm, humid air, you have the illusion that each private court into which you glance is a corner of a botanical garden.

This being so, it is no wonder that the Royal Botanic Gardens, established in 1818 beyond the Savannah along part of its northern edge and reaching back into the hills, is the finest experimental plantation of its kind in the Caribbean region. Those of Cuba, Jamaica, and Puerto Rico threaten to surpass it, but that day is not yet. Government House occupies a corner of the gardens. They fascinated Charles Kingsley, the author of *Westward Ho!*, when he visited Trinidad in 1869, and he devoted to them many pages of glowing description in his book *At Last*. Kingsley lived in a small cottage on the premises, as a guest of the governor. Bamboos that exceed one hundred feet in height grow close by. There are immense banyans and baobabs, cannon-ball trees, samans like stupendous umbrellas, and examples of that singular growth called the strangler vine. The latter twines itself around some tree, which it proceeds slowly and methodically to smother while its own spirals become thicker and thicker until they are able to stand by themselves. The tree in the middle dies, and the vine lives as a mass of coils each one of which is as thick around as an anaconda. "The Scotsman choking the Creole" may seem an overlong name, but that is what West Indians call the strangler vine, and it is so expressive that it would be a pity to shorten it. They say it reminds them of the Scots factors who used to come to the islands, get a job representing some lazy Creole, and end up by owning the property.

There is a superb orchid house in the gardens. A private individual started the collection and gave it to the state. It is being steadily enlarged.

As might be expected in a land where nature is so opulent, birds are plentiful not only throughout Trinidad, but among the trees and flowers of Port-of-Spain itself. The most noticeable is the kiskedee (a corruption of the French *qu'est-ce-qu'il dit?*—what does he say?), so called because its incessant cry mimics those sounds to perfection. It is a variety of tyrant flycatcher, but differs considerably from other members of the family found in the Antilles. Large and chunky, with a yellowish breast, the kiskedee is seen and heard in every garden, and like other tyrant flycatchers it exuberantly chases rivals from the field. Motmots, jacamars, toucans, bellbirds, and parrots inhabit the woods on the outskirts. There are sixteen species of hummingbirds, many of them named for gems: the ruby-throated, the emerald, the topaz. The Carib name for Trinidad was Iere, meaning "Land of the Hummingbird."

A tourist commission functions actively, with Wilson Minshall as secretary; but its program is not so far advanced as that of the commission in Jamaica. Minshall is a great believer in the airplane as a stimulator of tourism. There are two schools of thought on this subject. The old-fashioned view is that travel for pleasure will always be a more or less unhurried thing, that when surface ships are available they will be preferred, and that those countries that can be easily reached by sea will get the cream of the business. The other school holds that the appeal of the airplane is by no means confined to the busy man. The vacationist, too, will fly because it will save time on the mere business of "getting there" and enable him to make a longer stay in exotic surroundings. Minshall points out that, for a crossroads point like Port-of-Spain, there is the additional advantage that an increasing number of persons will pass through by air, and by the law of averages a certain proportion will decide to stop over. At the time we talked, 388 seats per day were the capacity of Pan American planes alone that called at the airport, well in excess of the entire number of cabins on ships and seats in planes arriving on a gala day before the war.

The Trinidad Government Railway has a trackage of 123 miles from Port-of-Spain on main lines east and south. Its equipment is out of date, and I do not endorse it as a comfortable means of travel. But there are good motor roads. The interior is colorful and worth visiting, offering as it does the unique asphalt lake, forests covering half the island, and some exquisite mountain and coastal scenery. The drives in the immediate vicinity of the capital have charm. Any taxi driver will take you along the curving Lady Chancellor Road from which you look down on the city and harbor, or eastward to the Laventille Hills. The circular tour on the Saddle Road is longer, and it would be wise to arrange for a car by the hour.

The North Coast Road, opened in 1944, has been called Trinidad's "skyline highway." It crosses the mountain range that bisects the island from east to west, and from the central point 1,000 feet above sea level there is a fine view of the indented coast. Venezuela is often

visible on the left hand and the island of Tobago on the right. Maracas Bay, the terminus of the road, is as reposeful a haven as you will
find anywhere in the West Indies; its beach is excellent and is being
developed as a bathing resort. Near-by Balata Bay, the shore at
Blanchisseuse Bay, and many other points are almost equally attractive. From the scenic standpoint the best of Trinidad is in the north,
from Corozal Point to Galera Point, because of the combination of
mountains, forests, rivers, and a strand that is free of marshes.

Several miles inland the range attains an extreme height of 3,000
feet and forms some valleys of great beauty, notably the Maracas
Valley and the Caura Valley. The former has a waterfall that cascades down 340 feet of solid rock and throws off clouds of spray as
it descends. The rock on both sides is thickly covered with mosses,
ferns, and many tropical plants with leaves of varied hues from
emerald green to scarlet. There are natural swimming pools at the
base of the falls. The district is a center for the cultivation of cocoa.

Seven miles from Port-of-Spain and halfway to the entrance of
the Maracas Valley is the township of St. Joseph, the former Spanish
capital that used to be called San José de Oruña. It was founded
in 1577, and its oldest building is a church at least a century younger
where a tomb dated 1682 is shown. San José was never much of a
place. Close to the town is a plantation now used as a government
stock farm; in the drawing room of the residence the last Spanish
governor, Don José María Chacón, signed the capitulation that
yielded Trinidad to the English in 1797.

San Fernando, thirty-five miles down the shore of the Gulf of Paria
from Port-of-Spain, is the second largest city. It is of Spanish origin,
but gives little evidence of that fact today, being to a large extent a
Hindu community. The chief crop roundabout is the sugar cane,
and to serve both big and little growers the first central grinding
mills in the British West Indies were erected near San Fernando
more than seventy-five years ago. This system rejuvenated the sugar
business, both for the estates that had been operating at too high a
production cost and for thousands of peasant planters, who found
a market for their cane at the centrals.

South of the sugar district there are oil fields that make Trinidad
the chief source of petroleum in the British Empire. In money value,
oil accounts for two thirds of the island's exports. And on La Brea
Point, close to the sea, is that natural phenomenon the deposit of

asphalt known locally as the Pitch Lake. Sir Walter Raleigh, while in search of El Dorado in 1595, described his discovery of the lake as follows:

Besides our vessels were no other wherries, but one little barge, a small cockboate and a bad galiota which we framed in haste for that purpose at Trinidado, and these little boates had nyne or ten men apiece with all their victuals and armes. I myself coasted in my barge close abord the shore, and landed in every cove the better to know the Island, while the shippes kept the chanell. I left the shippes and kept by the shore the better to come to speack with some of the inhabitantes and also to understand the rivers, watring places and portes of the Island . . . from Curipan came to a port and seat of the Indians called Parico . . . from thence I rowed to anchor port called by the natives Piche and by the Spaniards Tierra de Brea. At this point called Tierra de Brea or Piche, there is that abundance of stone pitch that all the shippes of the world may be therewith laden from thence, and wee made triall of it in trimming our shippes to be most excellent good, and melteth not with the Sunne as pitch of Norway, and therefore for shippes trading South portes very profitable.

The area of the lake is 114 acres, smaller than the Savannah in Port-of-Spain, but it is 285 feet deep at the center, and while the tonnage of its shifting contents has never been accurately calculated, scientists believe that it can supply the world's needs for two or three generations. Some five million tons of asphalt have been removed in the past fifty years, and in that period the general level of the deposit has dropped only twenty feet. No matter how much is taken out at any given spot, the hole fills up and in a week or so all traces of digging have disappeared. A relatively small influx of pure asphalt is supposed to occur from surrounding territory.

The Caribs believed that a tribe named the Chayma once lived on the site of the lake. Following a triumphant campaign against their enemies, they celebrated by killing many hummingbirds, eating the flesh and adorning themselves with the plumage. But the hummingbird was sacred, and the Great Spirit punished the Chayma by causing the earth to open and engulf them, and then filled the valley with a noxious stuff that should serve to all eternity as their tomb.

The village and its inhabitants, the Caribs said, were locked in the asphalt and preserved at the bottom of the lake. Fossils and the bones of prehistoric animals are, in fact, often recovered by diggers. In 1928 a tree thousands of years old was slowly thrust in an upright position six feet above the surface, then tilted to one side, and in the course of a few days vanished again. Conceivably the Carib legend was founded upon the observation of such happenings.

A visit to the asphalt lake affords no feast of beauty. The mass is of a grayish black, the texture of which has been likened to the hide of a monster elephant. The irregular folds do suggest the creases in an elephant's leathery armor, or that of a rhinoceros. After the rains, these folds fill with water, creating an odd network of silver against the somber expanse. It is possible to walk anywhere on the surface, for although it feels spongy in places, your feet will not sink in more than a fraction of an inch. The best reason for going to La Brea is simply that nothing like it exists anywhere else in the world. A coastal boat runs down from San Fernando and discharges passengers at the asphalt company's long pier. Cruise vessels sometimes make a special call. The landing place with an eerie background is incongruously called Brighton; the English have a way of bestowing their beloved insular names haphazard in the colonies.

Because of the island's Latin and Catholic traditions, the carnival season before Lent is widely celebrated in Trinidad. The Negroes, influenced by the Spanish of the mainland, have added calypso music. The combination has resulted in a folk art that is getting to be known outside the little country. Typical are songs like "Jeremiah," "Rum and Coca-Cola," and the one celebrating the romance of Edward VIII and Wally Simpson, which have been broadcast by American radio stations and recorded for the phonograph. A calypso, strictly speaking, is a concert at which aspirants for carnival honors try out their songs before an audience that pays admissions and vociferously votes approval or disapproval. Both words and music are largely improvised. The curious rhythm employed has itself come to be known as calypso. It bears a relationship to jazz, yet has a flavor all its own. Read cold, the lines often appear disordered, senseless, but they come remarkably to life when chanted and shrieked to melodies you would hear under no other sun.

Carnival jollification in the streets of Port-of-Spain is noisy, gaudy, and marked by robust humor. But it is not well organized. Nothing in the class of the Mardi Gras parades of New Orleans is attempted. The Tourist Commission advocates the planning of "at least one spectacular ceremony with gay and colorful effects carried to the greatest conceivable limit."

Trinidad's early history followed a different course from that of the Antilles. Columbus discovered the island on his third voyage, in 1498, and named it for three low peaks he noted as he rounded its southeastern end. He met Carib Indians in a canoe in the Gulf of Paria, and when he tried to interest them by having some of his sailors dance on the poop to tambourine music the Caribs loosed "a great cloud of arrows." These were no gentle primitives such as the Spaniards had exploited in Hispaniola and Cuba. Though Columbus arranged a truce with them that day, he thought it prudent to give their island a wide berth and sailed on into the Caribbean through the strait he called the Dragon's Mouth. For a good seventy-five years afterward, Spain's claim to Trinidad was little more than nominal, but remained unchallenged by other European powers. The El Dorado mirage caused the forgotten colony to take on importance. Somewhere up the Orinoco River, in the heart of the continent, or far behind the low-lying Guiana coast, there was supposed to be a city named Manoa where gold nuggets and gems were as common as pebbles and where the cacique painted his body with powdered gold. Therefore, it was the land of El Dorado (The Gilded Man). Many adventurers had tried to find it, the chief of whom had been Gonzalo Jiménez de Quesada, the conqueror of Bogotá. When he died in 1579 he left all his property to his niece and her husband, Antonio de Berrio, with instructions to continue the quest.

Berrio took this legacy seriously. He concluded that Trinidad was the best base from which to work, so he induced the Crown to appoint him governor of the island, as well as of Manoa, if and when he should discover it. Berrio did some perilous exploring over a period of years, and then Sir Walter Raleigh came along in pursuit of the same illusion. The Elizabethan courtier's visit to the asphalt lake has been mentioned. He proceeded to the town of San José, captured Berrio, and burned the place. The aging Spaniard gave Raleigh sound advice about the difficulties ahead of him, but it did no good. Out of the failure of his first expedition, Sir Walter at least got a best-seller, which he entitled *Discoveries of the large and bewtiful Empire of Guiana*. He returned in 1617, an old and desperate man, landed again in Trinidad, and then plunged into the wilderness, where he met with overwhelming disaster. King James I committed him to the Tower of London and had him tried for treason and beheaded. "This is a powerful medicine," said Raleigh, smiling, as he tried the edge of the ax, "but a doctor that cures all ills."

As soon as Trinidad ceased being a jumping-off place for El Dorado it sank back into a state of neglect that kept it for a century and a half one of the poorest, if not the most destitute, of the Spanish possessions. The value of the asphalt deposits was not understood. Small quantities of sugar, coffee, and cocoa were produced, and that was all. In 1740 the settlers complained that they could go to mass but once a year and then only in relays, because they had to borrow articles from one another to complete a decent costume. An old chronicler says that the members of the *cabildo* had a single pair of dress trousers among them. Curiously enough, neither the English nor French made a serious attempt until late in the eighteenth century to capture this fertile colony, though they were perpetually disputing ownership of insignificant islets farther north.

In 1780 a Frenchman from Grenada named St. Laurent visited Trinidad, saw its possibilities, and pulled wires at Madrid to get permission for himself and some of his friends to take up land there. Surprisingly, in view of Spain's policy of excluding foreigners, he was successful. Two separate decrees were issued under Carlos III, a fairly liberal monarch, inviting immigration to Trinidad, which at that time had only 300 white inhabitants. The majority of those who came were Frenchmen, though almost as many Spaniards soon followed suit. The Gallic touch that distinguishes the life of Port-of-Spain dates from this period. At the end of fifteen years, the white population had increased to 18,000.

A riot ashore in 1796 between English sailors and French privateers offended the Spanish authorities. It was one of the reasons given for the declaration of war by Spain on England the following year, and thus indirectly it sealed the fate of the colony. A strong British expedition under Sir Ralph Abercromby set out from Martinique, overawed the weak Spanish garrison, and obtained the surrender of Trinidad without bloodshed. A mass flight to Venezuela of most of the French settlers occurred, but after the Napoleonic Wars a good many of them drifted back.

Trinidad has known none of war's alarms since it became a British possession, unless you want to include the fact that the biggest United States base on leased territory in the West Indies was established there during the recent struggle. Politically, the colony has had a peculiar story. The property-owning class was not allowed to set up a limited form of self-government after the model prevailing in Jamaica, Barbados, etc. Instead, the Spanish code was retained and modified slowly by laws originating in London. The type of crown-colony rule applied to most of the British West Indies after the Jamaican riots of 1865 may be said to have been worked out here. When a legislature was set up, it consisted of officials and a varying number of other persons appointed by the governor. Later some of the seats were made elective. A greater degree of popular representation was granted recently, but Trinidad is still behind Jamaica in this respect.

The English did not find many Negroes on the island, and as the slave trade was abolished shortly afterward it was necessary to import free labor. Demobilized colored veterans who had fought against the United States in the War of 1812 were sent to Trinidad. These preferred to become small settlers and the problem remained unsolved. Chinese were tried with unsatisfactory results, for the Chinaman in an alien country usually succeeds in cutting loose from gang labor and setting himself up in business. Then Hindus and Moslem East Indians were brought under contract to stay for seven years. The policy was continued for decades, and a large proportion of the indentured Orientals elected not to return to Hindustan at the end of their terms. This accounts for East Indians forming almost 35 per cent of the population today.

In 1898 the island of Tobago, twenty miles to the northeast, was incorporated with Trinidad governmentally. Its area is only 116 square miles, its length 26 miles, and its greatest breadth 7½ miles. Yet for two centuries it was a perpetual bone of contention, having been taken and retaken by the British, French, and Dutch more often than any other West Indian island. The Spaniards also long laid claim to it, and for several years it was owned by the Duchy of Courland, a semi-independent Baltic state. Tobago was the "desert island" described by Daniel Defoe as the scene of Robinson Crusoe's adventures, though the original from whom the character was drawn admittedly was marooned on Juan Fernández in the Pacific. And it is the one place in the Western world where birds of paradise can be seen outside of cages. With so many titles to distinction, it merits special attention.

Tobago can be reached only from Port-of-Spain. Steamers that run two or three times a week take nine hours to make the trip. But there is a plane five times a week that does it in thirty minutes. You land in one case at the government pier at Scarborough, the capital, and in the other at a well-appointed midget airfield a mile or so away, near the southerly tip of the island. A little coastal boat circles Tobago once a fortnight, to deliver goods and take on cargo, and this constitutes a scenic pleasure jaunt of much interest.

Scarborough is a characteristic British West Indian seaport village, with no structures of historical importance, but a lovely tropical setting for its couple of thousand inhabitants, most of whom are Negroes. They tell a gruesome tale about the old prison. In 1801 there had been a slave revolt and the outnumbered whites were beleaguered, though they had had the luck to take the ringleader. Him they proceeded to hang in full view of the crowd. When he was dead the body was lowered, only to be hoisted back to the gallows tree a few minutes later. Again it was lowered and again hauled up, a dozen times in the course of an hour. The slaves supposed that many of their number had been captured and that all would be put to death. They stole away, disheartened. It was easy after that to subdue them.

There is a small but good botanical garden. On the north curve of the bay stands Fort George, and on the south the Robinson Crusoe Hotel, the most elaborate on the island. One other hotel and three or four guest houses offer accommodations in and near Scarborough. The foundations of a building are shown where in 1769 John Paul Jones, naval hero of the Revolutionary War, was tried in vice-admiralty court for killing a man. Jones, aged twenty-two, was then master of a Jamaica slaver. He was accused of beating his black carpenter so severely with a belaying pin as to cause his death. Jones explained that he had been lying ill with fever when he learned that the carpenter was plotting a mutiny and it had been necessary to subdue him. He had not intended to kill, for if that had been so he would have used the pistol he had handy. The Tobago judge acquitted him.

A scant three miles across the narrow southern neck of the island is Plymouth, a virtually deserted town, though decaying houses stand there and many of the street signs are still in place. It was the scene of fighting between the English and French. A tomb with a most cryptic epitaph, dated 1783, is shown in Plymouth: "Here lies Mrs. Betty [last name obliterated]. . . . She was a mother without knowing it, and a wife without letting her husband know it, except by her kind indulgences to him."

Tobago, as seen from one of its central heights, has been aptly compared by Heath and Jefferson Bowman in their book *Crusoe's Island* with " a shimmering green lizard, lazily sunning itself upon an immense blue carpet." Nearly all of it is accessible by automobile or on horseback. There is a reserve of virgin forest along a ridge in the northwest. Around the shore you will find innumerable bathing beaches, ten of which have been developed. A retired British naval officer, Lieutenant Commander C. E. R. Alford, who has lived there since 1931, has become the island's modern chronicler and chief enthusiast. In his pamphlet *Tobago,* which can be had from the Tourist Commission in Port-of-Spain, he meticulously describes seven excursions that enable the visitor to cover everything of interest. Space is lacking to give the details here.

But I must emphasize the feature that rejoices naturalists and is a great attraction for some tourists: the business of the wild birds of paradise. The fauna of Tobago, like that of Trinidad, is South American. Why, then, the presence of this creature, the most spectacularly beautiful of all birds, which in a state of nature is confined to New Guinea? Actually it is found not on Tobago itself, but on an islet east of its northern tip, formerly called Little Tobago and now Ingram Island. The latter is star-shaped, about a mile across in either direction; it is thickly wooded and rises to a height of nearly 500 feet. It was owned by the late Sir William Ingram, who in 1909 imported twenty-six pairs of a gorgeous variety of birds of paradise from Dutch New Guinea and set them free. Climate and other conditions proved satisfactory and they multiplied.

After the death of Sir William in 1929, his sons gave the island to the colonial government on the condition that the birds there be protected and a supply of food and water maintained for them. It has been a general bird sanctuary ever since. Trees that bear fruits and seeds liked by the birds of paradise have been planted at intervals in the woods. Basins attached to the branches are kept replenished with water. Wardens keep a watch for hawks and destroy them.

Anyone may go to Ingram Island from the port of Speyside, where you pay a modest sum for transportation on a boat with an outboard motor. The government charges a landing fee of two shillings (forty cents). There is no way of telling how many birds of paradise there are, for they are extremely timid and seldom appear in open glades where they could be counted. The visitor will be lucky if he sees one or two at a distance, while the spectacle of the males "dancing" before the females at the mating season is the rarest of privileges. Commander Alford rather optimistically tells what you may hope for, as follows:

Guides take you along the tracks to the points where the birds are generally to be found. You will hear them calling. Keep still and watch the treetops. A shadowy form sweeps across from one tree to another. Walk like a woodsman and try to spy a patch where the sunlight strikes through the trees. You hear the quaint little call again, and then a splash of yellow as a cock goes overhead. It is the cock bird, of course, who has the glorious yellow plumage. The spray of golden feathers, which are long and thin and like silk to touch, come from under his wings (not the tail) and when "dancing" they are thrust upward by the raising of the wings.

Alford warns that this sex play is seldom witnessed, then quotes the only party of whites who, to his knowledge, had been present at a demonstration on Ingram Island:

Four males were perched on a branch by themselves in a small clearing, while the females flew up and down on either side of them continuously, sometimes swooping in close to their suitors to obtain a better view. The males uttered loud cries, and then threw up their wings, displaying the full arc of their magnificent plumage, so that their bodies were covered with a golden mantle which they kept in a state of vibration. They then proceeded to strut up and down along the branch in a sort of side-step dance, cocking up their tails every now and then and displaying their golden side feathers to the full.

Tobago has been the discovery of the few, to date, in modern times. It is bound to become more and more of a tourist resort.

CHAPTER 10

"LITTLE ENGLAND" AND GUIANA

BARBADOS and British Guiana are not close relations. As colonies under the same flag and in the same region, they can be rated as cousins. Sisters, no. Barbados was uninhabited when pre-empted and settled by Englishmen; the first Scots, Welsh, and Irish brought there were bondsmen, and Negro slaves added the only other racial strain. The island was never occupied, even briefly, by a rival power. It nurtured sober English customs, which the blacks themselves came to share, and this in combination with its placid scenery justified its nickname of Little England. British Guiana, on the other hand, is a slice of South America, composed of mountains, primeval forests, and a strip of swampy coastland. Its population is a hodgepodge second only to that of Trinidad, with the special feature of tribes of untamed Indians. It has known several sovereignties.

In stressing the above differences I am perhaps indulging a bit in literary license, for the modern economic and political problems of the two places do draw them together. But I must offer an excuse for presenting Barbados and British Guiana in the same chapter, and paradox will serve as well as any. From the transportation standpoint, the easiest way of reaching both of them is via Trinidad.

Before the war Bridgetown, Barbados, was a regular port of call for steamship lines from New York, New Orleans, and Canada, and it was often on cruise itineraries. Today you have your choice of transferring at Port-of-Spain from Pan American Airways to a British plane or a small interisland passenger boat. This applies to North American travelers. Surface communication between England and Barbados has not been interrupted.

146

When you sight the island you are struck by its fully cultivated, trim, almost parklike appearance, so different from that of other West Indian countries. The hills are low and rolling, with comparatively few trees. The land at all elevations is richly green under its blanket of cane and other crops, but mostly cane. There are no real cities, but many townships and villages. Even in the rural districts the houses are numerous, bespeaking a dense population. Bridgetown stands on a roadstead rather than a harbor, and for so small a port the activity in normal times is astonishing. Laborers and peddlers swarm on the docks. The water is covered with little craft of every description, fishing boats setting forth or returning with the catch, bumboats trying to beat the competition ashore by hawking provisions from ship to ship. Scores of divers, naked except for breechcloths, clamor for the chance to show their dexterity in retrieving coins.

On my first visit I felt at once that the divers indicated something significant and puzzling about Barbados. At St. Thomas and elsewhere, the calling was pursued by colored boys. Here adults, some of them oldish, outnumbered the boys, and more surprising still, there was a sprinkling of whites among them. The game was played with the desperate intensity of men whose livelihood depended upon it, rather than as a sport that would yield a little pocket money to the lucky. I soon learned that making ends meet was harder in Barbados than in any other Caribbean island, because it has over eleven hundred inhabitants to the square mile, a ratio exceeding that of Puerto Rico. As for the white divers, they are so-called "Red Legs," descendants of Cromwellian bondsmen who formed a class that has never succeeded in coming up in the world and has lived for centuries among the Negroes, though with a minimum of intermarriage. A few families of the sort exist in Jamaica, but in Barbados there are enough of them to attract attention.

The mouth of a stream has been widened to form the Careenage, a narrow inner harbor where small ships can dock. Passengers from larger vessels are put ashore there in lighters. No one could call the little town impressive. At the end of the Careenage is the center of things, Trafalgar Square and its statue of Nelson. The streets parallel with the shore seem to have been laid out on the principle of faithfully repeating the idiosyncrasies of nature, and this produces some odd curves. Many of the names are nice. There are Magazine

Lane, Literary Row, Flower Pot Alley, Maiden's Lane, Bachelor's Lane, Sober Lane, and Amen Alley.

Shopping in the two or three department stores and many smaller places is not unlike what it would be in an English seaside town, the imported goods being largely British. Ready-made clothes may be had, of course, but an outfitter of any pretensions calls himself a "bespoke tailor." A number of good hotels are available, most of them located in the suburb of Hastings, on the southerly shore about two and a half miles from town. Among them are the Marine, up to date and with more than 120 bedrooms; the Royal, the Balmoral, the Windsor, the Hastings, and the Ocean View. The most famous hostelry, Sam Lord's Castle, however, is a little over ten miles out on the Atlantic coast, and of this more anon.

St. Michael's, the Anglican cathedral, was rebuilt of coral rock after the original structure had been blown down by the great hurricane of 1780. Thirty years before, George Washington had gone to church there during the visit that he and his half brother, Lawrence, paid to Barbados in 1751. At the corner of Bay Street and Chelsea Road is the house where the two young men stayed. George had the misfortune to contract smallpox, and for a while his case was thought critical. He was in bed for a month. Yet he regarded the journey as one of the most pleasant incidents of his youth, and in the diary he kept he made the following comments on the island:

"We were perfectly ravished with the delightful prospects on every side. Fields of sugar cane, corn, fruit trees, etc., all wonderfully green. The view from each height is even better than those which are lower. . . . The Governor seems to keep a proper state, lives very retired and at little expense. . . . The healthfulness of the island is shown in the florid countenances of the country gentlemen, and it is said that they live to great ages when they are not intemperate."

He considered the $60 a month that the house with board cost him and Lawrence extravagantly high, adding that this was exclusive of liquors and washing, which "we provided ourselves."

All that Washington wrote in praise of Barbados holds good today. It is undoubtedly the most healthful of the West Indies, being free of malaria and some other maladies associated with the tropics. The water supply is exceptionally pure, because the subsoil through which it runs is a clean, porous coral, and there are no swamps. The climate is mild and uniform, the temperature varying only seventeen degrees the year round, from a low of seventy degrees to a high of eighty-seven degrees Fahrenheit. This is due to the little island's location in the Atlantic Ocean, definitely apart from the chain of the Lesser Antilles, and refreshed at all times by the trade winds. Barbadians like to point out that their home lies on the thirteenth parallel of latitude, which runs through Nicaragua, the Philippines, French Indo-China, the southern part of Hindustan, the southern tip of Arabia, and the Sudan, Nigeria, and Gambia in Africa, and that nowhere along that parallel is there another spot with so genial a climate.

But though "Little England" is beautiful, I find its aspect tame in comparison not with obvious scenic superiors, but with glittering Tobago, say, or savage St. John. The life, too, is undramatic: a pleasant country-club sort of existence, English style, for the well-to-do; the poverty I have mentioned for ninety-nine out of a hundred of the blacks. Golf is played over a fine nine-hole course, and sea bathing, yachting, and fishing are well organized for residents and visitors. Drive anywhere through the country and your emotions will be touched by the reverse side of the picture. I do not know of another rural population that makes such pitiful attempts to live by means of trading on a minimum scale. The stalls that succeed one another at short intervals often display nothing but half a dozen eggs, a few oranges, and a pint of beans. It would not be worth while to carry so small an amount to the Bridgetown market. But a passer-by just might be tempted to purchase. As in Puerto Rico, nearly all the fertile land is planted to cane, and employment on a sugar estate is seasonal. The peasant can scarcely grow enough to eat during the off season, and from the look of things he tries to sell the little that he does raise.

In the old days when sugar was a bonanza and the expression "as rich as a West Indian planter" was commonly employed in Europe, some magnificent houses were built in Barbados. A few of these still stand. Among them is Farley Hill, sixteen miles north of Bridgetown, erected by a forgotton nabob in a lovely wooded glade 800 feet above sea level and reconstructed by Sir Graham Briggs in the middle of the last century. Its garden was once described as "the wonder of the island." A handsome variety of fern called the Farliense was developed there.

Better known is Sam Lord's Castle on the southeast coast, which has been converted into a hotel. The founder was by all odds the most colorful figure in Barbados a century and a half ago. His family had long been affluent planters and owned several estates. When Sam's elder brother died leaving children, Sam nevertheless managed to get possession of every one of the plantations. This wealth did not satisfy him. He wanted huge sums with which to build a mansion such as the island had never seen. The story goes that he became a wrecker after the fashion of his Cornish ancestors. He strung lanterns in the coconut trees on the shore of Long Bay, and in foul weather ships would be lured into the supposed haven and go to pieces on the rocks. Sam would send out boatmen to save the passengers and crew, but at the same time would rob the cargoes. This may or may not have been the case. Records exist, however, showing that Sam Lord once had a price put on his head for perjury and forgery. He wriggled out of all legal complications, and around 1820 he achieved his castle.

It is a great square structure with four entrances approached by steps of black and white marble, and around the top are medieval battlements. Deep porches on both floors adapt this severe European architecture to the tropics. The thick walls have withstood many a hurricane. The interior of the building is handsomely decorated, largely in stuccowork, the ceilings being particularly effective. These decorations were commenced by an English soldier known to posterity only as Warren, and were finished by Italian and English artisans brought out by Sam Lord. The castle, as renovated by the present lessees, is richly furnished with antiques, some of which belonged to old Sam himself. It has pleasant grounds and a private beach. A mile or so away, on a cliff overlooking the sea, is the Crane Hotel, a worthy rival for the favor of travelers.

Of great interest in the history of West Indian education is Codrington College on the Atlantic, straight across the island at its widest point from Bridgetown. This is the oldest school of university standing in the British colonies. A planter, Christopher Codrington, who had served as governor general of the Leeward Islands and died in 1710, willed his estate for its founding to the Society for the Propagation of the Gospel. He was a mighty pious man for the eighteenth century to have produced, and in the lawless Caribbean at that. He specified that the professors and scholars were "all of them to be under the vows of poverty, chastity and obedience; who shall be obliged to study and practise Physic and Chirurgery, as well as Divinity; that by the apparent usefulness of the former to all mankind, they may both endear themselves to the people and have the better opportunity of doing good to men's souls, whilst they are taking care of their bodies." The successive principals of Codrington College have been clergymen, as seems only proper. But the curriculum has been broadened through the years, and many of the graduates have distinguished themselves in a variety of callings. The buildings are effectively located on the side of a hill overlooking the sea and with an artificial lake directly in front of them.

Anglican churches that charmingly reproduce the atmosphere of English parish worship are to be found throughout Barbados. In one of them, St. John's, is the tomb of "Ferdinando Paleologus, Descended from ye Imperial Line of ye last Christian Emperors of Greece," who died in 1678. Christ Church near Oistin's Town, however, is the one that draws tourists, because its graveyard was the scene of a mystery so remarkable that societies for psychical research have studied it. No plausible solution has ever been advanced for the following weird occurrences:

A vault belonging to the Elliot family, in which there had been no interment for over seventy years, was opened in 1807 to receive the wooden coffin of a woman. According to a contemporary account, the vault was found to be "quite empty, without the smallest appearance of any person having been buried there." Not long afterward a child's body and then a woman's, both in leaden coffins, were placed in the vault. In 1812, when another funeral was held, it was discovered that the two leaden caskets were not in their proper places; notably the one containing the child, which was standing nearly upright with the head down, against the opposite wall. The wooden coffin had not been disturbed. It seemed a clear case of vandalism, but the matter was not taken seriously for the moment.

Four more times, up to the year 1819, the vault was opened for funerals, and on each occasion the leaden coffins were in a state of wild confusion, overturned, thrown here and there. A particularly heavy casket, which it would have required eight men to lift, was found on the fourth step, blocking the door. Each time they were restored to their proper positions—to no avail. The last interment had been attended by the governor, Lord Combermere, and he could not get these bewildering circumstances out of his mind.

The vault had been partly excavated in solid rock, and for the rest was "closed with a double wall, from top to bottom, an inner and outer, not united." A ponderous slab of blue marble lay over the entrance, above the steps. Care had always been taken to cement this slab in place, and toward the end secret marks were made in the masonry. The cement remained unbroken and the marks intact until the gravediggers were ordered to pry up the slab for a new funeral. The walls, floor, and roof of the vault had been frequently tested, without revealing signs that they had been tampered with. The theory that earthquakes had caused the disturbances was untenable. Firstly, no seismic shocks had been felt in Barbados during the period in question. Secondly, an earthquake strong enough to shift the coffins like playthings would infallibly have leveled Christ Church itself to the ground. And why were the light wooden containers ignored and only the lead cases tossed about?

Public opinion, of course, favored a supernatural explanation. But that was not good enough for Lord Combermere. On April 18, 1820, some ten months after the last burial, he decided to make a surprise inspection of the vault. Accompanied by four gentlemen, including the rector, the Reverend T. H. Orderson, who wrote a report of the proceedings and had it attested by a notary, the Governor went to the churchyard and had the marble slab removed. Again the leaden coffins were found to be in disarray. Then, as previously, the obvious human motive of theft was discounted by the fact that there had been no attempt to violate them.

The rector, in agreement with Combermere, ordered all the coffins taken out and buried in separate graves. The vault was left open and may be seen to this day, an ordinary-looking subterranean tomb that the years have moldered, its floor bestrewn with dry leaves and twigs blown in by the wind. Oddly enough, ghosts were never reported to have appeared in connection with the above happenings. Nor have there been any phenomena since the consignments to mother earth. I should like, however, to have one of those leaden caskets exhumed. Maybe it would be discovered lying on its side, or off at some angle beyond the limits of the grave!

The formal history of Barbados contains little that is exciting. It was one of the few West Indian islands that Columbus did not discover. A Portuguese ship is believed to have come upon it in 1536, and the sailors called it Barbudos (bearded), from the fig trees draped with Spanish moss that they had seen in great numbers. As it is west of the longitude beyond which Portugal could not seize territory in the Americas, according to the famous bulls of Pope Alexander VI, it was left alone. Nor were the Spaniards interested, though they laid claim to the whole archipelago. The original Arawak inhabitants had been killed off by Caribs, who had failed to establish settlements of their own.

Sir Olive Leigh, en route to Guiana in his vessel, the *Olive Blossom,* went ashore at Barbados at a date believed to have been 1605 and erected a cross with an inscription on a tree, "James K. of E. and of this Island." He never returned, but on the strength of his act Barbados likes to consider itself the oldest British colony in the Caribbean. Possession was actually taken in 1627 by Sir William Courteen, four years after plantations had been started in St. Christopher by Sir Thomas Warner. These two adventurers obtained noble patrons in England. The Crown appears to have granted Barbados to both of them. Partisans of Warner, acting in the name of the Earl of Carlisle, won out after an armed struggle. During the Civil War the island took the royalist side, and Parliament sent out a squadron of ships with troops to subdue it. Resistance was offered, but the colonists were soon forced to capitulate as the result of a blockade that cut off their supplies. Except for a few slave uprisings and some riots in the days following Negro emancipation, bloodshed did not again occur on Barbadian soil. This record of civil strife only—and not much of that—is unparalleled elsewhere in the Caribbean.

A legislature that had been set up in 1639 was recognized by Cromwell, and thereafter power reposed in a governor representing the king, an appointed council regarded as equivalent to England's House of Lords, and an assembly elected by the freeholders (men of property) to function like the House of Commons. This archaic system, modified by various extensions of the franchise and recently a good deal liberalized, has persisted to the present day. Barbados did not lose its constitution in 1865, as Jamaica and some of the other colonies did. Responsible government, probably within the framework of a West Indian federation, is now being demanded by a large section of the people.

The name Guiana is generally thought to have been derived from an aboriginal Indian word pronounced something like *winna,* meaning "water" or "watery country." Be that as it may, the coastal territory of the three Guianas fits the supposed origin perfectly. Many rivers pour down from the interior. They and their tributary creeks fan out near the sea and traverse the alluvial plain with innumerable waterways. Some of the links are bayous that have no current. Man has extended the network, by digging 140 miles of navigation and forty miles of drainage canals. The sea itself is shallow for some distance offshore, but there are several main approaches for ships, channeled by the larger rivers. The country is not unlike the delta of the Mississippi, but more solid and with a richer vegetation. Netherlanders were the first to exploit the future British Guiana. They reveled in it, as far as they got, and no wonder! For it seemed to them a tropical Holland.

Lafcadio Hearn paid a visit in the late 1880's. That great stylist had an eye for the sort of scenic effects he found, and his description could not be bettered:

The atmosphere is heavy with strange mists; and the light of an orange-colored sun, immensely magnified by vapors, illuminates a greenish-yellow sea. . . . We are in the shallows, moving very slowly. . . . The water shows olive and ochreous tones alternately—the foam is yellow in our wake. These might be the colors of a freshwater inundation. . . . There is land in sight—very low land—a thin, dark line suggesting marshiness; and the nauseous color of the water always deepens.

As the land draws near, it reveals a beautiful tropical appearance. The sombre green line brightens color, sharpens into a splendid fringe of fantastic evergreen fronds, bristling with palm crests. Then a mossy seawall comes into sight—dull gray stonework, green-lined at all its joints. There is a fort. The steamer's whistle is exactly mocked by a queer echo, and the cannon-shot once reverberated—only once: there are no mountains here to multiply a sound. And all the while the water becomes a thicker and more turbid green; the wake looks more and more ochreous, the foam ropier and yellower.

It might be thought that a similar impression would not be got from an airplane. Yet the above, greatly intensified, is just what you experience. As I have told in connection with previous flights, all colors are sharpened, all forms solidified to essentials like the projections on a map in relief. The yellow and ocher and green become pools and veins on the background of that sea dimmed by the heat haze to a steely blue. You are aware of the bar, which is a full nine miles out from shore and now resembles a submarine island looming darkly. The coast is the same thin line at a distance that it was to Hearn, changing as if by magic to a luxuriant façade of fruit trees and palms.

The transitions are very rapid, of course. In a moment you are swooping over jungle, river, and dwellings to a landing at the near-by airport. Georgetown, the capital of British Guiana, is on the right bank of the Demerara River, and it also has a short ocean frontage. Since its average level is four feet below that of the sea, there is a protecting wall that starts at Fort William Frederick at the mouth of the river and runs for several miles along the coast. The houses often are built on brick or cement pillars, which lift them several feet above the humid soil. Some of the streets have open trenches or canals down their center in which aquatic plants float. Improved drainage, however, has made it possible to ignore Dutch devices in the erecting of modern homes and the laying out of suburbs. Georgetown calls itself the "Garden City of the West Indies." This is typical of British Guiana's attitude, for although the country geographically is not West Indian, it sets store on its political relationship with the island colonies and dislikes being classed as South American.

A garden city the capital undoubtedly is. All travelers have noted the abundance of palms—eight or ten common varieties, and many that are rare—colonnades of palms, groves of palms. Every tropical plant with brilliant foliage or leaves will flourish here, but most of them are cultivated. Outstanding is the victoria regia water lily, indigenous and one of the horticultural wonders of the world. Its leaves are often over six feet in diameter, lying close to the surface of pond or canal like monster platters, and its great rose-white blossoms are from twelve to eighteen inches across. The victoria regia and the naturalized Indian lotus grow on every hand. Superficially, there seems no need for an official botanical garden; but there is one that serves scientific ends and is an admirable show place.

The old downtown quarter is still called Stabroek, which was the name given the original town founded by the Dutch. The name Georgetown was adopted in 1812. The public buildings are adequate, but not particularly inspiring. Both the Anglican and Catholic cathedrals date only from the end of the nineteenth century. The museum is somewhat superior to those in other British colonies of the region, but there is no decent library. Hotel accommodations are poor from the standpoint of the expected boom in tourist traffic. Two pleasant little hostelries from days gone by, the Park and the Tower, stand on Main Street, a thoroughfare made attractive by the grounds of Government House. A building program is an urgent necessity.

The second city of British Guiana is New Amsterdam, farther east on the coast. Unless business takes you there, it is scarcely worth a visit. Other townships are all tiny and in the interior. The vast hinterland has a great deal to offer, but an explorer's zeal is required to see much of it, except the superb Kaieteur Falls, to which special transportation routes have been opened. The peculiar topography of the country must be borne in mind. There are three belts, the first being the coastal one, at or below sea level, extending inland for a distance of ten miles and in places more. This is the belt where sugar, rice, and some minor crops are grown. It was the whole of Guiana as far as the early settlers were concerned, and it is all that the average visitor to Georgetown sees. The second belt is of sand and clay, covered with scrub woods; its varying width rises slowly to a height of about 200 feet above sea level. Then comes the huge third belt, which consists of undulating plateaus that merge with forest-clad mountain ranges; it penetrates the heart of South America for three hundred miles.

Four principal rivers run from south to north, cutting across all the belts. The Courantyne separates British from Dutch Guiana. The next river westward is the Berbice, followed by the Demerara and the Essequibo. The three last-mentioned divide the territory into three provinces, or counties, each of which is named after a river. Georgetown, as we have seen, is on the Demerara, and up this stream deposits of bauxite are worked. The Essequibo, however, is by far the largest river, being six hundred miles long and broadening to an estuary that is fourteen miles across when it meets the Atlantic. Communication with the far interior is by way of the Essequibo, which leads to gold and diamond fields, and to inexhaustible reserves of balata (chicle) and hardwoods. On the Venezuelan border there is the Northwestern District, largely unexplored, where gold has been discovered.

The pleasure tripper will be unlikely to want to visit the mines. The occasional enthusiast can make arrangements with the exploiting companies, especially the Demerara Bauxite Company, which maintains a "model town" for its employees at MacKenzie. A journey to Mount Roraima, where the frontiers of Guiana, Venezuela, and Brazil meet, may be dismissed as a jaunt for none but an expedition elaborately equipped; it is the locale used by Conan Doyle for his bizarre romance *The Lost World*.

Kaieteur Falls, on the other hand, should be seriously considered. They can be reached from Georgetown in three days by rail and river steamer connecting with a fairly good driving road. Also, a privately owned seaplane that will accept passengers makes the hop now and then in an hour or two. The falls are on the upper branch of the Potaro, a tributary stream of the Essequibo, at about the geographical center of the country. They were unknown until 1870, when Barrington Brown, a government surveyor, stumbled upon them. The Potaro plunges over a tableland into a valley, the total drop being 881 feet, 89 feet more than the height of the Woolworth Building, twice the height of the Great Pyramid, and five times that of Niagara Falls. For the first 741 feet the sheet of water descends straight, then bursts upon a rugged slope and continues foaming for the rest of its downward course. In the effective words of Sir Edward Denham, a former governor of the colony, "the division of the waters gives the impression of silver foxes rushing in their millions to throw themselves off the rocks." The extreme width of the falls is four hundred feet in the rainy season, and about fifty feet narrower in the dry season.

Sir Everard im Thurn, an explorer, saw the falls in 1879. He lay full length on a cliff and gazed down at them. His description of the view from that angle was as follows: "An indescribable, almost inconceivable, vast curtain of water—I can find no other phrase—some 400 feet in width, rolled over the top of the cliff, retaining its full width until it crushed into the boiling water of the pool which filled the whole space below; and at the surface of this pool itself only the outer edge was visible, for the greater part was beaten and hurled up in a great high mass of surf and foam and spray."

Mrs. Mary Gadd, secretary of the Tourist Commission, regards Kaieteur as a unique drawing card for tourists. She points out that if you go by plane you land on the river above the falls and take off practically at the brink, "a thrill which no one having experienced it is likely to forget." Incidentally, it is gold country and workings may be seen near by.

The original Indian population of British Guiana was composed of Arawaks, Caribs, Guaraunos, and some minor tribes. As in the islands, the dominant race was Arawak until the far more aggressive Caribs came on their strange migration northward from a point of origin that is believed to have been in Paraguay. Wherever the Caribs went in Trinidad and the Lesser Antilles they exterminated the Arawaks, but the wide reaches of mountains and forests made that impossible in Guiana. Descendants of both races live as neighbors today. The Guaraunos are the swamp Indians, their habitat always having been the coastlands. A small tribe so pale in complexion as to lead imaginative explorers to call them white was discovered not many years ago in the back country. They are the Woyaways. Unfortunately they are dying out, partly because they are susceptible to lung diseases. There is a higher mortality among the males than the females. All the aboriginal races put together constitute a mere 2.5 per cent of a total population of some 365,000.

Dutch, Portuguese, and British settlers arrived in that order, but their descendants of pure strain and other whites account for only 3 per cent. The mass of the inhabitants are East Indians (43.45 per cent), Negroes (37.41 per cent), and mixed bloods (12.39 per cent). Note that the East Indians are present in an even greater proportion than in Trinidad. Guiana is the sole New World country where they outnumber the blacks. They were imported during the same period and for the same reasons that they were taken to Trinidad. The conditions suited them and few cared to return to their former homes when their terms of indenture expired. At their present rate of increase they bid fair to become the majority element in another generation or so. Their labor saved the sugar industry. Rice culture was second nature to most of them, and their efficiency in that line has made the colony the chief rice bowl of the Caribbean region. Many East Indians—Hindus, Moslems, and Parsis—are now established as peasant farmers.

This Orientalizing of part of the northern coast of South America is a development the founders could not have foreseen, an odd historical quirk. It is paralleled in Dutch Guiana, where Javanese have been introduced, and in French Guiana, where there are Annamese and Arabs. We shall look at the two last-named colonies in connection with the Dutch and French islands. But a perspective on the whole Guiana territory can best be obtained at this point.

It had been a no man's land between Spain and Portugal from the beginning, for neither power felt sure whether it lay east or west of the line established by Pope Alexander VI. Both said it belonged to them, yet hesitated to colonize it. Spain's claim was the more all-embracing. Portugal contented herself with encroaching on the southeasterly end where it touched Brazil. Holland was the first other European nation to trespass, when an attempt was made by a company of Zealanders to found a colony in what is now British Guiana in 1580. They were unsuccessful by and large, but were never quite uprooted. Raleigh arrived in 1595 on one of his expeditions in search of El Dorado, and it is interesting to recall that his flowery descriptions of a land "that hath yet her maidenhead, never sacked, turned, nor wrought, the face of the earth not torn, nor the virtue and salt of the soil spent by manurance," almost led the Pilgrim Fathers to steer for Guiana instead of Massachusetts.

Meanwhile, the Dutch had obtained the right, in one of the clauses of the truce of 1609, by which Spain acknowledged the freedom of the Netherlands, to trade for nine years in any part of the Western Hemisphere that had not yet been organized. They picked the Guiana coast and soon had stations at the mouths of the Demerara and Essequibo Rivers. Then the French thrust themselves in at Cayenne and started to build a colony, which the Portuguese resented. Nobody bothered about the central district, Surinam, until the English took it in 1652. Observe that what is now British Guiana was then Dutch Guiana, and what is now Dutch Guiana was then British Guiana.

They often attacked each other, slew garrisons, and plundered warehouses. In 1667, however, as one of the terms of the Treaty of Breda, the English made a fabulous swap. They gave Surinam to the Dutch in exchange for New Amsterdam on the Hudson, the future city of New York. Each colony had been occupied by the rival power during the war, and the agreement was reached that both nations were to keep their conquests. The ironic point is that the Netherlanders gloated over it as a good bargain.

All Guiana, except the French part, remained in the possession of Holland until 1780, when she became embroiled with England over the American Revolution. The English left Surinam alone, but seized the provinces of Demerara, Essequibo, and Berbice. They changed hands twice more during the Napoleonic Wars, and were finally ceded to England in 1814. A few years later they were united as a single colony under the name British Guiana.

The Dutch constitutional structure was retained for a long time. The advisory legislature was a complicated affair called the Combined Court, consisting of the governor, six appointed financial members, and a court of policy chosen by a college of electors. The people now elect representatives by direct vote. The modern self-government movement is not so advanced as it is in Jamaica and Trinidad, but it is strong.

CHAPTER 11

HOLLAND IN THE WEST INDIES

I N THE last chapter the part played by the Dutch in colonizing the Guianas was touched upon. I showed that they had left their mark on the section owned by Britain. Surinam and the half-dozen small islands that remained in their possession from the days of strife are now officially known as the Netherlands West Indies. You would expect these to differ in architecture and customs from places developed by the Spanish, French, and English. But the visitor is amazed at the extreme "Dutchness" that he finds, at least on the surface, a feeling shared even by modern Dutchmen from Europe. One of the latter in Curaçao told me so. The matter-of-course way in which the old burghers reproduced Holland wherever they went is no less striking in the Caribbean than it is in South Africa and the East Indies.

The two divisions of the domain are lopsided as to area. Surinam has 55,143 square miles. The islands—Curaçao, Aruba, and Bonaire off the Venezuelan coast; Saba, St. Eustatius, and St.-Martin in the Lesser Antilles—total only 384 square miles. Values based on size can be illusory, however, and particularly in this case. As with British Guiana, the narrow coastal strip of Surinam is all that has been settled. Willemstad, Curaçao, is one of the leading ports of the West Indies and causes the island to outweigh Surinam in commerce. Aruba is the scene of gigantic refineries for the oil of Maracaibo, while the other specks of islets are of no mercantile importance.

From the travel point of view, Curaçao is a great attraction because of its free port. Most cruise ships stop there, and airplane traffic via Ciudad Trujillo and other transfer points is increasing. Paramaribo, the capital of Dutch Guiana, is visited by a few pleasure seekers; still fewer have the luck to see the extraordinary volcanic cone of Saba. The rest are simply not tourist territory. Yet every one is interesting. Let us steer an arbitrary course around them, beginning with Curaçao.

Columbus never sailed that way. In 1499 Alonzo de Ojeda set out on an independent voyage, with royal permission but well aware that he would encroach on the preserves of the "Admiral of the Ocean Sea." Ojeda looted the pearl fisheries that Columbus had observed near Trinidad, then proceeded west along the coast afterward known as the Spanish Main. Amerigo Vespucci, the man who was to give his name to both continents, was a member of the party and is often credited with having been the discoverer of Curaçao. He landed there, at all events, and wrote a highly fanciful account of his experiences. The place was the home of a race of giants, he averred, and went on:

> We beheld in a valley five of their huts, which appeared uninhabited: and we made our way to them and found only five women, two old ones and three girls, so lofty in stature that we gazed at them in astonishment: and when they saw us, so much terror overcame them that they had not even spirit to flee away: and the two old women began to invite us with words, bringing us many things to eat, and they put us in a hut: and they were in stature taller than a tall man. . . . We were all of a mind to take away the three girls from them by force: and to carry them to Castile as a prodigy: and while thus discussing, there began to enter through the door of the hut full 36 men much bigger than the women: more, so well built that it was a famous sight to see them: who put us in such uneasiness that we would much rather have been in our ships than in the company of such people.

No harm came to Amerigo. He and Ojeda reported the island to Queen Isabella as a new jewel in her crown. But the Spaniards did not attempt to colonize it until about thirty years later, when they lightly occupied Curaçao, Aruba, and Bonaire. They used the three for raising cattle in a desultory fashion, the beasts being allowed to run wild. No fortifications were built. For a hundred years this indifference continued. Spain could scarcely be expected to bother about a group of arid little islands when she had limitless fertile and unexploited provinces on the mainland.

In the early seventeenth century the Dutch were eager to obtain a permanent foothold in the New World. We have seen how they began operations on the Guiana coast. A port within the Caribbean Sea was regarded as an absolute necessity, partly for trading purposes and partly as a base for the sea rovers who flew the flag of the Dutch West India Company. Two expeditions, one of which was against Puerto Rico, met with failure. Then four ships invested Curaçao in 1634 and the Spaniards surrendered without a fight. Thereafter, the Hollanders held it against all comers. The buccaneers menaced it several times. Henry Morgan himself surveyed, in 1666, the formidable defenses that had been erected, and concluded that it would be unwise to attack. The French were twice repulsed. On a third occasion the corsair Jacques Cassard was on the point of succeeding when he agreed to accept, instead, a ransom of 600,000 louis d'or.

One of the first governors of Curaçao was Peter Stuyvesant, the famous peg leg, stubborn and shrewd, who did much to build up the port of Willemstad and was then promoted to be governor of New Amsterdam (New York).

This island that the Dutch have always so greatly prized is about forty miles long and from three to eight miles wide. Its foundation is volcanic rock, upon which coral reefs formed in prehistoric times. Low hills run down the middle of it. The windward shore has been pounded smooth by the surf and has no harbors. On the leeward side the sea broke through the reefs at intervals and formed a series of landlocked havens by filling what once had been valleys. The largest of these is the Schottegat, at the entrance of which Willemstad was placed and around the shores of which it has since expanded. The result is one of the most curious ports in the West Indies.

The narrow channel into the Schottegat is called St. Anna Bay, and a ship entering it passes straight through the city. On the right hand lies the Poenda district, which was the original town; and on the left is Overzidje, a name that means literally "other side." St. Anna Bay is spanned by a pontoon bridge, which because of the heavy traffic by water is open a large part of the time. A launch transports passengers, but automobilists in a hurry are often forced to make the circuit of the harbor to get from Poenda to Overzidje or vice versa. In the old days there was a toll for pedestrians crossing the bridge: two cents if a person wore shoes and one cent if he wore sandals; but if he was barefoot it was assumed that he was a pauper, and he passed free. Facing this bridge is the old and popular Hotel Americano.

Poenda has a medieval appearance, the houses being huddled close together and the streets even narrower than those in the most ancient Spanish-American town. There is a rather quaint explanation. The Dutch pioneers, it seems, decided that in that hot climate it would be well to imitate the Spaniards and have balconies. But their thrifty souls could not bear the waste of all that space. One after the other, the owners built walls to connect with the balconies and enlarged their houses at the expense of the roadway. If it were not for the many open doors and the glimpses of tropical potted plants, you could imagine yourself in an old quarter of a Netherlands city.

Overzidje, of course, is a good deal more modern. It is in no sense less Dutch. The salient buildings have stepped gables and dormer windows, even chimney pots for show. The windows are divided into many small squares, the glass framed with lead or tinted putty. The eighteenth-century Government House is a burgomaster's mansion to the last detail; it stands close to frowning Fort Amsterdam. One concession has been made to the Torrid Zone: houses are of various colors—blue, saffron, and pink for the most part—it being against the law to create a glare by painting any building white. Other colonizers in the region, by the way, have never had this rule, though the Spaniards favored tinted walls. White structures are to be seen all over the Caribbean, too many of them in some cities. I approve of the Dutch notion.

Willemstad is a free port, longer established and larger than Charlotte Amalie, U. S. Virgin Islands, its only rival in the West Indies. The Dutch followed this policy from the beginning and they made it pay big dividends. The shopping district is a market where the goods of all nations are admitted without customs duties, or in a few instances at a very low tariff. French perfumes and wines, jewelry, silver, and gaudy Oriental silks consistently outsold the products of Holland, and will again. The profit lies in a quick turnover, which makes for general prosperity and is subject to local taxation. Since the recent war a small sales tax has been imposed. Some of the stores are among the finest in the region, outside of Havana.

High finance is controlled by Portuguese Jews whose ancestors fled the Holy Inquisition. A branch of the Maduro family, bankers, boasts of having settled in Curaçao four hundred years ago. If such be the case, they were there long before the Dutch. Under the terms of the surrender the Spanish obtained a pledge that all the inhabitants would be transferred to Venezuela. Tradition has it that an exception was made in the case of a group of seventy-five Indians, and this ruling might well have been broadened to include certain Jews. The policy from then on was to allow freedom of religion and of enterprise, and virtual freedom of immigration. More Portuguese Jews came from Brazil. Traders and artisans from most of the European countries drifted in. Negro slaves were brought in large numbers from Africa. In recent years Chinese, Syrians, and other Orientals appeared. The claim is made that the descendants of forty-five nationalities live there today.

Papamiento, the speech of the masses, is a language rather than a patois. It contains Spanish, Portuguese, Dutch, English, French, African, and Indian words. Very simple but expressive, it has been called a spontaneous Esperanto. Two weekly newspapers are published in Papamiento.

I drove about the countryside during my short stay in Curaçao and confirmed my previous impression that it had almost no agricultural possibilities. A few plantations, which depended on the uncertain rainfall, existed in the past, but they long ago exhausted the thin soil. The natural vegetation is mostly of the cactus species. Sunbaked and brown, the undulating land is devoid of charm. Chinese gardeners succeed in cultivating vegetable patches by the industrious use of watering cans. A limited irrigation system keeps alive small groves of oranges, from which the liqueur known as Curaçao is manufactured. An attempt was once made to run an ostrich farm, since the big birds did well in parched areas of South Africa, but the climate proved to be too dry for ostriches. This island is more arid than even St. Thomas.

The Dutch, however, never had the illusion that they could plant there successfully. Curaçao, to them, was primarily an entrepôt, and in their steady way they clung to the idea through bad times as well as good. For a hundred years after the Napoleonic Wars the colony suffered a slow decline. Only the fact that it was a free port kept Willemstad going. Then the exploitation of the Lake Maracaibo oil fields sensationally restored the status of the island and gave it a prosperity greater than any it had known. Royal Dutch Shell was the first foreign concern to operate at Maracaibo. There was no deep-water harbor in the lake or within easy reach on the coast. Furthermore, Venezuelan political conditions were unstable, and Shell did not care to risk capital on building a refinery in the republic. Curaçao was barely two hundred miles away. It was decided to enlarge facilities at Willemstad and send the crude oil there for handling.

The first refinery was completed in 1918, but did not reach its full capacity until four years later. A continuous stream of tankers came to the Schottegat. Smokestacks and huge storage tanks became the most prominent features of the landscape. Then Royal Dutch and Lago Oil, the latter a subsidiary of the Standard Oil Company, extended operations to the near-by island of Aruba. New oil towns were built—Emmastad on Curaçao, St. Nicolaas on Aruba—hideously ugly, but representing solid and growing wealth. The concentration of petroleum interests is the greatest in the Western Hemisphere. During the war it was the chief source of supplies of the Allied nations. When Holland was overrun by the Germans in 1940 the United States landed troops to safeguard the refineries. It was necessary to repel one attack by submarines that surfaced and bombarded Aruba.

This brings us to the two lesser units of the colony, Aruba and Bonaire. Both were occupied by the Dutch at about the same time as Curaçao. They have had no history worth mentioning, and it is not on record that either of them was ever visited by a tourist. Aruba is flatter, barer of vegetation, and—if that be possible—drier than Curaçao. A little gold was once sifted from its marly soil; the ruins of a mine and a smelter may be seen on a desert plain. A few cattle and goats are raised. The desolation of the scene and the poverty of days gone by mean nothing to modern Aruba. The developments in connection with oil have put it in a class by itself. There has even been a substantial increase in the population, labor for the refinery and docks having been brought from adjacent countries. The Netherlands Information Bureau maintained in New York tells me that there is a project, unrealized as yet, to build hotels on Aruba, and also "bungalows for writers, poets and composers." That last is something to think about. Blatantly oil-minded Aruba, of all places, as a retreat for practitioners of the arts! I'll credit it when I see it.

Bonaire (the original Spanish name was Buen Aire—good air), the most easterly of the three islands, remains extremely primitive. Though it is flat, sandy, and without streams, the people manage to live by means of dry farming and the raising of goats. The uncultivated areas are thickly overgrown with cactus. It used to be a penal colony, the prisoners being set to mining the salt that exists in large deposits in crystallized form. The old salt pans are still worked commercially. A bluish pillar on the seashore by which sailing ships formerly steered is composed mainly of salt. Scarlet flamingos frequent the Pekelmeer, an extensive lagoon to the south of Kralendijk, the principal town. There is color on Bonaire for those who do not shrink from its isolation.

Six hundred miles to the northeast lie three infinitesimal remnants of empire, the islands of St.-Martin, Saba, and St. Eustatius, on the edge of the group that Columbus named for St. Ursula and her eleven thousand virgins. The combined area of the three is under thirty square miles and the population under five thousand. Yet each can lay claim to unique characteristics and to its special page in the tumultuous history of the region.

St.-Martin is divided between Holland and France. It is the only island in the Caribbean to be so shared by colonial powers. The story goes that a Dutch captain and a French agreed that they would walk in opposite directions around the island and draw a dividing line from the place where they met back to their starting point. The Dutchman was fat and could not walk so fast as his rival, but he astutely headed in the direction where the more fertile land lay, and he was content to accept the smaller district for his country. You may attach what weight you please to this yarn. It is a fact that Poincy, the first governor general of the Antilles in the French interest, sent an agent to occupy St.-Martin. Finding some Hollanders already on the spot, the agent agreed to a partition, and the two parties signed a pact in 1648. By its terms the French and Dutch settlers on St.-Martin formed an offensive and defensive alliance, which they observed no matter what relations might happen to prevail between their home governments. St.-Martin was attacked several times by buccaneers and pirates, but as sugar was about all it produced it got off lightly.

St. Eustatius, or Statia as English-speaking mariners have always called it, has played a melodramatic role that its present forlorn condition but serves to emphasize. The area is eleven square miles of barren land rising gradually to the cone of an extinct volcano called the Quill. The tiny port of Oranjestad barely keeps going, yet it has known a day when its main street and the beach on either side of it constituted one of the richest marts on earth. The Dutch took the islet in the 1630's shortly after they had seized Curaçao and started to create a free port as a complement to the one at Willemstad. At first black ivory was the chief commodity at Statia, and the success with which the trade was developed excited the envy of the French, the English, and the buccaneers. Between 1664 and 1674 the islet changed hands ten times. The marauders looted its warehouses and passed on, supposing that the port would not be able to revive in that unprotected spot. The tenacious Hollanders invariably returned, and their trading center came to be regarded as an international convenience in the eighteenth century. The sobriquet "The Golden Rock" was applied to St. Eustatius.

Janet Schaw, a traveler who passed that way in 1775, wrote about it as follows: "The town consists of one street a mile long, but very narrow and most disagreeable, as every one smokes tobacco, and the whiffs are constantly blown in your face. But never did I meet with such variety . . . From one end of the town of Eustatia to the other is a continued mart, where goods of the most different uses and qualities are displayed before the shop-doors."

The following year the American Revolution broke out, and in a short while St. Eustatius became the principal clearinghouse for contraband for American, French, and Dutch merchants, and even for the British in the near-by West Indian islands. Trade quintupled. In 1778 and 1779 the number of ships that anchored in the roadstead reached the amazing total of three thousand. London concluded, rightly enough, that the thirteen colonies were getting most of their military supplies from this free port. What is more, Yankee privateers who had seized English vessels at sea brought their prizes to St. Eustatius and sold them to the highest bidder. Dutch sympathies were obviously with the revolutionists. On November 16, 1776, the fort at Oranjestad had fired the first salute ever accorded the American flag in a foreign port.

England declared war on the Netherlands at the end of 1780. As soon as Admiral Rodney, in command of the West India fleet, received his instructions to that effect, he descended on the "nest of vultures," as Lord North had called the merchants of Statia, with two squadrons and a large armed force and demanded the surrender of the island with "everything in and belonging thereto." As his defenses were negligible, the Dutch governor complied at once. More than 150 ships of all classes were taken in the port. Thirty others, heavily laden, which had left a few days before under a naval escort, were overhauled at sea and brought back. The value of the booty obtained exceeded three million pounds sterling. By keeping the Dutch flag flying for a month, Rodney tricked large numbers of additional vessels, mostly privateers, into coming under his guns.

When he had completed his inventory, he distributed some of the stores among British colonies that had been suffering from shortages. The rest he auctioned off at the biggest bargain sale the West Indies had ever seen. No distinction was made between the property of English contrabandists and goods that had belonged to the enemy. This was the end of St. Eustatius as an emporium. The French seized the island for military reasons shortly after the departure of Rodney. Again it was tossed back and forth. The empty privilege of owning it was finally conceded to the Dutch. Other than officials and the crews of trading schooners, no one goes to St. Eustatius today.

Saba is not to be judged by ordinary standards. It is an extinct volcanic cone rising sheer from the sea to a height of 2,887 feet. The area is about half that of Manhattan Island. There are no ports, and landings have to be made through the surf on the narrowest of shingled beaches. The only town of importance is in the crater, at an elevation of a little more than 1,000 feet and invisible from the ocean; yet its name is Bottom. In days gone by, Bottom could be reached only by climbing a succession of ladders, while goods were hauled up the face of the cliff in baskets and nets. A good road, which winds incredibly, now makes the ascent possible on horseback. The population of 1,229 is preponderantly white, being descendants of the same families that settled the island three centuries ago. Saba has virtually no economic importance. A little agriculture is practiced in the crater and on the steep, boulder-strewn exterior slopes. The men are expert sailors and they build a few boats for sale. The women have a reputation for their lace and linen drawn work.

The freebooters pillaged Saba now and then. Treaties solemnly provided for its capitulation, notably at the time of the crushing of St. Eustatius by Rodney. But no enemy troubled to occupy it effectively. The great cruise ships find it impracticable as a stop. An occasional passenger vessel called there in the past, however, and always the hardy venturers were in ecstasies over the journey up to Bottom and the odd Dutch village they discovered there. One thing is sure: there can be no landing of planes on Saba unless the helicopter should be perfected for long-range flights. The more reason for the promoters of surface tramp trips to bear the little island in mind. It is an unspoiled novelty.

Physical first impressions of British Guiana, as described in the last chapter, apply also to Surinam (Dutch Guiana is a designation not used by the Netherlanders), only more so. Here the entire belt of alluvial plain is below the level of the sea. Except where dikes have been built to maintain it, the coast can scarcely be identified, because the ocean rolls in at high tide and mingles with the swamps, and even at low tide the foreshore is a chaos of mudbanks and pools. Six main rivers bisect the country from south to north, and the orange-brown of their sediment is visible twenty miles out to sea. Bars form, melt away, and re-form in the shallows, so an approaching ship has to follow a tortuous course. When tangles of mangroves appear on either side you know that at last you have begun to pierce the continent.

Paramaribo, the capital, is located on a shell ridge on the west bank of the Surinam River some fourteen miles above its mouth. It is diked against the stream and has a crisscrossed system of canals and gabled houses looking down on the still waterways. Many of the fields in the immediate vicinity are polders, or land reclaimed from the water by encircling dikes. This is Holland in the deep tropics. How deep may be judged by the countless palms, the mahogany trees that line some of the urban avenues, the tamarinds with their clouds of feathery pinnate leaves and brown pods, the flaming scarlet poincianas, the bougainvilleas, and the ornate blossoming shrubs.

In true Dutch fashion, the central square has a ponderous name, the Gouvernementsplein. Here stand the governor's stately mansion and the administration buildings, with a statue of Queen Wilhelmina overlooking well-trimmed lawns. Close by, on the river, is Fort Zeelandia, which used to keep raiders at bay and once thwarted even the English. The only real hotel, the Palace, also is close to the square. The Waterkant (Riverside) follows the course of the Surinam; this is the finest residential street, and some of the houses on it are magnificent examples of plantation architecture in wood, stylized with dormer windows and gables to suggest the Old World. I cannot improve on the following, taken from a promotion booklet issued by the Netherlands Government Press Service:

Paramaribo has the dignified, respectable, somewhat portly aspect, which characterizes most Dutch provincial towns. The Dutch have a word for it, which cannot be translated or even adequately explained: they call it *deftig;* the nearest English equivalent being perhaps "genteel." Add to this that Paramaribo, apart from one or two business streets, has that air of sweet tranquillity which is generally identified with the minor cities of Holland, and that general neatness and cleanliness which foreign visitors to the Low Countries have marveled at for untold generations, and it will be realized that some of the charms of old Holland are faithfully reflected by this lonely capital city of the jungle.

The population is partly African, partly Oriental, with a sprinkling of wild folk from the forests and a very small percentage of whites. Yet it is noticeable how strongly the Dutch note emerges among all except the Asiatics and the aboriginal Indians. The officials behave according to a precise pattern observed in no matter what part of the world they are on duty, being correct, hard-working men who keep regular office hours and transact business with an air of great formality. The only difference is that in the tropics they wear spotless linen suits instead of broadcloth. Both sexes ride bicycles more generally than is the case among the whites in the colonies of other European nations, with the exception of British Bermuda. The Negroes and half bloods have adopted Dutch customs, with emphasis on those that are now a bit archaic. The *Kotto Missie* dress for women is still seen; this is a type of Mother Hubbard, the skirt full and coming to the ground, distended by petticoats and tucked into rolls about the waist; the blouse a sort of starched cape, the headdress a bandanna kerchief twisted to imitate a Dutch cap. Fortunately the Negro love of color causes the wearers of this stifling costume to select prints in vivid shades and designs. Wooden shoes are not uncommon.

Figures on the racial strains, as shown by the last census, are surprising. The element made up of half bloods and civilized Negroes accounts for 40 per cent; bush Negroes, 10 per cent; Asiatics other than Chinese, 45 per cent; and the remaining 5 per cent is apportioned among whites, aboriginal Indians, and Chinese. Of the Asiatics a little less than half are Javanese and the rest British East Indians. The same labor problem that confronted Trinidad and British Guiana led the Dutch to recruit indentured field hands in Hindustan over several decades of the nineteenth century. It was not until the 1890's that they decided to import workers from their own densely populated colony of Java.

Nieuw Nickerie, the second largest city in Surinam, is at the mouth of the Nickerie River, close to the British Guiana frontier, inhabited chiefly by Javanese and Hindus who grow rice. It has changed its location twice, the earlier towns having been undermined by the sea. Coronie, on the coast between Nieuw Nickerie and Paramaribo, is an older place founded by Scotsmen when the territory belonged to England. It, too, is a center of rice culture and has become thoroughly Orientalized. Albina on the Maroni River, which separates Surinam from French Guiana, is little more than a frontier post where the main excitement used to be the sympathetic handling of fugitives from the French penal camps of Cayenne and St. Laurent. Moengo, thirty miles away, has recently become important as a headquarters of bauxite mining. There are no towns in the interior of Surinam.

Like British Guiana, this territory has its three belts: the coastal plain already mentioned, the rolling savanna of clayey soil mixed with sand, and the mountainous, forested hinterland. But in Surinam there has been less penetration of the jungle. At approximately the center of the country is a geological phenomenon, the Tafelberg, a triangular and almost flat plateau 3,300 feet above sea level and about sixty-five square miles in area. To the south, overlooking the plateau, are the Wilhelmina Mountains, the highest peak of which rises to 4,200 feet. Few white men have visited the Tafelberg, and much of the surrounding jungle is so dense that it is uninhabited even by Indians.

Gold is mined here and there, with diminishing returns. The discovery of bauxite in 1915, however, created an industry that has become so important that the Dutch feel the economic future of the country depends upon it. The largest deposits are on the Cottica River about one hundred miles from the sea and can be reached by boat. Production more than tripled in the twelve years before the war, and thereafter it attained huge figures that have not yet been revealed. The United States established a naval and air base in Surinam as much to safeguard the flow of bauxite, a basic war material, as to guard against a possible German coup from the west coast of Africa.

I have traveled on the freighters of the Alcoa Line that ply between New Orleans and the bauxite mines of Surinam. Prior to 1939 these boats took a maximum of twelve passengers, who enjoyed a round trip of about three weeks, calling at several ports and finally mounting a South American river accessible to travelers by no other means. The freight service was maintained without interruption, but there could be no catering to pleasure trippers during the war. Now Alcoa is building new ships and probably will offer greater comfort on a voyage that has unique attractions.

Surinam's history after the cession by England in 1667 was one of recurrent struggle against privateers, followed by a series of slave insurrections. There was a direct relationship between the two phases. In 1689 Jean-Baptiste du Casse, soon to be a brilliant French colonial administrator but at the time still a buccaneer, assailed Surinam unsuccessfully. Some attempts by lesser adventurers also were foiled, and the colonists believed that their position was impregnable. Then in 1712 came Jacques Cassard, he who extorted a ransom for sparing Curaçao, with thirty-eight ships and about three thousand men, a formidable piratical outfit backed by certain merchants of Marseilles. He swept past the defenses, laid siege to Paramaribo with part of his force, and sent the rest up the river to loot the plantations. The governor ended by buying him off with all the available gold and silver, as well as jewelry, cattle, sugar, merchandise, and slaves.

The lasting change brought about by Cassard occurred in the interior. There his lieutenants freed many Negroes, who helped the French to plunder the estates and as a reward were given arms and left to their own devices when the expedition withdrew. Previously a few blacks had escaped into the forest, where they had maintained themselves much as the Maroons did in Jamaica. These were now joined by thousands who feared the return of their masters. They had a whole continent into which to retreat, and the task of rooting them out was beyond the powers of the Dutch. A general slave rebellion took place in 1730. It was suppressed, but a considerable number of Negroes of both sexes got away. By the year 1748 a free society fifteen thousand strong had been built up. The term "bush Negroes" began to be applied to them.

An almost continuous state of war existed for fourteen years. White troops sent against the rebels were defeated; in some instances, whole parties were ambushed and massacred. The government finally sought peace with a large body of blacks in the Saramacca country, and though treaties were twice violated by the wild men, a settlement was at last reached in 1762. Semi-independence was conceded to this group. Other slave revolts led to a new "war" in the eastern part of the colony with the self-emancipated Negroes who came to be known as Djoekes and Aucaners. The Dutch brought in a brigade of European mercenaries commanded by a Swiss colonel. These troops succeeded in breaking the resistance of the blacks, but never actually conquered them. When the campaign ended in the 1770's, fewer than a hundred mercenaries survived and their foes had retired to more remote fastnesses. There was no treaty in this case. The forest men had been victorious in a negative sense, for their autonomy was taken as a matter of course and little by little got official recognition.

General manumission of the slaves in the nineteenth century did not tempt the bush Negroes to return to the lowlands and accept citizenship alongside their kind. They chose to remain in the woods and mountains, where they still live a tribal life that is a clear case of reversion to the ways of equatorial Africa. There are two main divisions, the Sarramaccaners and the Aucaners, which with three smaller tribes account for a total of perhaps twenty thousand souls. The name most commonly applied to all of them in the pidgin English of the coast is Djukas (a corruption of Djoekes), but bush Negroes is preferable.

At the head of each tribe is a chief called a *granman*, a title that means just what it seems: "grand" or "great" man. He is selected by the family groups, and then receives his formal appointment from the governor of Surinam. Under him are the captains of his villages, each of whom has a staff of trusties. There is a potentate recognized as being head granman over all the tribes, and if one wishes to be romantic this chief may be termed the King of the Bush Negroes. His authority is extremely tenuous. The governor makes him a yearly gift, which some describe as a tribute. On the other hand, the granman carries a cane with a silver knob, the traditional symbol of the acceptance by his people of Dutch suzerainty.

The League of Nations took cognizance of Granman Jankoeso in the 1920's as the head of a minority people, and his successor, Ah Tu Den Du, expressed annoyance at not having been invited to send a delegate to the Pan-American Conference at Havana in 1940. This last may be a myth, but so 'tis said.

During the century and a quarter from the end of the Napoleonic Wars to 1941, Surinam was a financial liability to the Netherlands government. A yearly subsidy had to be granted to balance the costs of administration. A system not unlike British crown-colony rule prevailed for both Surinam and the more prosperous Curaçao territory. The governor and the members of his advisory council were all appointed. A second council called the Staten was composed of five men nominated by the governor and ten elected under a franchise rigidly limited by property and other qualifications. The Staten had the right to amend the budget and the governor's ordinances, subject to a veto by the Crown. Voters in Surinam numbered only 1 to 1.5 per cent of the population, and in Curaçao about 5 per cent.

Surinam has no provincial or municipal bodies chosen by the people. Even the city of Paramaribo is without a mayor and council, but is administered by a commissioner under the direct authority of the governor. The provinces are run by commissioners appointed from the Dutch colonial service.

This backward state of affairs makes all the more interesting the changes promised by the Dutch government in exile while the war was still raging and given deeper meaning by the successful armed revolt of the Indonesian nationalists. It was declared that the kingdom of Holland would consist of three coequal partners: the Netherlands, the territories in the East Indies, and the territories in the West Indies. The two last-named did not "belong to" Holland, any more than Holland "belonged to" them. Fully autonomous governments would gradually be created for them. The policy was broadened in 1946 to recognize Indonesia as a commonwealth, similar to a

British dominion, which after a given period of time would have the right to withdraw from the partnership and become independent, if it so wished.

There is no reason to suppose that Surinam and Curaçao will be given the same status as Indonesia. But they are due to obtain real self-government on the basis of becoming integral parts of the kingdom, just as some French colonies are now integral parts of the French Republic.

CHAPTER **12.**

FRANCE IN THE WEST INDIES

I HAVE said little about the red tape connected with travel to the places described in the last three chapters. It was not onerous. An American citizen had to show a passport before he could land in any of those British or Dutch colonies, and a certificate of vaccination against smallpox was required. British Guiana had a nuisance rule that a passenger must obtain the governor's permission to disembark at the Georgetown airport; it did not apply to sea travel. But the policy was to ease all regulations. Officials recognized the fact that to capture a share of the tourist business they must make it as simple as possible for foreigners to come and go, and I was assured that the small annoyances still prevailing would soon be abolished.

When I sought a visa for the French colonies of Martinique and Guadeloupe I ran up against a totally different attitude. The consular service and the colonial authorities seemed to be in a conspiracy to keep out the inoffensive voyager. I had had much experience with French officials and had found them liberal in making exceptions for a writer carrying proper credentials. In this case, nothing of the kind. The trouble began in New Orleans, where the consul stated that before he could give me a visa the consent of the two local governments would have to be obtained. I asked why. He answered evasively that though the war was over, a state of peace had not yet been declared in the colonies and old prohibitions were still in force. Yes, he would write or cable at my expense to the governments, but there was no telling how long they would take to reply. Since I was going first to Cuba, it might be a good idea to get the matter handled from there.

The French consul in Havana was displeased at having had the

177

buck passed to him. More frank than his colleague, he explained that food and housing shortages in the colonies had led Paris to instruct that would-be visitors should be discouraged. It was all right for a cruise vessel to call for a day at Fort-de-France, Martinique, because the passengers would eat and sleep aboard ship. But a person making a stopover of indefinite length might run into difficulties. I said I was willing to take a chance on that; from France's standpoint my trip should be facilitated, because her colonies would presently be in a position to entertain tourists and would be clamoring for them. This was no time to hamper the gathering of material for a book that proposed to tell what Martinique and Guadeloupe had to offer.

The other shrugged. He said that I must present a letter to him from the American consul in Havana vouching for me personally. The American consul correctly took the stand—and phoned the French legation to that effect—that my passport vouched for me and as fully as the State Department ever vouched for an American private citizen. The French consul then became noncommittal. He did not say that he would query the West Indian governors, and he did not say that he would not. Finally, by dint of delays and shuffling, I was brought to the point where my itinerary did not allow me to wait any longer in the hope of getting a visa. It was an absurd performance, which I ascribe to the confusion over national politics, as well as uncertainty about their own jobs, felt by most underlings of the French provisional government at that period.

Luckily I was familiar with the islands from previous travel. A French friend had recently spent several weeks in Martinique and Guadeloupe, and I interviewed him to check up on present conditions.

Martinique has always counted for more in the West Indies than its area and economic resources would ordinarily warrant. It lies at the center of the arc of the Lesser Antilles, which begins at Puerto Rico and ends at Trinidad. The channels to north and south of Martinique were the best for crossing the arc and entering the Caribbean in the days of sail, because they were deep and in the direct path of following winds from the Atlantic. These circumstances gave the island great strategical importance. It was—and is—well suited to the culture of sugar cane. Manifestly a lovely unit of the archipelago, it also had a good climate. So the trespassers on Spain's preserves disputed it with ardor, and it was only by a series of miracles that France emerged as its permanent owner. Terrific natural phenomena have shaken Martinique. For one reason or another, it has managed never to be out of the news for long.

The formation is mountainous, rising to an extreme height of about 4,500 feet, but there are many low valleys and pockets of coastal plain where the soil is extremely fertile. The upper slopes are covered with rain forest, except at the southern tip, which is semiarid, a district given over to agaves and cacti like the plateaus of Mexico. In the north stands Mont Pelée (properly La Montagne Pelée), a volcano that has erupted more than once in historic times, notably in 1902, when it destroyed the city of St.-Pierre. It is never wholly quiescent.

The capital and chief port of entry is Fort-de-France, formerly Fort Royal, on an excellent though small landlocked harbor in the southwestern quarter facing the Caribbean. Coming by sea, you pass between the crumbling gray walls of Fort St. Louis on the right, sheering up from the water's edge like a miniature morro castle, and on the left a secondary fortress. These were strong defenses in the eighteenth century. Admiral de Grasse lay behind them in perfect safety until he led his huge fleet out to the calamitous battle with Rodney. The city never had any claim to architectural distinction. Two buildings hold the eye, but it is for their oddity; a church with a skeleton steeple of ironwork, and the rococo Bibliothèque Schoelcher. The steeple is so constructed as to resist earthquakes; the average visitor mistakenly thinks that it is a case of a job having been left unfinished. The library, erected as a memorial to the French statesman who brought about the emancipation of the slaves in 1848, serves a good purpose no matter how nightmarish its appearance may be. There are four fair hotels, of which the best is the Hotel de la Paix.

La Savane, a wide park adorned with palms and tamarind trees, has the one monument that every stranger in Fort-de-France wants to see: a marble statue of the empress Joséphine. She is represented as a somewhat thick-waisted beauty, garbed in the neoclassic style associated with her day of glory, her head and arms posed with conventional grace. The monument is of small artistic merit, but its association value is great. Marie-Joséphine-Rose Tascher de la Pagerie, called Yeyette as a child and Joséphine in her maturity, was born near the village of Trois Ilets across the harbor. Her father was a ruined sugar planter whose sister became the mistress of the Sieur de Beauharnais while the latter was governor of Martinique. His legitimate son, Alexandre, was born on the island, but was removed to Paris too early to have played with little Yeyette, as the romancers love to tell. She grew up half wild, her companions poor white and Negro children.

But Beauharnais had taken his mistress, her aunt, with him to France, and it was to this scheming woman that the glittering career of Joséphine was due. For the aunt first succeeded in marrying her lover, and then persuaded him to send for one of her nieces as a wife for his son. Joséphine's younger sister was chosen, but she had died before the letter reached Martinique and the elder was substituted. The future empress went to Paris in 1779 at the age of sixteen, was married to Alexandre, whom she did not even pretend to love, and bore him two children. His head rolled during the Terror. After she had spent some time as a prisoner herself in the shadow of the guillotine, she met the young Corsican officer who swept her up with him to the heights.

Napoleon's infatuation for Joséphine long enabled him to overlook her infidelities. But he was without illusions as to her background and her greed. "There, little Creole!" he said, as he led her into the royal suite at the Tuileries. "You now have the chance to sleep in the bed of your masters." He sent a picture to the church at Trois Ilets where she was baptized, and this can still be seen at the right of the altar, as well as a memorial tablet to Joséphine's mother at the left. The statue by Vital Debray was an inspiration of the colonial government and erected many years after her death.

It is impressive, that statue, as a reminder of the strange caprices of the Goddess of Fortune. By moonlight under the dark velvet of the tropic sky bespangled with enormous stars, the marble silhouette assumes a magic beauty. In the wet season, when La Savane is green, it appears lush and triumphant like the Empress in her glory. But when a film of dust lies upon it in the dog days and the surrounding grass is scorched, it has a forlorn look as though it would feel more at home at Malmaison. Joséphine once revisited Martinique for family reasons, but left as quickly as she could and never showed concern for the island's fortunes. All traces of the Tascher de la Pagerie plantation buildings at Trois Ilets have vanished.

The name of another royal consort is connected with Martinique. Françoise d'Aubigné was brought there as a child a century earlier, and spent several years there. On her return to France she married the dramatist Scarron. He died and she became first the tutor of Louis XIV's illegitimate children and then his mistress. He bestowed upon her the title of Madame de Maintenon, and when the queen died he made her his wife at a secret ceremony.

Fort-de-France is the only real city on the island. It has more than doubled in population in the past forty-five years, a fact largely due to the elimination of St.-Pierre, which previously had held first place by a wide margin. The location of St.-Pierre on a bay within a few miles of Mont Pelée was as perilous as that of Pompeii in the shadow of Mount Vesuvius, but its residents had always refused to believe it. They were not overly disturbed even in 1851, when the volcano exploded, rained ashes for days, and tore a gap in its summit that filled with water and became a lake that sight-seers enjoyed visiting. The sulphurous clouds that formed above the peak were thought picturesque, and the occasional rumblings added to the excitement of an ascent.

The town was built mainly of stone, and it climbed upward from the water front in a pattern of charming narrow streets with peaked roofs of red tile above walls for which the favorite tint was a clear yellow. The sidewalks varied in width from one to three feet. Awnings of vivid colors almost met across the roadways. For nearly two centuries St.-Pierre had been a flourishing port. The banks and the big shops of Martinique were there. It had 26,011 inhabitants in 1902, and some 4,000 more lived in the immediate neighborhood. Lafcadio Hearn has left us the best descriptions of St.-Pierre. He spent nearly two years there in the late 1880's and reveled in the place. Gauguin, the artist, paid a visit at about the same time, and in his less articulate way expressed equal delight. The women of mixed blood were exceptionally comely, and the manners and customs were carefree, marked by a graceful voluptuousness.

Such was the city overwhelmed utterly, in less than a minute, on the morning of May 8, 1902. There had been warnings for a month: earthquake shocks, the seeping of noxious gases through fissures in the rocks, and an abnormal flow of hot water in the streams. A factory in the village of Prêcheur collapsed after having been undermined by subterranean disturbances. But the people shrugged all this aside. The governor issued a soothing proclamation and brought his family to St.-Pierre to prove his confidence. At 7:52 A.M., as we know from scores of partly incinerated clocks and watches recovered later that had stopped at that moment, Mont Pelée blew its head off and a tide of red-hot lava surged down with incredible speed, blasted the city out of existence, and buried it. The ships in the harbor were burned, with the exception of one that limped to sea and finally reached Castries, St. Lucia. Prêcheur was wiped out. A broad band of the countryside disappeared under a blanket of lava, and zones in other directions were overrun by lesser torrents that had poured from the cone. Approximately one fifth of the island was devastated, and much of the rest showered with cinders.

Fine ashes carried to an immense height drifted on the winds and fell over a radius of roughly a thousand miles. Its presence in the air caused murky crimson sunsets. I can recall seeing these manifestations as a boy in Jamaica.

The loss of life was about forty thousand. Many on the outskirts escaped with wounds, but even in obliterated St.-Pierre there was one survivor, and according to some accounts, two. The authentic case was that of a Negro prisoner locked in an underground cell, the ventilation passage to which remained open by some freak of fate. The man was dug out and lived, though he had been frightfully burned. It is said that a shoemaker, who had run from his shop and leaped across the edge of the lava's path, also was saved. Still another authority argues logically that several who escaped instant death fled to the woods and to small villages. The first rescue parties found no one alive in the city except the prisoner in his dungeon, and so reported that he was the sole survivor.

Science was vastly interested in the Mont Pelée eruption, some aspects of which had never been paralleled in modern times. France sent out a commission headed by Dr. Alfred Lacroix, who published an exhaustive study. Not long afterward an American volcanologist, the late Dr. Frank Alvord Perret, made Mont Pelée his specialty. He built a station on the spot, collected data over a long period of years, wrote a book, and founded a local museum. For at least a decade no one thought it possible that St.-Pierre could revive as a town. The ruins appeared to be buried too deeply for that, and the matter that covered them had hardened as it cooled to a rocklike consistency. No trace of vegetation persisted. But life in the tropics is tena-

cious and enterprising beyond belief. Cracks appeared in the black-
ened crust, and presently fig seeds that had been carried by birds
germinated there. Other plants of the type that will grow even
among the stones of ruined buildings began to spring up. Then men
returned, cleared away the debris, and put up shacks on the old
foundations of houses. Three or four streets, including the rue Victor
Hugo, the former main thoroughfare, were restored for several con-
secutive blocks. Part of the water front was salvaged and a wharf
built.

St.-Pierre today has a population of between three and four thousand. It is by far the most popular place in Martinique for sight-
seers. Atop a low hill stands Dr. Perret's Musée Volcanologique,
which contains many curious relics found in the ruins. These comprise melted glassware and metal objects twisted into new and often
beautiful shapes. What once was a bottle of perfume may now be an
opalescent ball with a stain of sediment at its core. There are car-
bonized loaves of bread, fragments of looking glass that still reflect,
and books burned to a crisp yet as legible as the typing on a piece of
carbon paper. Dr. Perret treasured an electric light bulb he had discovered in a bed of ashes that worked as well as ever thirty years
after the disaster.

A good restaurant exists near the market in St.-Pierre. At the village of Le Carbet close by is an unpretentious, clean little hotel of
the bungalow style. The volcano can be ascended for the greater
part of the distance on muleback. However, the average visitor contents himself with looking at it from St.-Pierre. Smoking at intervals, muttering spasmodically, old Mont Pelée dominates the scene
no matter where you stand, so long as your back is toward the sea.
That it will explode again someday is as certain as anything can be,
but the dwellers at its foot feel quite sure that this will not be in their
generation. Man is incurably optimistic. He has tempted Vesuvius
and Etna and other great volcanos since the dawn of history, and he
will doubtless continue to tempt Mont Pelée for thousands of years.
Lafcadio Hearn was charmed to hear Martinique called by its people
Le Pays de Revenants. He insisted that the literal meaning, "The
Country of Those Who Return," was truer than "The Country of
Ghosts." St.-Pierre would seem to be a case in point.

The rest of the island has many scenic attractions in the forms of
palm-fringed beaches, winding mountain roads, and splendid views

that often range from the Caribbean to the Atlantic. At Didier, in the hills a little north of Fort-de-France, the mineral waters are regarded as curative and the place is patronized as a summer resort. A small beach five miles from the capital has been improved. The hotel there, Le Lido, is the finest on the island at present, but there is no bus service and it can be reached only by taxi or private car. Better transportation is one of the "musts" if Martinique is to get the tourist business for which it professes to be eager.

Lamentin on the east coast is a fairly important township commercially; marshes in the vicinity give it a bad climate, but serve as a feeding ground for water fowl, which sportsmen from all over the island come to shoot. At Ste.-Anne are salt mines and a petrified grove. This eastern, or windward, slope is where the largest cane plantations are located. Sugar and rum are easily the most important products. The secondary crops—coffee, cocoa, and vanilla—are raised in the mountains.

Martinique suffers from one scourge of Nature, which it shares solely with St. Lucia in the Antillian chain north of Trinidad. The deadly fer-de-lance serpent is common in its woods and fields, and despite the antivenom serums that are now employed this snake continues to take a toll of life among the cane cutters each season. It also stings pedestrians who stray from the main roads, but not in comparable numbers to those attacked during the harvest season. The dry cane leaves that fall to the ground give the fer-de-lance its favorite cover, and when the plants are cut in wholesale fashion the results may be imagined. The mongoose was introduced from Asia about seventy-five years ago to combat the serpent, and fair results were obtained. Riki-Tiki-Tavi, however, is a pest himself; he prefers chickens to snakes and hunts the latter as a sporting proposition—when he does not happen to be hungry.

There are said to be eight varieties of the fer-de-lance, the commonest being dark gray speckled with black. The divergencies are chiefly those of color and markings. No more than two or three actual subspecies exist in all probability. The head is flat and triangular, hence the name. Père Labat, the early chronicler of the French West Indies, wrote that he had seen a fer-de-lance nine feet long and five inches in diameter, but his imagination must have been heated at the moment. A length of four feet is usual, one of six feet exceptional. That much serpent, malignantly aggressive and charged with a poison of great virulence, is bad enough in all conscience. The fer-de-lance has the unpleasant habit of striking at human beings without warning or provocation, which is not true of most ophidians.

Why this creature should be found in Martinique and St. Lucia, while the rest of the Caribbean islands are free of poisonous snakes, is an enigma. But the fact must be taken seriously by travelers, who are warned to keep out of the bush. People have been bitten, though rarely, even in the botanical gardens of Fort-de-France.

The population of Martinique is over 90 per cent Negro, the descendants of the slaves with which France exploited the island at high pressure. Following emancipation in the middle of the nineteenth century, the same labor problem that affected all West Indian countries materialized. The blacks preferred to cultivate their own small patches of land or to live in the towns by some trade. So the planters experimented with importing British East Indian coolies, as in Jamaica, Trinidad, and the Guianas. The plan never was a success in Martinique, though a few of the Orientals remained as settlers. The Negro birth rate increased until there were more inhabitants to the square mile than in any of the neighboring islands, except Puerto Rico and Barbados. This forced a sufficient proportion of labor to return to the plantations, which pretty generally have remained in the hands of a white and light-colored minority known as Les Bequets. Ten families are credited with being the only rich persons, and their membership constitutes an exclusive social set.

Guadeloupe, separated from Martinique by the British island of Dominica, is the other French colony in the Lesser Antilles. It really consists of two islands: Guadeloupe proper or Basse Terre, which, mocking the term basse (low), is ruggedly mountainous; and the almost level Grande Terre. A very narrow arm of the sea, called the Rivière Salée, runs between them. Guadeloupe also has five dependencies: the near-by Iles des Saintes, Marie Galante, and La Désirade; the French half of St. Martin and tiny St. Barthelémy, up by the Virgins. This colony has been neglected by writers in favor of Martinique. The historians have a sound excuse, since Guadeloupe has made less history. Its topography and the life of its people are more varied, however, and the seekers of exotic impressions have missed a bet there.

Basse Terre may be described as an oval-shaped massif with a series of volcanic cones down the middle, of which the highest, La

Soufrière, at the southern end, soars to 4,900 feet. The capital, which is on the southwestern coast, is called Basse-Terre, too, but with the words hyphenated. Let us get straight on this terminology, which has been misunderstood by practically every commentator in English. There are a number of Basse-Terres or Basseterres in the West Indies, all of them on the inner or Caribbean side. For the early French voyagers used the name with a peculiar twist to mean "protected" rather than "low," whereas exposed stations on the Atlantic became Capesterre, or headland, with the implication that they were whipped by the wind. The idea was to distinguish between safe and dangerous anchorages, so you will not find any ports called Capesterre. In the case of Guadeloupe, the designation given the town was later extended to the island.

Extraordinary scenery, verdant for the most part but sometimes somber, is characteristic of the massif. The aptly named peaks—Les Deux Mamelles, Le Morne sans Toucher, etc.—are often veiled in clouds, and this is particularly true of the great Soufrière. The latter erupted in 1902 shortly after the Mont Pelée calamity. There was a manifest connection between the two events, but luckily the damage done by the Guadeloupe volcano was slight. It had shown its power in 1797 when, accompanied by earthquake shocks, it destroyed wide areas of fertile land. There are several vents, of which the most active is known as Echelle. Scientists believe that the Soufrière is a slowly dying volcano, but capable of many a convulsion before the end comes. The whole central part of the island is too precipitous to be tamed to the uses of the planter. On the lower slopes and the ring of coastal plain grow coffee, cocoa, vanilla, and bananas.

The city of Basse-Terre is small but picturesque. It is built like an amphitheater on the roadstead, the streets set back in tiers to a height of over 500 feet. A cathedral church, the Basilique, dating from 1694, is prominent. There is no harbor, and boats of any size have to anchor some distance out and put their passengers ashore in lighters. The permanent residents, who are all colored, live in a happy-go-lucky manner and transact a minimum of business. The scores of government officials, among whom a few whites are included, are birds of passage, at least in the higher ranks. They have requisitioned the only good hotel. The hill suburb of St.-Claude a few miles away is a pleasant resort. There are no other towns worth mentioning on Basse Terre island.

Grande Terre offers a radical contrast. Its surface undulates slightly, but generally speaking it is a plain of rich soil a few feet above sea level, and more than half of it is solidly planted to cane. This is the source of the sugar and rum that always were the mainstay of the colony. The inhabitants are more hard-working than those of Basse Terre. They have the reputation of being gloomy, but that has not been my own observation of the folk from any part of Guadeloupe.

On a bay approached through a channel between reefs at the southern entrance of the Rivière Salée is Pointe-à-Pitre, the commercial port and industrial center of the colony, as well as much the largest city. From the quays you look beyond islets covered with vegetation to the mountains of Basse Terre in the west. The back streets merge with country roads that run between tall stands of cane and are bordered by palms, bamboos, and scarlet poincianas. A few good buildings surround the central square, but Pointe-à-Pitre was severely damaged by the hurricane followed by a tidal wave that swept Grande Terre in 1928, and it has never been adequately restored. The market is its most colorful and animated spot. On fete days you still see the celebrated Guadeloupe costume for women, which consists of a short-waisted dress with a flowing skirt in startling patterns and bright hues, a dazzling kerchief folded across the shoulders, necklace and earrings, and a Madras turban with a long bow tied over the right temple. A similar and equally attractive costume has been largely abandoned in Martinique. Both colonies are greatly addicted to the celebration of Mardi Gras, with the city of Pointe-à-Pitre holding first place in the matter of the preservation of old traditions.

In view of its fifty thousand inhabitants and activity as a port in normal times, one notes with astonishment that there is only one hotel worthy of the name, the Hotel des Antilles. Official Guadeloupe, so far, has not been tourist-conscious. I am informed that the government has no plans for building new hostelries or making other improvements to entice visitors.

What I wrote about the people of Martinique applies also to Guadeloupe, except that the latter has about half the density of population to the square mile. Authorities point out that the tendency toward an abnormal increase is marked. The total has doubled in the last fifty-five years. Immigration from the dependencies has occurred, but not from any foreign country. The birth rate alone will assuredly lead to overpopulation in the next half century. The problems of Barbados, Puerto Rico, and even Martinique may be averted here, because there is relatively more fertile land and a greater diversity of crops. It has been pointed out that every peasant here, including the plantation wage worker, has his own patch of land, and he will tolerate no system that attempts to take that away from him.

Marie Galante is an almost round island twenty-two miles to the southeast of Pointe-à-Pitre, fifty-eight square miles in extent and composed of a series of low plateaus and plains. It bears a general resemblance to Grande Terre. About half the arable land is planted to cane, and in recent times a considerable number of cattle and sheep were raised. Deforestation for the sake of hardwood timbers and fuel has led to soil erosion and dried the streams to mere trickles. There is not a single sheltered harbor, the coast being either shelving sandbanks or defined by abrupt cliffs. Grand Bourg, the landing point and seat of government, is a township straggling along an unindented beach.

La Désirade, off the east end of Grande Terre, is a good deal smaller. It has been described as a long limestone block that has the appearance of a moored boat, its prow and stern upcurved. A few hundred peasant farmers and fishermen are recorded in the census as residents. A leper hospital is maintained by the government on the north shore. La Désirade (a corruption from the Spanish *deseada*—desired) has one claim to fame. It was the first land sighted by Columbus on his second voyage, 1493.

The Iles des Saintes, off the southern tip of Basse Terre, consist of two inhabited islets and half a dozen rocky cays. All are recent volcanic fragments, bold in outline and with many little basins guarded by reefs. The anchorage at Terre d'en Haut is protected from most winds by the towering bulk of Basse Terre and by Marie Galante to the east, and sailing craft used to take refuge there. France valued it as a naval base in the eighteenth century. No crops are grown on Les Saintes except for local consumption. The islets were long a favorite resort of week-end trippers from Guadeloupe.

I have seen the above three—Marie Galante, La Désirade, and Les Saintes—only from the air. My French informant painted a disparaging picture of them under postwar conditions. He told me:

"The small islands close to Guadeloupe are hardly more civilized than Pacific atolls. They are overrun by wild goats and pigs. The Negro inhabitants, gendarmes, and customs officials all live wretchedly. But there are two or three smugglers who have a good deal of money and are the real rulers of the dependencies." I gathered that the contrabandists had their field day when Martinique was blockaded in 1940–43 and was close to starvation.

St.-Martin, treated in the last chapter in connection with Holland's part ownership, is of little economic consequence. The French district was settled chiefly by Normans and later received some Scots settlers. The majority of the population is white. St.-Barthélemy, commonly called St. Barts, is doubtless the smallest and the most insignificant of the ancient bones of contention in the Caribbean. It is smaller than St. John. France took it over from buccaneers, traded it to Sweden in 1784, and brought it back for 400,000 francs in 1877. The people of St. Barts are even more predominantly white than those of St.-Martin. Both islands breed sturdy seamen who rove throughout the archipelago and speak English in preference to French. Their schooners bring salt from St.-Martin to all the French colonies in the West Indies.

The colonies of Martinique and Guadeloupe are the survivors of numerous possessions that France once held in the Lesser Antilles. An adventurer named Pierre Belain d'Esnambuc, whose sister was an ancestress of the empress Joséphine, was the pioneer when in 1627 he divided the island of St. Christopher, better known as St. Kitts, with the Englishman Sir Thomas Warner. The enterprise had the backing of Cardinal Richelieu. Seven years later, Esnambuc was ordered to proceed to the conquest of Martinique, while one Charles de l'Olive and a partner took over Guadeloupe. Both islands were inhabited only by Caribs. Spain had never attempted to make good her claim to them.

The work of subduing the Indians was performed efficiently by Esnambuc, and before long Martinique was receiving settlers from France. Olive met with setbacks, largely because his methods were so barbarous that the natives retaliated vigorously and preferred death to surrender. After the tribes had been crushed at last, the stronger warriors slipped away in canoes to Dominica, St. Lucia, St.

Vincent, and Grenada. The French had their eye on these four islands also, and eventually occupied them in the face of stiffening Carib resistance.

Richelieu sent out, in 1639, the illustrious Philippe de Loinvilliers de Poincy, grand cross and bailiff of the Order of the Knights of Malta, as proconsul of all the territories seized and about to be seized in that region. He made his headquarters on St. Kitts, where he built a grandiose chateau, from which he ruled for the twenty-one remaining years of his life. He installed lieutenants in Martinique and Guadeloupe and often visited the two islands. His military operations against the Caribs and at times against European opponents were generally successful. The flamboyant tree was renamed poinciana in his honor.

After the passing of Poincy, the English and the Dutch, but especially the former, disputed Martinique and Guadeloupe so often with the French that it would be impossible to record the details in the space available here. Père Labat gives a lively account of a successful defense of Guadeloupe against the English, in the course of which he tucked up his priestly robes and fought a battery at the point of greatest peril in Basse-Terre. But subsequent clashes were not always so fortunate. Both islands were occupied by the English during the Seven Years' War, and it was assumed that they would be annexed. At the peace of 1763, however, they were returned to France because the sugar interests in Jamaica and Barbados did not want the competition of their products in the London market. France lost Canada at that time, and her statesmen declared it would have been a greater blow if Martinique and Guadeloupe had been taken. Such was the effect of the sugar bonanza upon the policies of nations in the eighteenth century!

The two colonies constantly changed hands between that date and the end of the Napoleonic Wars. Rodney won his victory over De Grasse off the Iles des Saintes in 1782. Without doubt this was the greatest and most decisive naval action ever fought in the Caribbean Sea. If England had lost, all her island possessions would have fallen to France, and she would have been forced to accept less favorable terms at the peace that ended the American Revolution the following year. The black insurrection in St.-Domingue (Haiti) led to similar uprisings of the slaves in Martinique and Guadeloupe, but these geographical units were so small that success or failure depended upon the stand taken by outsiders. After hesitating, the English moved in. They were driven from Guadeloupe by Victor Hugues, the French revolutionary commissioner, who chanced to arrive with troops at about the same time. But they held Martinique from 1794 to 1800 and used it as the headquarters of all British forces in the West Indies. Napoleon regained both islands under the terms of the Peace of Amiens and pacified them. Two years later France and England were at war again.

Close to the southern end of Martinique is an isolated hulk of rock, Le Diamant, shaped like a huge castle, which rises some 200 feet from the level of the sea. This became the scene of one of the spectacular flourishes in which the British navy of the Nelson era delighted. Admiral Hood noted that French ships evaded him by running between the rock and the Martinique coast. He laid his seventy-four, the *Centaur,* alongside and sent a scaling party to the flat top of the rock to attach a hawser. By this means five cannon were hoisted and solidly emplaced, some of them in caves. Ammunition, food, water, and other stores were hauled up. A crew of 120 men and boys, commanded by Lieutenant J. W. Maurice, was assigned to duty and the unit became H. M. S. *Diamond Rock,* a stationary "battleship." Maurice held his position for nearly eighteen months, greatly hampering the traffic in and out of Fort-de-France and repelling attacks.

Then came Admiral de Villeneuve on his famous cruise to the West Indies with the whole French Mediterranean fleet, undertaken for the purpose of decoying Nelson from the shores of Europe. Villeneuve was astounded at the successful fortification of the rock. He told off a squadron to lay siege, and as he caught Maurice at a juncture when food and ammunition were low, he forced a surrender. The English sank three of his gunboats before they struck their flag. Villeneuve passed on, dodging Nelson in American waters, but was fated to lose all at the Battle of Trafalgar on October 21, 1805.

Diamond Rock is not a place one visits. It is pointed out to surface passengers, who never fail to be thrilled by its dramatic story. The planes north from Trinidad streak overhead. On my last trip I happened to look down at the right moment, and against the faintly luminous sea the redoubtable natural fortress had the appearance of Gibraltar itself. It made one of the most imposing spectacles that I had the luck to see from the air.

In the period between Trafalgar and Waterloo, England again took Martinique and Guadeloupe along with every other French colony in the Caribbean region. The two big islands were restored by the treaty that wound up the Napoleonic Wars, and the sovereignty of France has remained unchallenged to this day. Martinique, however, was a center of diplomatic and other intrigues during World War II. Upon the collapse of France, 1940, the aircraft carrier *Béarn,* with new planes purchased in the United States, detoured from her course to Europe and took refuge at Fort-de-France. Shortly afterward the cruiser *Emile Bertin* arrived with an immense consignment of gold belonging to the Banque de France, the value of which has been estimated at close to one billion dollars. The planes and the gold were stored on land. On the pretext of guarding against a Nazi coup, a British naval force rigidly blockaded Martinique for several months, preventing the importation of food and halting even the mails. The British cordon was replaced toward the end of 1940 by a milder United States blockade.

Marshal Pétain's government appointed Admiral Georges Robert high commissioner for the French Antilles, with headquarters at Martinique. This ruthless Vichy partisan stamped out a local De Gaullist movement and blocked normal relations with the democratic countries for almost three years. Following the invasion of North Africa his position was gradually weakened, and in the summer of 1943 a Free French administrator succeeded him. Under the constitution of the Fourth Republic the islands are an integral part of France. They had enjoyed wide political liberties since 1875, electing senators and deputies to the French legislature. Now they are completely organized as departments instead of colonies. They take pride in this status and there is nothing resembling a separatist movement. The trend among the Negro masses is toward the Communist party, and at the last elections Reds topped the polls. My French friend believes that the attitude is, in his own words, "more theoretical than practical. The voters respond to the personalities of candidates rather than to their programs. But antiwhite feeling has cropped up in Guadeloupe, and in Martinique public opinion is

against the Bequet millionaires who own a large part of the island
and monopolize its industries."

French Guiana, often referred to as Cayenne after its capital city,
is the most easterly of the three colonies carved by the rivals of Spain
and Portugal from the then unclaimed coast below the mouth of the
Orinoco River. Its general characteristics are the same as those of
British Guiana and Surinam. But although the French made an
early start, their penetration of the hinterland has been the least profound. Cayenne was founded in 1626 on a flat island of the same
name lying close offshore between two rivers. It barely kept alive
until 1643, when reinforcements came. Settlements were established
on the mainland and spread very slowly to right and left along a
swampy strip not more than ten miles across at any point. Paris neglected the colony for a century and a quarter. In the 1760's the Duc
de Choiseul, chief minister, recalled its existence because he had a
pet scheme. Its population was then some five hundred whites, a few
thousand Negro slaves, and an unestimated number of Indians in
the forests.

France having lost Canada as a result of the Seven Years' War,
Choiseul felt it was essential to develop some other large New World
colony as a source of lumber, salted fish, and minor staples. The
Guiana holding had been saved, so why not try there? No preliminary study of the possibilities was made. The lesson that should
have been learned from the tragic blunders committed in Louisiana
only forty-five years before, at the time of the Mississippi Bubble,
was calmly ignored. Choiseul did as John Law had done. He poured
eleven thousand settlers into Guiana in three years and took it as a
matter of course that they would tame the wilderness. The project
was an utter failure. Most of the green Europeans died of fevers, and
the rest could not solve tropical problems fast enough to suit the
Minister. When he threw up the enterprise there were fewer than a
thousand survivors, and many of these straggled back home.

Guiana was forgotten again until the French Revolution. It was
then used as a place of exile for criminals and political offenders.
Mordantly, the victims invented for it the name of the "Dry Guillotine," because of every batch of deportees at least one third died
quickly of yellow jack or malaria and another third perished in a
few months. The sinister reputation of penal colony and death hole

has clung to French Guiana ever since. Napoleon III instituted the policy of sending out only convicts who were serving long terms, and who agreed to become free settlers under a pledge that they would never leave the colony. Some ten thousand arrived over a period of years, but the plan was not a success. Too many succumbed to the climate or broke their paroles. The transporting of white convicts was discontinued. The Arabs and other Orientals who were sent instead adapted themselves well enough to the life, and their descendants formed a useful addition to the country's peasantry.

Under the Third Republic the penal system was again expanded. The whites shipped from France were either desperadoes or men whom the government wished especially to isolate. Newcomers were placed on some small islands west of Cayenne, one of which is called Devil's Island. The name caught the imagination of journalists and lurid stories were spread as to the cruelties practiced there. Actually the islands were used as a station for screening the prisoners. Those who behaved quietly were transferred to the mainland, in and about Cayenne and St. Laurent, where they lived and worked under light restraint. The incorrigibles undoubtedly received rough treatment. There were cabins on Devil's Island where prominent exiles were held in what amounted to solitary confinement. Such was the case of Captain Alfred Dreyfus, who had been wrongly convicted of selling military secrets to Germany. He was not maltreated by the wardens and hard labor was not required of him, but he suffered intensely from the isolation. His honor was at last fully re-established.

Escape from Devil's Island was an impossibility; the term figured widely, nevertheless, in newspapers and books, where it meant an evasion from any prison camp in the colony. It was quite common for convicts to get across the Moroni River into Surinam, or to make their way in rowboats along the coast to Brazil or other foreign territory. Very rarely were they turned back to the French authorities. Shortly before World War II, it was announced that no more prisoners would be transported to Guiana. The Vichy administration reversed this order, but the Fourth Republic has finally decreed the abolition of the penal settlements and the closing of all jails except those needed to take care of local offenders.

Cayenne is a backward city that has attracted few visitors from the outside world. But it is on the direct air route between Port-of-Spain and Rio, and it may yet develop possibilities as a tourist resort.

CHAPTER 13

WINDWARD AND LEEWARD ISLANDS

T HE words "windward" and "leeward" have always figured in the nomenclature of the Caribbean. Originally
they were nautical terms, the first meaning the point or side from
which the wind blows, and the second simply standing for the opposite. The prevailing winds in that region, whether the trades of
everyday or the storm currents of the hurricane season, come from
the Atlantic and blow either straight west or from southeast to northwest. The east coast of any given island, therefore, was windward
and the west coast leeward. But groups of islands were soon distinguished by these convenient names. The Spaniards called the entire
chain of the Lesser Antilles the Islas de Barlovento, and the Greater
Antilles the Islas de Sotavento. The French accepted the system;
they spoke and wrote of the Iles du Vent and the Iles sous le Vent.
Then along came the English with a modification of their own. They
left the Greater Antilles out of it, and they divided the Lesser Antilles into the Windward Islands and the Leeward Islands. It was most
illogical, for the line was drawn below Guadeloupe and the southerly group did not differ from the northerly in the matter of expo-
sure to the winds.

Keep the above in mind, according to the nationality of the au-
thors, when you read books about the West Indies. The English divi-
sion eventually grew to be political, applying to territory under their
flag. The Windward Islands today are a colonial entity composed of
Grenada, the Grenadines, St. Vincent, St. Lucia, and Dominica. The
Leeward Islands are composed of Antigua, Montserrat, Nevis, St.
Christopher (St. Kitts), Barbuda, Anguilla, and the British Virgins.
They are of unequal interest to the traveler. Only one, Dominica, is

extraordinary, and in consequence I shall give that island the lion's share of attention. But all the others have something to offer. Let us take them as they come, proceeding from south to north.

Grenada can be reached from either Trinidad or Barbados by small interisland schooners or motorboats. The best plan is to transfer at Port-of-Spain from Pan American to one of the comfortable "hop planes" of British West Indian Airways. My fancy happened to be caught by a homely craft named the *Silver Arrow*, larger than the boat that had taken me from St. Thomas to St. John, but catering to a similarly mixed lot of passengers. She made Grenada from Trinidad in a little better than twelve hours, then circled back with calls at St. Vincent and Barbados.

Writers without number have praised the harbor of St. George's, the capital of Grenada. I have read of it as "well-nigh perfect," "the finest in the West Indies," "the most beautiful," etc. These encomiums seem highly exaggerated to one who knows Santiago de Cuba, Kingston, or any of a half-dozen lesser rivals such as Port Antonio or Charlotte Amalie. But St. George's *is* an admirable and a curious haven. The town is built on a peninsula, and there are really two ports: a shallow exterior bay and the deep inner, almost landlocked harbor called the Careenage. Around the latter the mountains rise steeply, for it is nothing less than an extinct volcanic crater arrested in the process of either rising or sinking in some convulsion, and with the seaward side blasted away. Seismic disturbances have rocked its waters in historic times.

All Grenada is of purely volcanic origin. The Grand Etang, a mountain lake six miles inland and 1,740 feet high, is another dead crater. Mount St. Catherine, 2,749 feet, the point of greatest elevation, is covered with earth now and forested, but it was active a few centuries ago. The valleys are fertile. Streams flow down most of them, and generally speaking Grenada is a favored isle. It used to produce sugar, but turned through luck or good judgment to less competitive crops. Spice trees, particularly nutmegs, were introduced from the Orient with excellent results. A good variety of coffee was grown. The principal article of export for many years was cocoa. Eventually the plantations were broken up and most of the land passed into the hands of small cultivators. These give the impression of being better off than is the case in the average British West Indian colony.

The town of St. George's is picturesque, with its old fort at the tip of the promontory and its hilly streets rising abruptly from both water fronts. On the central ridge three churches stand out—Catholic, Anglican, and Presbyterian. There are no other buildings of distinction, except Government House on a slope overlooking the town and harbor.

Grenada was founded as a colony by the French. Jacques Dyel du Parquet, a nephew of Esnambuc, came there from Martinique in 1650 with two hundred men, found it to be a Carib stronghold, and waged a war of extermination with the Indians. The Morne des Sauteurs on the northern coast is shown as the cliff from which the last surviving band of warriors threw themselves into the sea rather than submit. The English call it the Caribs' Leap. During the ensuing centuries Grenada changed hands frequently. The bloodiest incident was in 1795 when Victor Hugues came south from Guadeloupe and waged what is known as the Brigands' War. He seized Grenada with the aid of colored insurrectionists, and a general massacre of the whites followed. The governor, Sir Ninian Home, was slain with forty-seven others in a single coup. Following its recapture the following year the British did not lose the island again.

The Grenadines, which are strung out in a northeasterly direction for sixty miles, consist of half a dozen fair-sized islets and many rocky cays. They are administered by Grenada. Dry and of small economic value, they attract the enterprising foreign sight-seer only once in a blue moon. One of the tiniest of the group if known as Kick-Em-Jenny, which quaint appellation is believed to be a garbling of Caye-Qui-Gêne (Troublesome Cay). Another rock is called London Bridge, and a third World's End Reef.

Roughly the same size as Grenada and resembling it physically is St. Vincent, the next unit of the Windward Islands. Here we have another totally volcanic formation with a spine of mountains, deep valleys widening into plains at lower levels, and a ring of narrow beaches. The proportions, however, are bolder and the subterranean forces by no means quiescent. The Soufrière, 3,500 feet, the most northerly peak, is a volcano that has often erupted disastrously. A terrible earthquake smote Caracas, Venezuela, in 1812, at the height of a revolution led by Simón Bolívar, and was held by the ignorant to be a supernatural intervention. At the same moment the St. Vincent peak exploded and showered cinders, ashes, and boiling mud

mixed with lava over a wide area. Again in 1902 the monster broke
loose sympathetically with Mont Pelée, Martinique, and this time
the calamity was on a giant scale. Torrents of lava poured down at
intervals for three days. Nearly a third of the island was devastated
and two thousand lives were lost, including the inhabitants of one
of the two last remaining Carib reservations in the West Indies.
Spasmodic volcanic activity continued for ten months.

Kingstown, the capital of St. Vincent and its only important town,
is on a broad open bay on the southwest coast. You will find nothing
memorable in the way of architecture, but many of the houses are
pretty against the verdant hillsides, because of the un-English practice of tinting the walls in gay pastel shades. The small botanical
garden on the outskirts is the oldest in the Caribbean and, it is said,
the first ever founded by Europeans in the tropics. Captain William
Bligh made his famous voyage on the *Bounty* for the purpose of
obtaining plants for this garden. The mutiny of his crew caused the
loss of the specimens. But a second ship was fitted out for Bligh,
and in January 1793 he arrived at Kingstown from the South Seas
with 530 species of cuttings, tubers, and seeds, including the breadfruit and the mangosteen. All the botanical gardens in near-by colonies stem from this one, and it was instrumental in establishing
many staple crops. Yet St. Vincent itself adopted the arrowroot,
which is indigenous to the West Indies, when sugar ceased to be
profitable. More than half its export trade today rests upon the lowly
arrowroot.

The island was first claimed from the Spaniards by the French.
Shortly afterward Poincy recognized it, along with Dominica, as a
neutral refuge for the Caribs. This solution was ratified by England
and Holland, but before long the English violated it and took possession. The French then renewed their claim. The ownership of
St. Vincent was tossed back and forth. During the Brigands' War
the Caribs became such violent partisans of Victor Hugues that after
his forces had been expelled they continued to oppose the English
in a struggle waged without quarter. Inevitably they were crushed,
and the tribe was deported to the Bay Islands off the coast of Hon-
duras—all save a handful, whose descendants were fated to be
wiped out a century later, as we have noted, by the Soufrière.

St. Lucia manifests a logical progression of the volcanic submerged Antillean mountain range. Its highest point is a few hun-

dred feet lower than the apex of St. Vincent. But the ribbed back-bone of its larger area contains many peaks resembling those we have just surveyed, as well as some of bizarre form. Here, too, there is a Soufrière—a generic French name, incidentally, that means a sulphur mine or a place that belches forth sulphur. St. Lucia's sample has a saucer-like crater about three acres in extent. South of it and close to the shore are the two Pitons, isolated cones so evenly molded that they look like monuments. The Gros Piton is over 2,600 feet, and the Petit Piton about 200 feet shorter. Sailors set their course by them in the old days. Hot springs bubble up at various spots. The terror beneath has been dormant since the arrival of the white man, but it often mutters. There is something uncanny about the sulphur and alum that sift out of crevices and form deposits on patches of heated ground.

I flew to St. Lucia from Port-of-Spain. The start had been made from Piarco Airport a little after dawn, and there was magic in the resulting panorama of new impressions. The forests of Trinidad were clotted darkly, with lakes of mist here and there. Only the palm trees stood out, miniature but precise, their fronded crowns in some cases seeming to be afloat on the mist. The light spread in a rosy haze from an irregularly clouded east. Soon we were soaring over the northern mountains, and a line of surf as tenuous as a thread of wool appeared below, running from horizon to horizon. Suddenly the whole sky was golden with sunshine. The sea assumed the pale, pure blue of distance and shimmered faintly like shot silk. We had left the Land of the Hummingbird behind.

It was hard to keep track of the islands that emerged. Grenada may have been sighted, but at so great a distance that I was not able to identify it. We did pass over several of the Grenadines and traversed part of St. Vincent. I noted a phenomenon that was dupli-cated farther up in the Lesser Antilles. The windward coasts of many of the islands had long stretches of low but steep cliffs, pounded to smoothness by the waves. I could see rank after rank of breakers smashing against them, pouring in some instances into caverns at sea level and foaming out again. This was a vivid illustration of the dif-ference between windward and leeward, for on the latter or Carib-bean side you will find no cliffs. It is not necessary to be a geological expert to realize what has been happening through the centuries. When the formations first came into existence they were symmetrical, but the Atlantic washed away some of the lower slopes and created bastions that in turn are being undermined. No wonder the best harbors are all to leeward.

Our descent on St. Lucia was made several miles from Castries, the capital. The surroundings of the airport are dreary. The gnarled terrain of the island had offered few choices. Level ground that would accommodate runways chanced to occur in a desert spot, and the engineers were thankful to find it. Within ten minutes by car, however, a beautiful tropical shore commences to unfold. St. Lucia is comparable for scenic effects with Grenada and the Basse Terre half of Guadeloupe. Castries is on a magnificent circular bay approached by a deep channel with headlands on either side. This is one of the best protected lesser havens in the West Indies, and the French and English each did their share in fortifying it. It was a naval station for many decades. When the tides of war ebbed from the Caribbean, Castries became a coaling port. The fuel was brought from Cardiff and heaped in pyramids along its docks. Travelers were wont to gape at the spectacle of ships being coaled by the hand, or rather head, labor of women and girls. Men shoveled the stuff from the piles and filled huge baskets, which the women balanced on their pates cushioned only by a ring of twisted banana fiber called in the West Indies a *cotta*. The speed and energy with which these female workers kept up an endless chain between the dock and the bunkers was impressive. They seldom earned more than twenty-five cents for an eight-hour day.

Times have changed. The increasing use of oil as motive power ended the importance of the Castries depot. There are mechanical devices for the little coaling that is still done, and wages have gone up. But I ascribe the ugliness of the present water front to the grimy traffic that dominated it for so long. No one has troubled to furbish up the drab warehouses of the past.

Back of the docks the town has beauty, although there are no interesting public buildings. The older homes are on narrow streets showing the French influence; others mount the incline of the 800-foot Morne Fortuné. Halfway up the latter is a broad terrace on which Government House is located, commanding a sweeping view of town and harbor. The military garrison once had its encampment on the very summit of the Morne as a precaution against the fevers that decimated raw troops from Europe. Eight hundred feet was not high enough to get away from the mosquitoes, and before the present century yellow jack took its toll. Fer-de-lance serpents swarmed in the woods around. The soldier's life in Castries was not a happy one. Nowadays the serpents are less plentiful.

Also on the Morne Fortuné stands the Hotel Antoine, an excellent hostelry with a good cuisine. The Unique, in town, has its merits. Castries is better equipped in this respect than most small West Indian ports.

A few miles up the coast near the northern end of St. Lucia is the fishing village of Gros Islet with Pigeon Island opposite. One of the two hills of which the latter is composed was Admiral Rodney's lookout on the eve of the Battle of the Saintes. The French fleet lay at Fort-de-France (then Fort Royal), and the English fleet at Castries. But Rodney had stationed frigates strung out in a line to within sight of the Martinique port, and every day he climbed to a parapet on Pigeon Island to watch for action. When De Grasse emerged at last, Rodney knew it within a few minutes by relayed signals, and he ordered immediate pursuit. This was one of the great chapters in the history of a colony that experienced little but turmoil for three centuries.

After Sir Olive Leigh had called at Barbados in 1605, he proceeded to St. Lucia and landed a party that attempted to found a settlement. The English were driven out by the Caribs in less than a month, and when a similar effort was made in 1638 the Indians again were victorious. The French came twelve years later under one Rousselan, who met with better success as a result of marrying a Carib woman and negotiating a pact of amity with her tribe. Soon the English were back, and the seesaw of sovereignty that was the rule throughout the Lesser Antilles took on a particularly frenzied character here. St. Lucia changed hands more frequently than any island except Tobago. It was among those restored to France at the Peace of Amiens in 1802, only to be again captured when the Napoleonic Wars started up again. Great Britain obtained it permanently at the final division of spoils in 1814. It is the site of one of the United States naval and air bases established on leased territory during World War II.

Martinique and Guadeloupe were described in the previous chapter. Between these two lies Dominica, the most northerly of the

Windward Islands group owned by the English. As I have implied, it is the nonpareil of the archipelago, the spot where the traveler will have his richest surprises if natural beauty is what he seeks rather than historic monuments or social entertainment.

In the first place, Dominica is the culminating massif of the so-called Antillean Andes as distinguished from the new range that rears up from a broader base in Puerto Rico, Hispaniola, Jamaica, and Cuba. Its Morne Diablotin is a little over 5,000 feet high; that much in an island that is only twenty-nine miles long by sixteen miles wide! The curve descends through Guadeloupe and the outcroppings beyond until it subsides in the Virgins. Dominica is *all* mountains; more, it is the tops of mountains, bold, serrated, with intervening chasms, yet opulent everywhere with the noblest tropical forests, or banks of shrubbery that include ferns in infinite variety. The lower reaches of the formation are under the sea.

Streams abound in this paradise. It is said, half seriously, that there are 365, one for each day of the year. Many of them plunge in feathery waterfalls from one level to the next. The pictorial effects are simply astounding. Lest I seem to rave, I shall quote one or two of the eulogies that have been written about Dominica. Though he never lived there and saw it from the deck of a ship in passing, Lafcadio Hearn poignantly felt the island's magic. He made the following comment in his *Two Years in the French West Indies:*

We are steaming on Dominica—the loftiest of the Lesser Antilles. While the silhouette is yet all violet in distance, nothing more solemnly beautiful can well be imagined: a vast cathedral shape, whose spires are mountain peaks, towering in the horizon, sheer up from the sea. We stay at Roseau only long enough to land the mails and wonder at the loveliness of the island. A beautifully wrinkled mass of green and blue and gray—a strangely abrupt peaking and heaping of the land. Behind the green heights loom the blues; behind these the grays—all pinnacled against the sky-glow—thrusting up through gaps or behind promotories. Indescribably exquisite the foldings and hollowings of the emerald coast. In glen and vale the color of canefields shines like a pooling of fluid bronze, as if the luminous essence of the hill tints had been dripping down and clarifying there. Far to our left, a bright green spur pierces into the now turquoise sea; and beyond it, a beautiful mountain form, blue and curved like a hip, slopes seaward, showing lighted wrinkles here and there, of green. And from the foreground, against the blue of the softly outlined shape, cocopalms are curving—all sharp and shining in the sun.

William Gifford Palgrave, the English writer and traveler of the nineteenth century, stated the case more succinctly: "In the wild grandeur of its towering mountains, some of which rise to 5,000 feet above the level of the sea, in the majesty of its almost impenetrable forests, in the gorgeousness of its vegetation, the abruptness of its precipices, the calm of its lakes, the violence of its torrents, the sublimity of its waterfalls, it stands without a rival, not in the West Indies only, but, I should think, throughout the whole island catalogue of the Atlantic and Pacific combined."

Several writers have called Dominica the Tahiti of the Caribbean, than which there is supposed to be no higher praise. I have never seen Tahiti, but to judge from the classic descriptions of the latter I should say that the comparison was just. As a matter of fact, there are districts of almost equal size in the mountains of Hispaniola, Jamaica, and eastern Cuba that match the beauty of Dominica. The latter is none the less superior, because it is a unit with the ocean on all sides to enhance the wonder of the land. It is the loveliest single island in the West Indies, and it is without a flaw. There are no desert areas.

Like its immediate neighbors, Dominica is volcanic. Morne Diablotin is a dormant volcano, directly linked no doubt in the bowels of the earth with its two malignant sisters to the north and south: the Soufrière in Guadeloupe and Mont Pelée in Martinique. There is a crater not far from Diablotin in which sulphur bubbles perpetually and often spurts upward in geyser-like jets. The English have given it the prosy name of Boiling Lake. This, of course, is an active vent, which at any time might break bounds and precipitate a catastrophe. Hot springs occur in many other places. But there has been no major eruption for centuries, and to this circumstance we owe the uniform beauty and fecundity of the island.

The wholly mountainous nature of the country is caused by a series of spurs branching off to the sea from both sides of the typical backbone range. One district of about 20,000 acres grades down toward the leeward coast in undulating land that varies from 1,500 to 200 feet above sea level and is called, if you please, the Layou Flats. Low valleys and narrow coastal plains also occur. Only in such limited pockets could the staple West Indian crop, sugar cane, be commercially grown. So Dominica was never exploited by planters in a large way. Comparatively few Negroes were brought in as slaves, and the Caribs were not extirpated. A diversified agriculture grew up. The early French settlers did well with coffee, and a little of it is still produced. Dominica has long been famous for its limes; not only the fruit is exported, but by-products such as concentrated lime juice and the essential oil of limes. Oranges, cocoa, and spices reach the outside market.

All the above items add up to a trivial figure in the total trade of the Caribbean. The inhabitants of Dominica number barely fifty thousand, and most of them are poor but happy. They can live on what they cultivate themselves. That is one reason why the atmosphere of the place remains primitive, unspoiled. Weigh their lot against that of the Barbadians, who are four times as numerous in a much smaller island, and they must be considered the luckier people.

Roseau, the capital, lies on an open roadstead on the southwest coast. It has no urban dignity, but the environment is overwhelmingly fair. Roomy houses, generally of wood and too often with sheets of corrugated iron for roofs, stand amid trees so thickly planted that the residential streets are like paths through a grove. Decorative vines riot along the veranda rails, and the gardens are filled with a blaze of flowers. You see hovels, also, but in that setting even the simplest form of existence does not seem squalid. There are some adequate government buildings, a rather ordinary Anglican parish church, and a fine Catholic cathedral. The Roman faith has by far the larger following. An old water-front fort, dating from 1775, is now used as a police station.

Behind the town, at the lower end of the Roseau Valley, are botanical gardens founded less than sixty years ago, but ranking high among Caribbean rivals. A visiting French authority, P. E. Cadillac, pronounced them to be "worthy of a great European city." Morne Bruce, 500 feet, slopes sharply on the southwest side to a plateau from which a marvelous view of the gardens, the town, and the glittering coast may be had.

Near the north end of the island is Prince Rupert's Bay, a natural harbor sheltered by two hilly points, which would be a better location for a port than Roseau. The British once had a military station in the village of Portsmouth there. Other settlements, in the interior as well as on the coast, are mere hamlets. There probably never will be any building on a large scale in that leisurely Eden.

The possibilities for sight-seeing trips are endless. A drive anywhere in the island in an experience. After you have covered the new Imperial Road and the other fairly good motor highways, you will do well to hire a horse and explore the bypaths. The standard trips are to Freshwater Lake at an altitude of 3,000 feet, which is easily accessible at the end of superb forest trails; Boiling Lake in its "Valley of Desolation," already mentioned, a much more difficult place to reach; the waterfalls of Layou and Pagoua; and the Carib reservation eleven miles inland from Marigot. The last-named is the only spot in the West Indies where a self-contained community of aborigines can be seen. There are but a few hundred of them and it is doubtful if many, even of those who look Amerindian, are really of pure blood. Intermarriage with Negroes has been common. The prevailing cast of countenance is Mongoloid, with prominent cheekbones, somewhat slanted eyes, and a yellowish-brown complexion. The frames are stocky and short, the hair a coarse black mane. These Caribs earn a living at fishing, raising vegetables, and weaving excellent waterproof baskets. They still make the dugout canoes of their ancestors and manage them with the utmost skill in bringing their wares around the coast to the market place at Roseau.

Dominica's fauna is of special interest to naturalists. Birds are found in those volcanic fastnesses that occur nowhere else in the world. For instance, there are four indigenous parrots in the Greater and Lesser Antilles, and of these two are peculiar to Dominica. The more striking is the *Augusta imperialis,* as large as a fair-sized chicken. Its predominant color is a dark green, but the breast is purple, the head blue, and the tail a luminous bronze. The area it inhabits is believed not to exceed four square miles of wooded crags at the north end of the island. The local variety of solitaire, the *siffleur montagne,* is remarkable for having red plumage mixed with the regulation somber blue. Its sad, sweet notes equal the unearthly singing of the solitaire I described in one of my chapters on Jamaica. The hummingbirds are almost as numerous and varied as those of Trinidad. A species of tropical wren known as the *trembleur* has the peculiar habit of vibrating its wings after it has alighted, with the energy displayed by hummingbirds when these are poised before a flower.

Agoutis, or Indian conies, occur in the wildest parts of the central range. In the pools formed by mountain streams an exceptionally large kind of frog abounds. The legs of this "mountain chicken," as it is facetiously called, are valued as an epicurean delicacy. Iguanas are caught near the seashore and used for food by the Negroes and Caribs. But the woods of Dominica are absolutely free of the fer-de-lance serpent, the scourge of Martinique, only thirty miles away.

Dominica was one of the first islands discovered by Columbus on his second voyage, 1493, and the day being Sunday, he named the place accordingly. The Spaniards never attempted to take possession of it, and for more than a hundred years it was the chief Carib stronghold. The ranking cacique there was obeyed in emergencies by the seafaring tribesmen of the neighboring islands. King Charles I's "grant of all the Caribbees" to the Earl of Carlisle included Dominica. The noble lord's man on the spot, Sir Thomas Warner, waged a regular war with the savages, and by weight of superior arms he consistently beat them. But he left their headquarters alone, save on one occasion when a party of Caribs kidnaped his wife in Antigua and took her to Dominica. Warner dashed there in pursuit and obtained her release. A curious incident, any way you look at it. The Caribs were cannibals—the very word in both Spanish and English is a corruption of their name—and they were not given to sparing prisoners. Lady Warner seems to have been used as a hostage, with whom immunity was bought by the farsighted cacique.

The French tried to colonize Dominica a few years later and were bloodily repulsed. Then came Poincy's compromise under which it was a neutral island. The pact was honored longer in connection with Dominica than with the others, simply because the difficult terrain made military operations expensive. Gallic adventurers edged in, all the same, married native women, and got on such friendly terms with the tribes that the two peoples regarded each other as allies. Père Labat tells of visiting Roseau at the end of the seventeenth century and meeting a pure-blooded Indian woman, Madame Ouvernard, then a centenarian, who bore the courtesy title of Queen of Dominica. He gave her his blessing and two bottles of *eau de vie*.

Following the Treaty of Aix-la-Chapelle, 1748, the French de-

cided that they must have the island since it lay between their flourishing colonies of Martinique and Guadeloupe. Their planters in-
filtrated without serious objections on the part of the Caribs. Using
this as a pretext, the English proclaimed during the Seven Years'
War that the neutrality agreement no longer held. They seized Dominica in 1759 and had their title confirmed at the peace table in
1763. All the accessible land was surveyed and sold by commissioners in London in lots for about $1,500,000, but not many of the new
proprietors took over. Several thousand slaves were imported.

The game of hauling down flags and hoisting them again proceeded merrily through the American Revolution and the Napoleonic Wars. In 1778 French troops under the Marquis de Bouillé
raided from Martinique and took the island after a brief resistance.
An observer records that the town of Roseau was entered "in most
regular and solemn order, the drums beating a slow march, and the
soldiers with small boughs and flowers in their hats." Rodney's victory at Les Saintes reversed that decision. Victor Hugues landed
from Guadeloupe during the Brigands' War, but was expelled. In
1805 a French fleet bombarded Roseau into submission and disem-
barked four thousand soldiers. The governor, General Prevost, re-
treated to the old fort at Prince Rupert's Bay, and when called upon
to surrender or be annihilated he replied nonchalantly: "My duty
to my king and my country is so superior to every other considera-
tion that I have only to thank you for the observation you have been
pleased to make on the often inevitable consequences of war." That
time the invaders withdrew after collecting a ransom of $60,000.

Of all the little islands that have been alternately French and English, Dominica is the one in which the Gallic influence has persisted
most strongly. The nearness of Martinique and Guadeloupe doubtless has had a great deal to do with this. But the geographical form
of the island has also been a factor, because it discouraged the plantation system and led to isolated communities that clung to the first
impress of civilization received. The language of the common people
today is a French patois. French family and place names are far more
numerous than English. Costumes, fetes, manners, and superstitions
resemble those of other Gallo-Negroid communities in the New
World. A native-born writer of real distinction, the poet and essay-
ist Dr. Daniel Thaly, does his best work in French.

Administratively, Dominica was one of the Leeward Islands until

1937, when it was transferred to the Windward Islands group, with which it obviously has greater kinship.

How different they are, those Leewards! Just as volcanic as the islands we have been considering, but much less lush. They suffer, many of them, from a shortage of water and resulting aridity. The case grows steadily worse until we reach the Virgins, the problems of which have already been told. Yet all the islands in question started out with sugar cane and enjoyed prosperity during the golden period of that crop. The trouble is that they cling to sugar, even though it cannot be profitably cultivated in small units under modern competitive conditions. They are very poor, but can boast of some beautiful scenery and are pleasant to visit.

Antigua is the seat of government. It is only 108 square miles in area, roughly oval in shape, and surrounded by coral reefs. Its principal attraction is the coast line, indented by several deep harbors approached by channels broken through the reefs. St. John's, the capital, is on a bay two miles long by three quarters of a mile broad. English Harbour and Falmouth are almost as commodious. If only the interior lived up to the winding tropical shore, it would be a wonderful island. But its low hills are as brown and baked as those of St. Thomas, and it is with the greatest difficulty that the cane fields on the flats are kept alive when the rains fail. There is a single stream, while a certain amount of water is stored in cisterns. The greatest elevation in the southerly volcanic section is under 1,000 feet and no clearly defined cones are visible.

The town of St. John's has an Anglican cathedral a century old, but no other fine buildings or interesting ruins. English Harbour is where Nelson refitted his fleet after Villeneuve had eluded him in 1805. Admiral's House at the ancient dockyard has been preserved and contains relics of the greatest of English sailors. But Nelson loathed the station on account of the heat and mosquitoes. He wrote that if it had not been for the company of a certain lady, "who is *very, very* good to me, I should hang myself in this infernal hole." He could not have cared for scenery, because the harbor has undeniable charm. One of the new United States naval bases was built in Antigua.

St. Kitts, to use the name that has long been general for St. Christopher, lies to the northwest. It is a notably more interesting island than Antigua, being fairly well watered and blessed with fertile soil on the lower levels. The aboriginal name was Liamuiga, which means fertile. Roughly oval-shaped, the southern end narrows to a peninsula with a round head bearing a salt pond in the middle like an eye. The purely volcanic mountains culminate in a peak about 4,000 feet high called Mount Misery, the crater of which shows signs of activity though there has been no eruption for centuries. On the leeward side the range forms a semicircle enclosing a rich plain, where the capital, Basseterre, stands on an open roadstead. Ten miles from the town is a precipitous mound of volcanic rock named Brimstone Hill, which in the old days was heavily fortified. Also near by is Monkey Hill, so called because simians were released there and multiplied. Monkeys are not indigenous to the Antilles, and this is the only place where they are found wild.

Basseterre, founded in 1627 by Esnambuc and adopted by Poincy as his capital, was often damaged in the strife that raged for the possession of the island. In 1867 it was totally destroyed by fire and rebuilt in Victorian style. It has nothing to offer the sight-seer except a fairly good botanical garden. There are no other towns of importance, but at the parish church of Old Road is to be seen the tomb of the original English colonizer, Sir Thomas Warner, with its flamboyant epitaph. Excursions among the heights and along the shore afford many delightful views. The sugar estates look comparatively flourishing.

Tiny Nevis, across a two-mile strait from St. Kitts, is a single volcanic cone sweeping up to a height of 3,596 feet. The narrow coastal plain, however, saves it from an isolation such as Saba's. The island once had a vogue as a resort of fashion. Its hot springs were believed to have special curative merits, and visitors from Europe flocked there in the latter half of the eighteenth century and the early years of the nineteenth. The old Bath House Hotel, employed as a setting by Gertrude Atherton in her novel *The Gorgeous Isle*, was renovated in 1909. Nevis was the birthplace of Alexander Hamilton. Nelson's marriage to Frances Herbert Nisbet, a widow, took place there in 1787 with the future King William IV as best man.

Anguilla, which like Nevis is administered from St. Kitts, is a flat and barren island where a few cattle are raised and a little salt is washed. Barbuda was formerly the property of the Codrington family, who got rich on sugar but were a good deal more interested in the fallow deer and pheasants they introduced from Europe and the guinea fowl brought from Africa. They turned the island into a game preserve. A handful of Negro peasant farmers and fishermen live there today. The deer became naturalized and permits are occasionally issued to hunters in Antigua.

Montserrat contains three groups of volcanic mountains in its thirty-three square miles. The highest peak, 3,000 feet, is a semiactive Soufrière. The northern part is desolate and dry, but in the south streams make the soil cultivable. Sugar cane, citrus fruit, and sea-island cotton are grown. The first settlers in Montserrat were Irish. Their names have come down, being easily the commonest among the modern colored population. The local dialect is still marked by a faint brogue. As to the British Virgins, the little that need be said about them has been said in a previous chapter.

The history of the Leeward Islands centers about St. Kitts rather than Antigua, though political leadership has passed to the latter. The reasonable division of St. Kitts arranged by Esnambuc and Warner did not long endure. The French were the first to gain the upper hand under Poincy, while the English consoled themselves with Antigua and Montserrat. But in the course of the next two centuries, St. Kitts changed hands over and over. There probably was more heavy fighting within its restricted area than in any of the other small islands. Detailed accounts have been kept of the campaigns, because both the French and the English had a sentimental attachment for St. Kitts as the "mother" of their West Indian colonies. In 1782 the Marquis de Bouillé landed with eight thousand men and assailed the Brimstone Hill fortress, which was garrisoned by only six hundred. The bombardment, which lasted for a fortnight, reached an intensity seldom known in those days, and the defense was considered so honorable that following the capitulation the Marquis loaded his captives with favors. He released the commanding general, Fraser, without a parole, declaring that his gallantry had earned him the right to fight the French again as often as he pleased. The lower officers and men were to be exchanged, but Bouillé sent them home at once and left it to the English to return an equivalent. Such were the amenities of war in the elegant eighteenth century.

St. Kitts, along with all the other Leeward Islands, remained permanently under British sovereignty after Rodney's naval victory.

They were not affected by the black revolution in St.-Domingue, molested by Victor Hugues, or attacked by Napoleon's navy. For the last century and a half their sole despoiler has been the Carib god Huracán, lord of the circular tempest, across whose favorite pathway they unfortunately lie. The English word hurricane and the French *ouragan* are said both to have been adapted from the aboriginal tongue in St. Kitts.

CHAPTER 14

THE LAND OF
CHRISTOPHER COLUMBUS

I FLEW to the Dominican Republic from Antigua, with a change of planes at Puerto Rico. On my way down through the archipelago I had by-passed the two countries that share the island of Hispaniola, my seemingly perverse reason having been that they were of major importance and interest. Having just revisited Jamaica and Cuba, I thought it better to seek impressions in some smaller places before I wound up my trip with Hispaniola. It should give me a more balanced picture for the purposes of my book. I felt now that this had been a sound idea. After several weeks of rapid exploration, a leisurely view of Christopher Columbus's own land awaited me, and the prospect was stimulating.

The Dominican Republic and part of Haiti, meanwhile, had been shaken by a great seismic disturbance that originated in the Brownson Deep, reached the land mass with diminished power, but set tidal waves in motion that swept the coast repeatedly. One township near Samaná Bay had been wiped out, but the loss of life had not been heavy because the preliminary shocks had served as a warning and most of the population had fled. Amazing phenomena were reported in the newspapers. It was said that a field of growing corn had been shifted for ninety or a hundred yards, the surface soil remaining intact so that the crop was not harmed. A spasmodic trembling of the earth had occurred almost every day for a month, and no one could imagine when it would cease. Yet buildings had stood up against it remarkably well.

Mona Passage, which separates Puerto Rico from Hispaniola, is an extension of the Brownson Deep. This is a strange thing, for the mountains of the Greater Antilles clearly form a single chain below the sea as well as above it. The profundity of the Mona Passage means that two masses of stupendous peaks were cleft assunder in prehistoric times. Blair Niles has aptly said that to the ocean creatures living on the floor of the Brownson Deep, Hispaniola is higher than Mount Everest. I might add that Puerto Rico would appear just as imposing to these problematical beings. Contemplated from the foot of the Himalayas, a variation of five thousand feet at the top would make little difference.

You cannot judge submarine depths from the air. Even if there should appear to be a tone of darker blue, this may be owing to idiosyncrasies of the light or to the shadows of clouds. Knowing what I knew, however, I was astonished to find the eastern end of the Dominican Republic a map in the lowest relief. I had sailed past it in a ship, and it had not seemed so flat then. It was typical sugar country, like that of central Cuba, with endless squared-off fields of cane rolling gently between occasional stands of timber and dotted by sentinel palms. Broad new roads intersected the region, an improvement over comparatively recent days when the transportation system of the republic was one of the poorest in the West Indies. General Rafael L. Trujillo, the dictator, is justly proud of his road building.

We swept over the towns of La Romana and San Pedro Macorís, and soon the ancient capital at the mouth of the Ozama River loomed up. It was founded in 1596 by Bartholomew Columbus at the orders of his brother, the Admiral, and is the oldest city in the New World. They named it Santo Domingo, but since 1936 it has been Ciudad Trujillo. This is the outstanding instance of the chief's having been glorified by a change of names. Let the point pass for the moment. The airport is conveniently located on the outskirts of the city. When I arrived, the immigration department honored American passports without a Dominican visa if the traveler had come direct from United States territory. They handled the formalities with courtesy and dispatch, and issued a permit good for a couple of weeks. A law has since been passed under which nothing is required except proof of identity. A tourist card for a stay of up to sixty days costs a dollar.

I checked in at the Hotel Jaragua in the newer, western section of the city. Without question, this is the finest hotel of the international type to be found in the West Indies, with the exception of the Nacional in Havana. Of these two the Jaragua has the advantage of being much newer and equipped in more modern fashion. It was built by the government—"under the personal direction" of President Trujillo, the publicity folders are careful to inform you—and opened at the end of 1943. The management is American. Standing in broad grounds, the hotel faces the tree-lined Avenida Independencia, while its rear is on the Avenida George Washington, a magnificent driveway, or *malecón*, that follows the shore of the Caribbean Sea. The only drawback is that no bathing beach exists at this spot. The Jaragua has its own swimming pools. I do not particularly care for the extreme modernistic architecture that has been employed, or for the glaring white of the exterior. But this is a personal reaction. I heard no unfavorable criticisms by the public.

The verandas and outdoor terraces for recreation are spacious, all the public rooms luxuriously appointed, and the bedrooms the last word in comfort. It should be understood that the Jaragua is not truly Dominican. It is a hotel designed to cater to rich foreigners, and the few natives you see there are decidedly of the ruling political caste or from the ranks of the well-to-do. But unlike the English colonial hotels that I have criticized, the Jaragua goes on the principle that its guests want a taste of things Dominican. Local foods and drinks are featured along with standard dishes. One evening while I was there the whole menu was native, and the tourists loved it. Prices are kept below the astronomical figures indulged in by some luxury hotels. But the Jaragua is not cheap. It would be difficult to get by for less than $15 a day, on the basis of a single room, *à la carte* meals, and the customary tips.

I followed my policy of not remaining too long in agreeable resorts of fashion where one gets only a limited view of the life of the country. The place to which I moved turned out to be semiforeign also; but it provided an interesting angle. It was the Hotel Chechoslovakia on the Calle Seybo, run by a Jewish man and wife who had met in the republic as refugees. There is a farming settlement called Sosua in one of the northern provinces, where "displaced persons" from Europe were admitted by President Trujillo as early as 1940. He donated part of an estate he owned there, and announced that he would find homes for a maximum of 100,000 anti-Nazis. At the end of the first year there were 300 colonists at Sosua. The population mounted to about 500, and then shipping was cut off by American participation in the war and the German submarine campaign on this side of the Atlantic. Success had already been registered. In 1943 Sosua had an income of $20,000 in milk products alone.

Not all the *émigrés*, however, were satisfied to be farmers. Some of the professional men and merchants among them drifted to the cities and made a go of it. No obstacles were placed in their way by the authorities. My hosts at the Hotel Chechoslovakia were examples of the enterprise shown. They had a nice little family pension, the charges being $5 a day for room and board. Many of the guests were Americans and Puerto Ricans. The dining room, which occupied a veranda on three sides of the house and looked upon a small but attractive garden, was open to the public. Dominicans often dropped in for meals, as did a certain number of refugees, and the atmosphere was cosmopolitan.

The numerous other hotels in Ciudad Trujillo are Spanish West Indian in character, similar to the smaller hostelries of Havana but a shade less expensive. Theirs are the principal restaurants. Apart from these, the eating places are unpretentious, most of them being of the café type. Some are run by Chinese. The multitude of bars, which sell fruit juices and coconut water as well as alcoholic drinks; the pastry shops and ice cream parlors, which feature tropical flavors; the street vendors of cigarettes and flowers; all combine to give the feeling of a Latin milieu where nature's gifts are enjoyed to the full. On the Caribbean shore are pleasant beach clubs shadowed by coconut palms, and in many cases with tables at the rear set out under thick-foliaged almond trees. Licensed gambling goes on at one or two of these places. Incidentally, there is an elaborate gaming casino in the Hotel Jaragua itself. Horse racing may be enjoyed at the Perla de las Antillas track, recently opened.

An active tourist commission functions under the direction of an American, H. W. Goeggel. It has its offices in the Palacio del Partido Dominicano, Avenida George Washington, one of the gleaming white buildings erected under the Trujillo regime. Goeggel is the man to consult if you do not quite know how to set about your sight-seeing. He will draw up an itinerary and get you a taxi with an English-speaking driver. He placed a car at my disposal for a day, and though I knew the city well enough from a previous visit not to need a guide, the courtesy proved most helpful. For one thing, my chauffeur was a rare personality, a fellow with sound information about the country and its history on the tip of his tongue, and one who knew how to adapt himself to my special interests. His name was Diógenes Moreta. He was of native birth, but had lived and worked for twelve years in Haiti and had a perfect command of both French and English in addition to Spanish. Intelligent and eager to do more than was asked of him, this Moreta. In less than an hour I had the feeling that we were old friends. He had had previous experience in taking a writer around, for in Haiti he had been engaged for a long tour through the republic by Mabel Steedman, an Englishwoman. She mentions him appreciatively in her book *Unknown to the World*.

We drove first to the heart of the original city. Crowded into a few square blocks of the land that slopes up from the west bank of the Ozama River stand the most venerable buildings in the Western Hemisphere: the ruins of the Alcázar de Colón, the cathedral, occupying one side of the Parque Colón, the Torre del Homenaje (Tower of Homage), all dating from the early sixteenth century; and a number of mansions scarcely less ancient, converted now to public purposes. It should be said that these structures and half a dozen others on the Calle Isabela la Católica and neighboring streets are the sole survivors of the hurricane of 1930, which leveled the capital. Ciudad Trujillo has been rebuilt and greatly extended in the past seventeen years. The channel of the river has been dredged so that liners of deep draught may enter and dock at a magnificent system of new piers. Yet the historic core has lost none of the character that it would have been so easy to harm by the juxtaposition of crude modernity.

I had been here in 1936 and had carried away memories that made this second visit doubly interesting. A soldier in a linen uniform met me at the ornate carved stone gateway of the Alcázar de Colón, or Columbus Castle, and showed me through the place, which has been cleaned up just enough to make inspection easy. It was built by Don Diego, son of Christopher, when he was appointed governor general with authority over all the territory then held by the Spaniards in the New World. Completed by 1514, it served as his residence and viceregal court, and was occupied by his widow, Maria de Toledo y Rojas, called the Virreina, who long outlived him, by two of his sons, and by some of his successors in the governorship. It was an edifice of solid stone blocks, built like a medieval castle. There were two stories with a reception hall, banqueting hall, several bedrooms, and quarters for guards and servants. The walls were immensely thick, but had embrasures through which guns could be fired for its defense. Impregnable in its days of glory, it lasted with only slight damage until the beginning of the nineteenth century. Vandalism on the part of the Haitians when they conquered Santo Domingo is largely responsible for its present partially shattered and roofless condition.

Across from the Alcázar is the National Museum, housed in what used to be a noble mansion. Professor Felix M. Pérez Sánchez, the director, received me and exhibited his treasures with a thoroughness that left me convinced of their value. The relics of heroes of the republican period are appropriate enough in a collection of the kind. I enjoyed looking at them, though I saw none that would have a striking appeal for strangers. The Arawak pottery and other artifacts, however, are clearly the most important that have been assembled in any Caribbean museum. This race of Indians once inhabited the whole West Indies chain. At the time of Columbus they had been almost exterminated in the Lesser Antilles by the Caribs. But the latter had not yet reached Hispaniola. It was with the gentle earlier race that the Spaniards had to deal, and we know how they were destroyed. The white conquerors were as ruthless in their own way as the Caribs would have been.

The Arawaks left no written word. They loved to sing and dance, but none of their songs have been recorded. A few fables of the simplest oral type are all that have come down to us. We can appraise them today only by their craftsmanship. They are supposed to have been incapable of working in metals, and the examples of their beads and pottery that have been discovered are fairly primitive. Clay was the material they utilized best. They embellished their earthen vessels with intricate patterns. Of the many objects pointed out to me by Professor Pérez, the one that I thought the most advanced was a stamp cut in stone with which they impressed a design on an otherwise finished artifact while the clay was still soft. Also, there was a message in hieroglyphs on a tablet, as yet undeciphered. The array of idols and grotesque models of men and beasts in this museum is fascinating. Visitors to Ciudad Trujillo who have the least interest in archaeology should not fail to see it.

The Torre del Homenaje toward the mouth of the river was the first fortification erected in the city and was finished in 1510. The tradition that it was built in honor of Columbus is hardly credible, for he had died neglected in 1506 and his reputation was at its lowest ebb. Later generations dedicated it to him more or less consciously. The pile is massive, squarely posed, and in a remarkable state of preservation. It serves as a Dominican army post. The quarters where Oviedo wrote his *History of the Indies* are shown with dubious authenticity. That he worked and died somewhere in the fortress is sure.

No doubt attaches to the honors paid the Columbus family in the cathedral, started in 1523 and completed in 1540. By that time Don Diego's governorship had restored the prestige of the name. The Discoverer had expressed a wish that his last resting place should be in Santo Domingo City. So as soon as the cathedral was finished the bones of both the First and Second Admirals, as father and son were called, were removed from Spain and buried side by side in a vault below the altar. Subsequent interments of relatives and descendants occurred in the same general location.

The cathedral was the first erected in the New World. It is an imposing example of a Spanish-Romanesque basilica, with three large naves and fifteen chapels. The style is not uniform. Central design and interior are inspired by early Gothic, but the façades with their rich frescoes are in the Andalusian Renaissance style. Depredations by spoilers, especially Sir Francis Drake when he captured the city in 1586, have left their mark upon the building. Terrible "El Draque" camped in the cathedral itself, looted much of its plate, and damaged monuments. A great treasure in the way of relics, sacred vessels, jeweled ornaments, and paintings has nevertheless been built up; it can be seen on request. The walls show cracks caused by earthquakes. Inside and out, the stone has been softened by time to a tint of golden gray. There is no building in all the Western Hemisphere where one is conscious of the past so poignantly.

In the central nave not far from the western door stands a mausoleum of white marble shaped like a temple, open on the four sides to reveal a bronze sarcophagus supported by a pedestal. Once a year the casket is thrown open for the benefit of the public and is seen to contain a small leaden chest. The latter is the original coffin of Christopher Columbus, and it still guards his bones. For many years the Spanish and Cuban governments tried to create the impression that this was some sort of hoax, but one hears less and less of their version of the story. Careful investigation has satisfied historians that the Dominican claims are correct. The following is the extraordinary sequence of events that began with a blunder and ended in a fortuitous discovery:

As mentioned in one of my chapters on Cuba, when Spain gave up her half of Hispaniola to the French in 1795 she refused to part with the remains of Columbus. The family vault was hastily opened and the right leaden casket removed, as they believed, for burial in Havana Cathedral early the next year. The people of Santo Domingo City themselves assumed that that was what had happened. It probably was a matter of no consquence to them at the time, for they were menaced by the slave revolution in St.-Domingue and decades of misery lay ahead. The country fell under the domination of the blacks. Independence as a republic was not won until 1844. The cathedral had escaped violation, but records of the Columbus graves had been lost.

In 1877 the rector, Padre Francisco X. Billini, took up a collection among prominent citizens for a fund to repair the building. Everyone was hard up and he obtained only a trivial sum. A legend that money had formerly been hidden in a wall of the structure was called to his attention, and in desperation he authorized a trusted agent to dig at the spot indicated. Instead of gold a coffin was uncovered. It bore the name of Don Luís Columbus, the grandson of the First Admiral. This caused much talk over a period of months, and at last the high dignitaries of the archbishopric instructed Padre Billini to conduct a search for the purpose of locating all possible graves of the illustrious family. On September 10 several churchmen and statesmen, including the Minister of the Interior, were watching a single laborer break into a closed vault that had been noted the day before. As the wall gave way a leaden casket was seen and pulled out. When the dust had been scraped off the lid, the astounded witnesses read an inscription extolling Christopher Columbus.

"There can be no doubt about this!" exclaimed a monsignor. "What a treasure!"

Ironically, the workman supposed that the gold of which he had heard rumors had been found. "Good!" he said, throwing down his tools. "Then you can pay me off and let me go." He was disgruntled at being handed fifty cents, the total that the pockets of the on-lookers yielded.

The coffin was opened later in the presence of officials and members of the foreign diplomatic and consular staffs. A deposition was prepared by a notary, in which the company declared it was their unanimous opinion that the remains were truly those of the First Admiral. As the casket of Don Diego, the Second Admiral, was *not* discovered, in spite of an exhaustive hunt, it has been since taken for granted that his bones were the ones that the Spaniards had transferred to Havana and subsequently to Seville.

The Columbus cult has grown enormously in the Dominican Republic in the seventy years that have elapsed. All the nations of the Pan-American Union are to share in the supreme monument, which has not yet been built. This is to take the form of a gigantic recumbent cross, with beacons for the craft of sea and air. It will be located in a water-front park on the eastern side of the Ozama River, the spot first chosen by Bartholomew Columbus as the site of the city and abandoned shortly afterward for the west bank.

Dominicans have a flair for reverently patriotic entombments. In the early years of the present century, the government collected the bodies of those who had led the independence movement of the 1840's and placed them in a chapel of the cathedral. It was felt that this did not sufficiently honor the three greatest—Duarte, Sánchez, and Mella—and in 1944, on the hundredth anniversary of the revolution, their remains were removed to a pantheon that was given the name of Altar de la Patria. It had been the Puerta de El Conde, one of the chief gateways of the ancient city wall and the spot where the heroes raised the cry of liberty. Restored and improved with symbolic additions, it makes an effective monument. The tomb lies under the center of the arch, with a military guard on perpetual duty.

Another "first" in Ciudad Trujillo is the University of St. Thomas of Aquinas, oldest of American seats of learning. The ruins of the earliest hospital are to be seen. Both institutions were founded during the governorship of the Second Admiral. College facilities are being widely extended by the present government, the emphasis being on medical and other scientific studies.

I asked Moreta to take me on a tour of the outstanding civic improvements about which one hears much talk in the republic. Space is lacking to give a detailed account of all I saw. I shall presently discuss Trujillo's policies as a whole. But the public market system must be cited as a special illustration. There is a large central building with several branches in different parts of the city. Unquestionably these markets are the most modern and hygienic, the most rationally conducted of any in the American tropics. They may be equaled in the United States, but not in the localities with which I happen to be familiar. The structures are airy and the cement floors, walls, and counters spotlessly clean. Vegetables and fruits of the country are displayed in the greatest profusion, at prices a good deal below those prevailing in the shops outside. The meat department is run along model lines. You are separated by glass from the butchers, who take their wares from a refrigerator and show them to you on a platter. After you have made your selection, the cutting and weighing is done with a minimum of handling. The order is wrapped in waxed paper and put in a compartment of a rotating drum, which is spun around to face you. If contamination occurs after you have accepted the package, that is your own fault. You have been able to see for yourself that the meat was delivered undefiled. Constant supervision by inspectors guarantees that the butchers do not fake their end of it.

In comparison with those of other Caribbean lands, whether independent or colonial, and particularly in contrast with Dominican conditions of days gone by, these markets are fabulous. They not only safeguard the health of the community, but encourage people to buy native instead of imported foods. The fees charged the stall holders are modest. The system is one of Trujillo's pet projects. He is proud of it, as well he may be. Let us note briefly the rest of his accomplishments.

He came to power in August 1930. Two weeks later occurred the hurricane that wrecked the capital as it had never been wrecked before. Trujillo declared martial law and set about the task of rebuilding with remarkable energy and imagination. It is a brand-new city today, and its growth westward along the Caribbean shore has been phenomenal. The streets have been widened, the public squares improved with landscaping. Many administrative structures have been raised, and although I find the tendency toward the modernistic style excessive, the interiors are well adapted to comfort in a hot climate. A huge capitol is in course of erection. There are no slums, but in their place an expanding series of low-rental workmen's homes built by the government. Beggars have vanished from the streets. Crimes of violence have been greatly reduced, and it is claimed that pedestrians may roam the city at night in perfect safety.

New schools have been opened throughout the republic and illiteracy reduced. Bridges as well as roads have been built wherever needed, irrigation canals dug to serve arid regions, and farming colonies established for thousands of the landless. Instead of importing rice, as was the case until a few years ago, the country now produces a surplus of this staple and sells large quantities of it abroad. A dozen up-to-date hospitals have been placed in operation, four of them in the interior. Regular payments are being made on the foreign debt, an obligation with which no previous native administration tried seriously to cope.

The above are not merely the boasts of a propaganda ministry. They are facts. It is obvious that the rank and file of the population have benefited materially, not only from the direct results of the efficiency program but from the ending of the political brigandage that used to be chronic. As far as I could tell, the majority were satisfied with the present regime. Moreta was a stout supporter. There is another side to the picture, however. Generalissimo Dr. Rafael Leonidas Trujillo Molina, Benefactor of the Fatherland and Restorer of the Financial Independence of the Republic, to give him some of his many titles, has been an absolute dictator since 1930. But one legal party has been allowed to exist during the period of transformation, and it is to be suspected that the President's recent advice to dissident factions that they organize and take part in public affairs will not result in a serious opposition. The press remains shackled; its editorials and news columns alike sing daily paeans to Trujillo and report nothing that might be termed even faintly critical of his government. Such Dominicans as disapprove of him either keep silent or leave the country. Several hostile juntas operate abroad, notably in Haiti, Venezuela, and New York.

The exiles violently attack the regime. They accuse it of murdering opponents, exploiting the poor, and collecting a rake-off on every new industry or important business deal. I consider it only fair to say that, on the spot, I heard none but unsubstantiated rumors to this effect, though there is probably much truth in the third of the charges mentioned. One matter, at least, I checked carefully. I had read in a Haitian newspaper that, "thanks to a brother of Trujillo (Pipi), the

Dominican Republic is today the very home of venereal diseases, on account of the innumerable houses of prostitution run by this Pipi." The assertion is a falsehood, or let us say a wild shot in the dark. Medical reports state that the V.D. rate in Ciudad Trujillo is below the average of West Indian cities. I inquired about commercial prostitution and was told there was very little of it. Then I asked my chauffeur, Moreta, to show me some of the best "houses." He replied that the capital had nothing of the sort to offer, that apart from gambling the night life was pretty tame.

Did he really expect me to believe, I countered, that there was no prostitution in a place the size of Ciudad Trujillo? He said of course there was some, but not conducted in a big way. A few amateurs who met in semiprivate establishments. He would let me judge for myself. So he drove me one evening to a place or two on the outskirts where women sold beer in their front parlors. A couple of naïve country girls always were in attendance, to drink with the occasional customer, dance to phonograph music—and succumb readily to blandishments, if invited. In no Latin-American city would the authorities dream of interfering with this sort of thing, but it bore little resemblance to the string of bordellos supposedly managed by the President's brother. Nor did I observe a single street-walker while I was in the republic.

I set out in this book to record travel impressions, and I am neither defending nor condemning any political faction. The reader must decide whether he thinks the great material gains are worth the price of the curtailment of Dominican liberty. Yet I must call attention to a bizarre phase of Trujillo's exercise of power. The General is a glutton for flattery. A few years ago a sycophantic official put up a huge electric sign in the capital, reading "Dios y Trujillo." Foreigners poked fun at it, and it has disappeared. The squares and avenues are strewn with memorials, nevertheless, the inscriptions on which laud the President in fulsome terms. They range from an obelisk on the Avenida George Washington, erected by the legislature in connection with the rechristening of the city, to various pillars, plaques, and street signs, official and unofficial. Public documents declare that this is the "Era of Trujillo." An approved likeness, photographic or in colors, hangs in literally every gathering place of the demos from government offices to barrooms. It is the same in provincial towns, and even along the country roads you see hand-lettered eulogies on boards standing in front yards or nailed to trees. Mussolini got plenty of that in his heyday, but not, proportionately, as much as Trujillo gets.

I had Moreta take me out to San Cristóbal, the President's birthplace, and to near-by La Toma, a plantation owned by Trujillo where a river that has been running underground emerges from a hillside and forms a celebrated bathing place. San Cristóbal is a provincial capital. It must once have been a little town of ordinary appearance, but special pride naturally has been taken in reconstructing it. The administration buildings, schools, police station, etc., are among the finest to be seen, and still more ambitious developments are planned. The new-fashioned streets are clean, and many a striking residence turns its back on the past. Except for bars, movies, and perhaps a cockfight, the casual visitor will not find anything there in the way of amusements.

La Toma is an estate of lordly proportions, irrigated in part, with thousands of acres planted to the standard crops of the region and lush pasturage for cattle and horses. All its activities are along the most modern lines, and the strains of beasts and plants are superior. It is intended to set a standard for emulation by private husbandmen. Whether the latter learn as much as they might from it I do not know. But the small farmers of the district gave the impression of being prosperous and contented. There was no crowding, and though the cabins were sometimes poor, each family had enough land for its needs. Observing this in conjunction with the manifest fertility of the soil, I formed a theory about Trujillo and his paternalistic program. He had been able to succeed mainly because the Dominican Republic is a thinly populated country; a naturally rich country, also; but the first of these two points was the vital one. The disorder and poverty that prevailed when he took charge had been only temporary obstacles. As soon as genuine order had been established, hunger ceased. It had been simple to go on from that point. Neither he nor anyone else could have obtained a quick solution in an overpopulated land; in Puerto Rico, for instance.

The baths at La Toma are in a marvelously beautiful spot. The water, purified and chilled by its passage through limestone rocks, gushes into a basin that has been squared off with retaining walls and then flows as a broad, low cascade into the river bed. Steep cliffs covered with tropical vegetation, including ferns and vivid blossoming creepers, form the background of the basin. Water lilies float on the far protected side, out of reach of the current. There are two bathing pools, one reserved for the President and his guests, and the other open to the public.

On a subsequent occasion I drove to San Pedro Macorís, which is about twice as far from the capital as San Cristóbal, in the opposite or easterly direction. This trip confirmed my feeling that the Republic was making admirable progress along economic lines, but I found no suitable accommodations for tourists. Plans are afoot for building hotels and developing new pleasure resorts. The opportunities are limitless. Samaná Bay, easily accessible from Ciudad Trujillo, is one of the finest protected bodies of water—a gulf rather than a bay—in the West Indies, and the fishing there is excellent. It cries out to be added to the itinerary of cruise ships, but the hotels and sport clubs must be promoted first. Samaná could rival Cuba's Cienfuegos and Jamaica's Montego Bay. I did not go to the north, where there are two important cities: Santiago de los Caballeros and Puerto Plata. Their exploitation as travel centers is for the immediate future, though both already have fair hotels.

Along the Haitian frontier, which runs north and south from the Atlantic to the Caribbean, several modern towns have been constructed on the sites of small villages that formerly existed there in a state of primitive isolation. They have been linked up with the national transportation system and furnished with good public buildings, schools, and libraries. The show place is Elias Piña, midway of the line. The Trujillo government has carried out the original idea of marking the entire border with an international road instead of a series of forts. This was done after 1936, when the 250-year-old boundary dispute with Haiti was settled. Tragically, the pact was marred in 1937 by a massacre of Haitian squatters on Dominican soil, which Trujillo countenanced.

I have deferred until now my trivial personal experiences with the earthquake alluded to at the beginning of the chapter. The day I landed in the country, I felt a few vibrations so slight that a person who had not been informed of recent events might have failed to notice them. Ciudad Trujillo, anyway, had been on the southerly edge of the zone affected and had suffered little or no damage. Cracks had appeared in one of the old administration buildings, and it had been thought wise to evacuate it temporarily. Here and there a brick wall had crumbled. No worse than that. By common consent, as in all places subject to earthquakes, no one volunteered a word about the affair. When I asked a certain lady to tell me what it had been like, however, I was given a lively story. She said that the shocks had come in waves, day after day, causing the woodwork of her house to creak and groan, ornaments to topple, and pictures to sway on their hooks. The motion had been undulating, and to such an extent that she had often felt definitely seasick. The effect was less nauseating outdoors. Her life had been one of rushing into the garden periodically, clinging to an orange tree, and wondering whether the house would suddenly take a dive in her direction. Domestic animals had been smitten with terror. At last the quivering had grown weaker and weaker, and she had ceased to worry about it.

I have been through minor earthquakes in San Francisco and elsewhere. The description of this one places it in a special class. Doubtless the convulsion at the bottom of the Brownson Deep was of cataclysmic proportions, for the shocks had had to pass miles upward through the towering bulk of Hispaniola. That they were relatively so feeble by the time they reached the surface is not surprising. On the north coast, of course, they had been sufficiently stronger to upset many of the apple carts of puny man.

My failure to visit the northern cities was due to this disturbance. The fact that the monster was still behaving rather formidably up there did not hold me back; I should have liked to see it in action. But transportation facilities had been thrown somewhat out of gear. I was warned that I might find myself marooned in some town longer than I cared to risk.

Being in a volcanic region, all the West Indian islands are subject to earthquakes. Fortunately a given place is not likely to be affected twice in a generation. Many have gone exempt for longer than a century. By the law of averages, Hispaniola has received its share for a considerable time to come.

History impinges so deeply upon everything connected with the Dominican Republic that it is impossible to write about any aspect of the country without referring to its past. In the preceding pages my notes on travel found themselves inextricably mixed with events ancient or recent. But some kind of separate résumé, however brief, is called for. I hold to the idea that you cannot fully enjoy sight-seeing in a land unless the national story is clear to you.

After first sighting terra firma in the Bahamas, going ashore on a couple of islets, and visiting the coast of Cuba, Columbus crossed the upper exit of the Windward Passage and discovered a great island that he called Española (modernized to Hispaniola) on December 6, 1492. He cruised along its northern shore, was wrecked in his flagship, the *Santa Maria*, on Christmas Day, and decided to form a settlement at the spot, though the latter was not well suited to his purpose. This was the lost township of La Navidad. Columbus left thirty-nine men there and sailed back to Spain with the *Pinta* and the *Niña*. When he returned at the head of a great expedition the following year he found that every one of his colonists had been killed by the Arawaks, these least bloodthirsty of savages having finally revolted against the cruelty of the Spaniards in enslaving them and violating their women. The Discoverer then founded a city farther east on the banks of a small stream, a few miles from the modern Puerto Plata, and named it Isabela in honor of the Queen. Here he ruled as governor for a little longer than two years, but spent part of the time in new voyages of exploration. He went back to Spain in March 1496.

During his absence his brother Bartholomew acted for him and transferred the capital to Santo Domingo on the south coast, as has been related. Columbus reappeared in 1498, to find insurrection raging. He had always been a poor administrator, and now he was not able to get things under control. The monarchs sent out an inquisitor, Bobadilla, who shipped Columbus to Europe in chains. The rest was anticlimax for the unhappy Genoese. He was forgiven and allowed to make a fourth voyage, but all went badly. On his way out he was forbidden even to take refuge at Santo Domingo, though a terrible hurricane was brewing. He fled to the Central American coast, where he was buffeted by incessant storms, vegetated without profit on the Isthmus of Panama, and was driven ashore in Jamaica, where he spent a whole year as a castaway. The governor at Santo Domingo finally allowed him to be rescued, but he was held a prisoner in his old capital, and when repatriated to Spain it was only to die as a discredited hanger-on at the court.

The colony flourished for its first half century under Nicolás de Ovando, Diego Columbus, and their successors. It was the place from which all conquests were governed until new viceroyalties or captain generalcies could be set up. Diego Velásquez left from here to take Cuba, Ponce de León for Puerto Rico, Juan de Esquivel for Jamaica, and Vasco Núñez de Balboa for Darien. Hernando Cortés and Francisco Pizarro both started out in Santo Domingo, but planned elsewhere their epical campaigns against Mexico and Peru. In addition to the first palace, the first cathedral, the first monasteries, hospital, and university, Santo Domingo was made the scene of the original *audiencia*, a sort of supreme court for the entire region, and this vastly enhanced the prestige of the city.

But there was very little gold in Hispaniola, and although it was productive agriculturally, its small area was overshadowed by the endless reaches of the continent. Men were soon emigrating from this pioneer colony to the mainland. The western end was never settled, or even properly explored, by the Spaniards, and it became the resort of corsairs and other lawless exiles. The virtual division of the island into two states was a fact at an early date. The French took advantage of this, brought the buccaneers under control, and by the end of the seventeenth century had developed by far the richer colony. They called it St.-Domingue (now Haiti), while usage extended the name Santo Domingo to the whole of the Spanish half.

Broadly, it may be said that for two hundred years Santo Domingo went gradually to seed as a result of neglect by its parent country, that it was plunged into wild disorder when the slave revolution broke out in Haiti, suffered long oppression by the invading blacks, and for generations after its birth as a republic was more scourged by revolutions than any other Latin-American country except Haiti itself. The Spanish colonists misjudged Toussaint l'Ouverture, backed him against the French, and were forced when he was victorious to submit to his rule. Spain then ceded the territory under pressure to the France of the Directoire, but the private hope that this would bring about liberation for the whites proved illusory. The army sent by Napoleon to reconquer the island met with disaster. The French held Santo Domingo for only a short while after they had to retire from Haiti. The blacks returned and reduced it to the status of a province, their absolute domination lasting for twenty years.

The War of Independence organized by Juan Pablo Duarte and his lieutenants, the Trinitarians, in 1844, was fought with Haiti and was swiftly successful. Military chieftains, however, thrust aside the idealistic Duarte and subjected the young Republic to decades of misgovernment, marked by frequent insurrections and new clashes with Haiti. One president actually negotiated the reannexation of his country by Spain in 1861, a solution that lasted for less than four years; while another did his utmost to persuade the United States to absorb it in the early 1870's. It would be tedious to review the rise and fall of dictators, the political murders, and the general chaos that prevailed thereafter until the period of World War I. The country fell hopelessly into debt to foreign bondholders, and intervention was threatened by five European powers. To forestall this, Theodore Roosevelt forced the Dominican government to accept a United States receiver of customs, who apportioned the revenue equitably.

Civil disorder was only slightly curbed by this measure. In 1916 Woodrow Wilson demanded that the treasury, army, and police, as well as the customs, be placed under the direction of American officials. Comprehensibly, the Dominicans resisted with passion. The upshot was the landing of a United States naval detachment. President and legislature were both ousted, and the military government that was established lasted for eight years. Policing was done by the Marines with the help of the native National Guard. One of the young officers in the latter, Lieutenant Rafael Trujillo, proved especially efficient and co-operative. Trusted by his American superiors, he was rapidly promoted, and when the occupation ended in 1924 Colonel Richard Malcolm Cutts, head of the constabulary, recommended that Trujillo succeed him. That proved to be the road to power for the Dominican.

A few years after the withdrawal of the Marines, Trujillo was commander in chief of the army. It is claimed that he did not participate in the revolution of 1930, but merely refused to order his troops to fire on the civilian mob that had marched against the government. Be that as it may, he emerged as the manifest "strong man" of the crisis, swept the polls in an election, and has not had to worry since about the outcome of his quadrennial referendums.

CHAPTER 15

HAITI: THE BLACK REPUBLIC

THE weather was threatening on the afternoon I left Ciudad Trujillo, and the departure of the plane was postponed several times. As I waited outside the airport building a faint tremor shook the earth, the first in a number of days and quite possibly the last flutter of the disturbance. I applied it to myself as a fitting gesture of farewell. When we took off at last the wind was blowing in light gusts, and the massed clouds had an ominous look. Seasoned travelers by air commented that this was not the kind of occasion that justified worry. Reports had been coming in and all the possibilities had been checked. If a storm brewed, we should be running away from it. There was the comforting realization that the cruising speed of a plane is greater than that of a hurricane. The dangerous voyages are those on which you run into the unforeseen.

We flew directly west along the coast at the start and then veered inland. The atmosphere was pretty somber, but I caught a glimpse in the distance of Pico Trujillo (a name of recent adoption), 10,319 feet, the highest peak in the West Indies; and shortly afterward we crossed over the lake called Enriquillo, which is 135 feet below sea level. The Haitian border skirts this lesser version of the Dead Sea, one of the strangest depressions in the Caribbean region and a startling contrast with the *cordillera* to the north. Beyond is the small Lac Azure, which I did not see.

Down fell the darkness, the transition appearing to be instantaneous and caused by clouds into which we had passed. It was a very opaque blue for a while, rather than black. Fog pressed close against the portholes of the clipper. We were over mountains now, and I didn't like the combination. Suddenly the transparency at the front end of the plane flashed the sign, "Please attach your belts."

This is an order given before every take-off and landing. The company does not tell passengers so, but in the event of an accident the belts would prevent people from jumping out of their seats or being thrown helter-skelter about the compartment. Belts in themselves could not save lives, only avert some broken bones, lessen confusion, and make rescues a bit more practicable. I had never before observed the sign on midway of a flight. What did it mean? Presumably that the pilot was not entirely happy about his position. Wooden-faced, we all attached our belts. In less than five minutes the order was flashed off and we relaxed. It went to show that no precautions can be overlooked by the men who guide passenger planes, for if there was danger it had been of the briefest duration.

We pitched considerably on the air waves, and I rate that voyage as the one I enjoyed least. Presently the lights of a town on Haiti's southern peninsula emerged from the gloom below. We turned north, struck across La Gonâve Channel, and glided to an easy landing at Bowen Field, Port-au-Prince, as the moon rose. There were special rules about entering and leaving Haiti, but the details were simplified for American citizens. I had had to get a visa beforehand, at a cost of three dollars. Courteous immigration and health officials now accepted my statements at face value and bowed me through. I must get an exit permit when ready to go, they informed me, and that too would be three dollars. Negroes every one of them, naturally, for this was the Black Republic; but Negroes with quite a different air from those of other West Indian countries. They were like French bureaucrats, formal, poised. At the least sign that the visitor had more than a superficial interest in their country, however, they eagerly met him halfway and their remarks were tinged with pride.

Being attached to the airport, these officials necessarily all spoke English. The fact that I could explain my mission in French clearly set me apart in their estimation. The doctor offered to call on me at my hotel and furnish me with data. He accompanied me to the door, chatting. The field was well situated within the city limits. A low fence separated it from a busy avenue, and although the hour was late, another Haiti from that of the suave functionaries clamored for attention across the fence. A row of black heads bobbed, their features indistinguishable. Hands flourished articles of the sort that are offered to tourists in every Caribbean port—sandals, mahogany trays, baskets—but the prices here were the lowest I had heard quoted. Haiti is an extremely poor country. Even the long chance of finding purchasers at night for their souvenirs had to be taken by the vendors.

I engaged a taxi and drove to the Hotel Splendid, traversing the downtown streets with a glimpse of the public market where small oil lamps still flickered here and there to mark a stall, speeding past the enormous presidential palace on the Champ-de-Mars, and mounting the slope of the residential quarter beyond. The Splendid is a converted mansion, built in the most comfortable, indeed lavish, tropical style. A broad veranda runs the whole length of the front and connects at one end with a cool, high-ceilinged dining room. There is a garden on three sides, a driveway that curves from an upper gate in the street wall to an exit lower down. A two-story annex has been erected parallel with the main house and starting from this second gate. Fruit trees as well as flowering shrubs fill the space between the two buildings.

The establishment is run by a French couple and a Belgian assistant manager. Once within its doors you may persuade yourself, if you wish, that you are living tourist-fashion, isolated from the extraordinary land to which you have come. But this will be an illusion. For $6 a day, true enough, you can have a room, meals, and service far superior to the general standard of the community. The regime will be tropical French, and the minority of Negro guests and visitors a natural part of it. Haiti crowds close, nevertheless, and why anyone should want to shut his eyes to it I cannot imagine. I have heard American whites at the Splendid congratulating one another that here, thank God, they could meet in an oasis of civilization—whatever they meant by that. They must have been blind and deaf if they did not perceive that the atmosphere that wrapped them round was unique, though not in the sense that they would have liked to believe.

I had arrived just before the dining room closed, so I sat down to a meal that met with my full approval. The cuisine was basically French, the best on earth when all is said and done, with Caribbean side dishes and an abundance of fresh fruit. Afterward I strolled over to the annex, where I had been assigned a room. A gallery with a low stone parapet ran along the second floor of the building on the garden side. I changed into a thin bathrobe, sought the gallery, and leaned on my elbows there, smoking. It was a brilliant moonlight night, very still, so that the silhouettes of the trees looked as if cut from a dark cardboard. The steeply pitched roofs of houses in nearby streets loomed still more solidly. Sweet, heavy odors of jasmine and orange blossoms permeated the air instead of seeming to drift upon it.

Though still, the night was not silent. The calls of birds, reptiles, and insects rang incessantly with the effect of a chorus. Those sounds were familiar to me: the deep booming of bullfrogs, the clattering of tree toads, the croaking of nocturnal lizards, the shrill sibilance of crickets, the occasional hoot of an owl. They belonged to tropic countrysides, I mused, rather than to a city. The thought possessed me all at once that there was a preternatural quality about them, here in Port-au-Prince. They were too loud. They fell into a sort of pattern at times, like a series of signals or even a cabalistic language. I listened more intently and could have sworn that some were not of animal origin, but clever imitations by human voices. Was I detecting scraps of a code? A mad idea perhaps, yet anything can happen in this country, which is full of secret societies a good deal less innocent than the Shriners or Elks.

Many travelers have written about the night sounds of Haiti, stressing in nearly every case the unescapable voodoo drums of the interior. They have not been analytical where the odd cries of beasts and insects are concerned. Up till that evening, anyway, I had read no such narrative. Later I discovered that Mabel Steedman, who also stayed at the Splendid, had received an impression similar to mine. Shivering, she had wondered what it meant: "the loud croaking of frogs, the strange whispering of the trees and, above all, curious patterings and shufflings for which I could not account."

By daylight Port-au-Prince reveals itself as a city of extremes, architecturally and otherwise. The well-to-do neighborhood where I lived has an inordinate number of the imitation châteaux of the type I saw at Port-of-Spain. All the peculiar features are more exaggerated here. The gables are often so narrow and tall that they resemble slices of pie with the wide ends down, and from certain angles they suggest steeples. Mansard roofs with dormer windows once had a vogue, as the survivors prove. Cupolas, observation platforms, and excrescences of various kinds abound. As the ground floor generally has an open veranda and supporting pillars, an absurd combination results. The trend is away from these monstrosities. Some

fine homes have been built in recent years by politicians and foreign businessmen. The tendency to adopt glaring white modernism
is not so marked as in the Dominican Republic, which works out to
the advantage of Port-au-Prince. A second hotel, in the same class
as the Splendid, adds to the attractions of the section. It is called La
Citadelle, and being higher up the slope it is ostensibly cooler and
has its tourist following. For my part, I prefer the greater accessibil-
ity of the Splendid.

The main section of the capital has little claim to beauty or historic
interest, for since the original revolution against France it has been
destroyed and rebuilt several times. The Champ-de-Mars at the center makes an imposing showing, but even there the edifices are of
the present generation. A few years ago the field was a dusty parade
ground where children, goats, and mongrel dogs roved when the
soldiers were out of the way, and on which a mean presidential palace fronted. It is handsomely landscaped now, and against a green
background the monuments to Toussaint and Dessalines no longer
seem forlorn. The old palace, gutted during a sanguinary incident
of which I shall say more, has been replaced by a pile larger than the
White House and of a calcium dazzle in the ruthless sunlight. A hall
of justice, equally livid, and other administration buildings stand at
right angles to the south. They would be more pleasing if tinted in
pastel shades. The barracks behind the palace demonstrate this with
their plaster surfaces washed a pale gold.

Near the Champ-de-Mars is another square faced by two cathedrals standing side by side. Both are Catholic, one old and one new.
Surely anywhere else the squat, undistinguished temple would have
been demolished after the completion of its tall successor with twin
spires and carved façade. But the Haitian masses, the inarticulate,
the poverty-stricken, proved tenacious in their love of the altar before which they and their fathers had knelt. Although it is in a state
of utter disrepair, it is opened for worship sometimes. Gradually,
meanwhile, the traditions have been shifting their habitat. A French
bishop presides over the official, new cathedral. Always in the
Black Republic the priests have been, for the most part, white and
French.

There are no other structures that demand attention for artistic
reasons. The downtown business streets are utilitarian and drab.
Even the water front, which usually has charm in tropical ports,

is in dire need of improvement. Sprawling inland and up and down the foreshore, the quarters of the poor consist of flimsy wooden houses, often unpainted and with obviously bad sanitary arrangements. At intervals there are ulcerous congestions of slums. But the seething life of Port-au-Prince is never dull, never stamped with the apathy that is so noticeable, for instance, at the La Perla squatters' settlement in San Juan, Puerto Rico.

Take the big public market under its iron sheds, of which I caught a glimpse the night I landed. It is not so picturesque as the ramshackle Colón Market in Havana, and certainly it is no competitor of the establishment in Ciudad Trujillo for efficiency and hygiene. On the other hand, the variety of the wares offered and its chaffering crowds, tensely competitive yet good-humored, give it a unique place among all the markets I have visited. The stone-paved area with arched supports for the metal roofs stretches over two square blocks, linked in the intersecting street by a nondescript tower. Except for the corridors, every foot of the floor space is packed tightly with stalls, and there is an overflow onto the steps, the sidewalks, and in spots along the very roadway. Meat, dairy products, vegetables, and fruit naturally head the list of offerings. Then come clothing, new and secondhand; shoes, sandals, and leather belts, the two last of native manufacture; artisans' novelties, from carved wooden utensils to baskets and crude pottery; and finally every conceivable object that a destitute population can turn to account. You see old Standard Oil cans on sale for a few cents, cans that have held American fruit juices or baked beans at several for a penny, Coca-Cola and beer bottles at a penny, burlap bags, rubber from old automobile tires, and twisted nails that have been drawn from discarded crates.

I observed a boy who was soldering strips of bent tin onto condensed milk cans to form handles, a bit of ingenuity that raised the value of his wares to two cents each. A girl shopped earnestly for material with which to make a skirt, her choice wavering between sacks that bore the name of a cement concern and that of a well-known brand of American flour. I bought for sixty cents a pair of heeled sandals cut from home-tanned hide. It was the heels that attracted me, for I don't like the flat, draggy sort. I found that those heels, as well as a piece to waterproof the soles, had been whittled with a penknife from the treads of a Goodyear tire. Mighty good sandals they were, too, if a trifle heavy.

The life of the market is gay on the whole, despite the cruel economic struggle you sense about you. Women ride their donkeys in from the country, or travel many miles afoot, with nothing but a few eggs and odds and ends of vegetables that would not bring a total of a dollar if all were sold. But these women do not think in the terms of profit on time and effort, there being no standard by which to estimate the latter. Their errand is to go through certain motions that may result in exchanging their goods for things they need more urgently and that cannot be grown on the soil—cloth, needles, and salt, maybe. Also, the market is a social center, a place of excitement where gossip can be exchanged. Even the haggling over a sale is a thrill they do not get at home, and every little episode that affects the individual or a competitor is dramatic. I stopped to buy a belt at a stall, but the black boy had none that would fit me. Disconsolately he announced, after persuading me to try on every one in his stock, that the fault was his; he should have had a more varied selection. I continued my ramble through the market and was at the other end, twenty minutes later, when he came charging after me. He had found the very belt, he cried. I returned with him, and as it proved to be the right length I paid him the modest eighty cents asked. At once the women at all the adjoining stalls broke into pleased laughter and clapped their hands. They had watched the transaction from the start and considered it an event of the day that there had been a lucky ending.

Saturday is, of course, the gala day of the week, but as far as I could see the market never was closed. Even on a Sunday morning, or at any hour of the night, you can discover a few hopeful lingerers. Until recent years there was another market in the square before the cathedrals, an informal, open-air display of goods spread on the ground, which drew so many thousands that threading one's way through the packed mob was a feat. I saw it on a previous visit. Upper-class worshipers had complained that the chattering of the hucksters made it difficult for them to follow the mass, I learned, and the government had abolished the market. Its place has been taken by three or four scattered centers for outdoor shopping—a vacant lot here, a stretch of pavement there—while no important street is without its handcarts at the curb and women crouching alongside the buildings, trays of novelties or cakes at their feet.

You wonder, with all this peddling, how there can be enough custom to support retail stores. Yet hundreds of the latter exist, from dealers in imported articles to the veriest tumbledown shacks where food staples and native liquor are sold. The more pretentious usually call themselves bazaars, no matter what their stocks may be. Haiti, incidentally, has had a preferential trade treaty with France since the Republic was first recognized by Charles X in 1825. As a result, Parisian perfumes and other French luxury products can be bought at lower prices here than elsewhere in the West Indies with the exception of the free ports of St. Thomas and Curaçao and the French colonies themselves.

Bookstores are surprisingly numerous, but that is of a piece with the excess of newspapers published. Both activities are due to the cultural and political fervor of the Haitian elite, whose passion for ideas is truly Gallic. The written word reaches an infinitesimal minority of the people, yet local authors who can scarcely expect to make a living from their work turn out books, pamphlets, and periodicals of which a much larger country could be proud. They have kept the idea of liberty vital through decades of chaos. In this restricted circle and among their more intelligent supporters there is also a deep interest in French literature and translations from the English.

The seashore outskirts of Port-au-Prince to north and south should be more attractive than they are. The setting is beautiful, but man has been careless in his use of it, and—with some exceptions—you are greeted by dilapidated mansions that are shamed by the noble trees among which they stand, and by straggling, unkempt villages. A sugar concern controlled by Americans maintains a colony, neat and sanitary, where its employees are well insulated from the adjacent squalor. I drove through it, but was not enchanted by the commonplace screened bungalows, the community club and tennis courts. The identical setup can be found from end to end of the Canal Zone, at Guantánamo, Cuba, or wherever else the Yankee tolerates brief exile in the tropics. The site, however, commanded a lovely view of the city and harbor.

The *haut monde,* native and foreign, turns to the hills that start directly behind Port-au-Prince and curve in a ridge that at a distance of ten miles has risen to almost 5,000 feet. Marvelously fine houses have been built by rich men up there where it is cool even in the dog days. The American ambassador's summer residence is one of the

best. Pétionville at a halfway stage and Kenscoff on a summit are
the capital's favorite resort towns. Everyone who drives a car spins
up to Pétionville of an evening for dinner and dancing at one of the
casinos *en plein air*. Kenscoff is some five miles farther, over difficult
roads that take you to a plateau with the climate of the Temperate
Zone. There are week-end cottages at Kenscoff, much patronized by
American visitors, who rejoice in the fact that blankets are in order
on most nights of the year.

Sight-seeing in Port-au-Prince and near-by points in the interior
was improved for me by my ability to talk colloquial French with
chauffeurs. I did not find the equal of Moreta, my Ciudad Trujillo
driver, but I was served by several knowing fellows who had the
privilege of waiting for patrons at the Hotel Splendid. They spoke
English of a sort, but I suspect they found it a bore and regarded
those who forced them to use it as legitimate victims. When they
heard French from alien lips they brightened, and from that moment
they assumed the role of friendly guides and bodyguards rather
than taxi chauffeurs.

One moon-faced black driver with a wisp of mustache and twin-
kling shoe-button eyes announced that he was resolved to show me
the night life of Port-au-Prince. We got around to it in due course
and he made it an amusing experience. Depending on the way you
view the matter, there is less night life here than in Ciudad Trujillo
—or a good deal more. No hotel approaching the class of the Jaragua exists to stage glittering social affairs and serve as a luxurious
background for gambling. Even the lesser beach clubs of the Dominican capital are not paralleled. But when it comes to low-down
cabarets and other sporting diversions, Port-au-Prince has it all over
its rival at the opposite end of the island. Gallic humor and Negro
robustiousness make quite a combination. I shall not list the places
at which I took a look, for they were probably ephemeral and
not of sufficient artistic merit to rate publicity. The side issues are
what dwell in my memory, anyhow.

The first place at which we called was a dance hall in a garden
starkly illuminated by unshaded electric light bulbs. Fortunately
the tables on the surrounding veranda were in shadow. I stepped out
of the cab, making no remark to the chauffeur, who had been engaged for the evening, mounted to the veranda, and ordered a
drink. A minute later he passed me with a reproachful glance,

bought himself a rum and Coca-Cola at the bar, and returned to seat himself beside me. I perceived my error. He was my cicerone and should have been invited in, while it stood to reason that the drinks were on me. Without apologizing in words, I corrected my procedure and all went merrily as he instructed me in the ways of the land.

The dancing was not very good. But after all, the chauffeur commented, dancing was not the chief function of those houris. Perhaps I would like to make the better acquaintance of some of them. If so, I had only to point out a girl and he would fetch her, but he must warn me that none of them spoke French or English. How did it happen that in this country they did not speak French? I asked, surprised. They were very ignorant, he answered, and seldom progressed beyond the patois; Spanish was universal among them, of course. I wanted to know why Spanish instead of French.

"My dear monsieur, it is plain you do not realize that these girls are from the Dominican Republic," he replied. "You will almost never see a *Haitienne* in the life. There may be some few of other nationalities, but we call them all *Dominicaines*. It is a compliment, not a rudeness, for we mean that only a Dominicaine is clever enough to get money for what a Haitienne is accustomed to giving away for nothing."

The poker face with which he made the quip was priceless. A national vendetta that had been on for generations inspired the smooth, sarcastic words. As a matter of fact, most *filles de joie* in Haiti *are* Dominicans, and for two obvious reasons: it is easy to bring them across a land frontier, and their light complexions score a hit in the pleasure resorts of a black country.

We made the round of several cabarets, one of which called itself the New Orleans, plain like that, in English, though no Haitian tongue could manipulate the name without accenting it heavily. Sailors haunted the garish New Orleans, which would have fitted into the picture at Zanzibar, Papeete, Recife, or any of the ultra-exotic ports. Here the dancing was excessively tough, but effective sometimes. At spots on a higher level I heard songs that contained good political satire, and others in the patois that were rich with honeyed, plaintive sentiment.

My next chauffeur was an utterly different type. I had engaged him to take me on an extended circuit of the countryside. As we drove through Port-au-Prince he reeled off guide information in a mechanical voice. I had heard most of it before, but I let him go on, and it was interesting when he pointed out to me the spot at the Pont Rouge where the emperor Dessalines was assassinated. It had been a suburban crossroads, perfect for an ambush. Now the runways of the airport approach within a few yards. The commemorative stele for Dessalines stands on the boundary of Bowen Field. Passengers can see it at a distance from the landing stage. Not one in a hundred ever asks what it is.

I said something to the chauffeur about Haitian rulers in general, leading up to comments on the existing regime. Was anything better really to be expected of the obscure Dumarsais Estimé, I asked, than of the deposed Elie Lescot, whom he had just succeeded as president? He answered me over his shoulder, speaking with growing rapidity and excitement. Yes, Estimé was the superior, because more of the people and more in touch with their needs. I replied that I doubted it for such and such reasons. This was too much for my man. He drew up the car at the side of the road, turned to me, and delivered a political speech of the greatest eloquence that lasted for twenty minutes. It made no difference to him that he was supposed to be driving me to Léogane and then round by Croix-des-Bouquets and Bon Repos. But I winnowed some facts from his fervid partisanship and thought the money I was paying him per hour well spent. He was, I discovered later, the president of the taxi driver's association and by way of being an active politico.

From that point on he took keener pleasure in showing me places and enlarging on their significance. We stopped at the Damien Agricultural College, which was developed during the American occupation, only to find it closed that midsummer afternoon. The chauffeur conceded it was a good idea to have such a college, but felt it had been run extravagantly and with favoritism. It would have been hard to discover a more ferocious democrat than he.

Léogane, site of the original French colonial capital of St.-Domingue, is a shabby, uninteresting port today with not one building from its era of glory standing. I should have liked to continue over the mountains to Jacmel on the Caribbean coast. The journey there and back would have lasted into the night, the road being a rough one, and it had to be postponed. We followed the route already decided upon, an ancient one known as the Grande Route du Cul de

Sac. Neither Croix-des-Bouquets, scene of a famous pact between whites and mulattoes in the slave revolution, nor Bon Repos proved to be more than drab villages. There are no cities in that southeastern region, but it was the life of the peasants that I had come to observe, and because the district is off the beaten track it was a good choice.

If Haiti were to adopt a homely symbol of the national life, it should be a donkey with loaded panniers. An overwhelming share of the transportation burden is carried by this beast. You cannot be on any Haitian road without passing donkeys coming or going, some almost buried under mountains of produce, others with a woman riding between the hampers. On the morning of market days they plod in an unbroken line toward the town, and toward nightfall they plod in the opposite direction. But there is no day when they fail to trudge in and out of Port-au-Prince, no day when a glimpse of a country vista will not reveal donkeys one at a time, or by twos and threes, as the outstanding feature of motion across the landscape. Women with baskets on their heads are to be seen also, a human element that you take as a matter of course. It is the donkeys that give you the feeling that you are in Haiti. They are used in the other islands, but nowhere else are they so numerous. Imported motor trucks offer negligible competition in this poor and densely populated republic.

Donkeys were all about me on the road to Bon Repos. I had my chauffeur drive slowly and studied the owners of the patient animals, as well as the wayside dwellers. They maintained the usual Haitian attitude of blank neutrality toward the white stranger. Many travelers have told that here you get exactly what you give in the way of recognition. If you call, *"Bonjour,"* the peasant returns the greeting and in the same tone that you employed. "Bonjour, monsieur [or madame]" rates you a title. If you laugh and wave a hand, the Haitian will do the same, and in that case with a more spontaneous amiability, probably, than you achieved. I noted for myself that so it was. On the other hand, there is little curiosity and no self-conciousness aroused by a white's presence. This makes it possible to get a just idea of how the people live.

The houses I saw were nearly all of one or two rooms, with wattle or mud walls and thatched roofs. Cooking was done outdoors, in some cases under a shed, in others by means of a pot balanced between the traditional three stones on open ground. Fruit trees, clumps of bananas, and vegetable patches were cultivated close to the houses. Scrawny chickens hunted for food around every dwelling. The more prosperous kept hogs and goats. Tethered where there was a little grass to crop would be the inevitable donkey, unless one of the women of the family had taken it to market. But the only pampered creature was an occasional game cock in a pen of its own and fed with corn, no matter what other mouths went hungry. The Haitians are even more devoted to cockfighting than the Cubans, if that be credible.

In fine weather the dusty yards were, I remarked, the centers of social activity. Chattering parties of both sexes had gathered in many of them, with half-naked children underfoot. Apparently no drinking was going on, because the men like to take their liquor at a village rum shop when there is money to spare for it. Nor any dancing, because that is a ritual for the night and the accompaniment of voodoo drums. These folk were content merely to chatter, now and then to laugh at jests no outsider could fathom. The men gave the impression of being supremely idle, whereas the women combined tasks with their merriment, fetching water in gourds, pounding corn in mortars, and moving from washing bowl to cook pot.

One yard, however, was the scene of a terrific hullabaloo. The women from several households had separated into factions behind two of their number. The leaders were capering with fury and pouring out denunciations in a rapid-fire patois that went clear over my head. At moments one would gain the ascendancy and attempt a rounded statement, only to be screamed down by her opponent, and at these junctures the partisans also leaped in the air, hooking their fingers like talons. I ordered the car halted and watched them, an attention that put no damper whatsoever on their frenzy. Side glances from a few of them was all I got.

The chauffeur informed me carelessly that it was a dispute over a trifling sum of money. Then he smiled faintly. "One of those women just told the other," he said, "that if it could be proved she was lying she would come out in the road and let this car drive over her."

That's Haiti for you! The only importance of the rare sight of car and foreigner was the chance it afforded to make a point in her diatribe. After the clamor had gone on for at least a quarter of an hour without action, I wearied of it and proceeded to Bon Repos.

A plain stone marker stands there on the spot where three Haitian engineers lost their lives co-operating with American troops during the Caco fighting in 1919. The Cacos were half-savage hill dwellers —some called them patriots and others bandits—who resisted the Yankee occupation. Close by was a barracks built by the Marines and now used by a garrison of the Garde d'Haiti, the only regular military force in the republic. Gloomily my chauffeur volunteered that the building was not kept in as good condition as it had been by the Americans.

On the way back I stopped at a village church, a simple structure of clapboards with a brick foundation. Although it was a week-day afternoon and no service was being held, the interior blazed with votive candles and many women knelt in prayer. I asked the chauffer whether the population as a whole could be considered devout Catholics. He answered that they were very pious, though worshiping in church was left mostly to the females. But of late some odd Protestant sects such as Seventh Day Adventists and Jehovah's Witnesses had been gaining adherents. What about voodoo? I inquired. He shrugged a shoulder. Well, people went in for that too, he admitted—a lot of ancestral foolishness, as the intelligent were aware. Seemingly he regarded Protestantism as being more subversive than voodoo, yet it was a matter about which it was impossible to pin him down.

Visiting writers have discussed voodoo to the point of tedium and I do not propose to add to the chorus, beyond making a few basic assertions that it would be an affectation to omit. As Dr. Price-Mars and other Haitian students have shown, voodoo is a primitive animistic religion and only incidentally a cult of sorcery. It was brought by African slaves, chiefly the advanced Dahomeans, and for centuries it has had a powerful hold upon the Haitian masses. The ritual has been modified in the New World, mixed up to a certain extent with Catholicism, and the devotees see no wrong in attending church one day and going to a voodoo ceremony the following night. That human sacrifices were offered in the past is a certainty, but nothing of the sort has occurred for many years. Instead there are animal sacrifices and orgiastic dancing in dim forest glades. It is all strictly against the law, yet is often winked at by the police. I have heard distant drums summoning the faithful (who hasn't, in

Haiti?), and at the same time I am as convinced as I can be of anything that foreigners who claim they have witnessed the real thing have simply been taken, for cash down, to some comparatively mild show got up for their benefit. For this statement I have the authority of Haitian intellectuals, who would not confess that they had ever participated themselves, but who probably had. Given the horror of voodoo in the white world, the native who would furnish sensational truth on the subject to seekers from abroad can hardly exist. The ignorant as well as the educated are proud Negroes who writhe when their country is portrayed as barbarous.

My second trip out of Port-au-Prince was to the north. This main route to Cap Haitien and the Citadel of King Christophe is the only one that the average tourist ventures upon. Indeed, the Citadel is the sole show place from the tourist point of view that the republic has to offer, and a unique sight it is. Nowadays you may fly from Bowen Field to Cap Haitien in an hour, be met at near-by Milot with horses for your party, inspect the Citadel, and get back to your hotel in the capital in time for dinner. The journey by car formerly took from two to four days (round trip), depending on the weather and the state of the roads. The latter had been put in better shape since my first visit to Haiti, and I chose the longer, more revelatory approach.

The first stop was the port of St. Marc, a place where much history was enacted during the slave revolution and successive overturns. A new prosperity has come to it as the shipping point for banana plantations established by American fruit companies in the past few years. Sand and broken sea shells make the unpaved streets glare whitely under the sun. It is not a place where there is much temptation to linger. From St. Marc the route strikes inland across the Artibonite Valley to Petite Rivière, which is a township of some interest.

The Palais aux Cent Portes, credited by some accounts to King Christophe and by others to Dessalines, stands at Petite Rivière. Restored, it is used as the municipal offices. While not extraordinary, it merits inspection. The many doors (considerably fewer than a hundred, be it said) and windows are all arched. A reception room, supposedly kept in its original state, contains a bust of Christophe inscribed with his motto, *"Je Renais de Mes Cendres"* (I Rise Again from My Ashes). A short distance away are the ruins of the Crête-à-Pierrot, a fortress defended heroically in 1802 against 10,000 French regulars by its garrison of 1,200 blacks who at the end of three weeks cut through the lines with a loss of half their number.

Curving northwestward, the road reaches the coast again at Gonaïves, the city where Toussaint l'Ouverture was treacherously seized at a conference by General Brunet and shipped to a jail in France to perish of cold. Here, the following year, Jean Jacques Dessalines tore the white strip from a French tricolor, retaining the black and red as Haiti's flag, and declared the country independent. From Gonaïves the way crosses the base of the northern peninsula, through Ennery, Toussaint's own town, through the fertile Plaisance Valley, and over the northern plain, where the dreadful massacres that inaugurated the black revolution took place, down to Cap Haitien on its splendid harbor.

The Cape, as Americans call it, is a more solidly constructed city than Port-au-Prince, though it has been destroyed as often, if not oftener. Many of the houses are of stone, somewhat Spanish-American in type and pleasingly tinted. There are a few second-rate hotels and at least one good store, the Altieri, which specializes in French perfumes and other imported luxuries. You will, of course, take a look at the debris of the reputed palace occupied by Napoleon's sister, the fair, frail Pauline, wife of that General Leclerc who failed to subdue Haiti and died of yellow fever. But there is nothing to hold anyone for long at Cap Haitien. It is the starting point for the Citadel, which in clear weather can be distinguished looming on the peak of Bonnet-à-Evêque (Bishop's Cap), 2,600 feet to the south. It will require a little less than an hour to drive to the village of Milot, where the ascent begins, and the nearer you approach the more astounded you will be by the gigantic, mad, and withal beautiful monument that the black king left behind him.

At Milot itself is the Palace of Sans Souci, or what is left of it. Christophe built several regal mansions, but this one was his favorite. The story goes that he modeled it on Pauline's palace, but I never could see that. Sans Souci was far more magnificent that the building pointed out in Cap Haitien. Its floors were of marble, its walls paneled in native hardwoods and draped with fine tapestries and velvets. A stream is said to have been turned from its course and the water distributed in channels beneath the structure to give perpetual coolness. All that remains now is a shell, to which access is gained through a great courtyard and a series of terraces.

As for the Citadel—properly La Citadelle de la Ferrière—which towers above, four miles by a zigzag trail from the foot of the mountains, it deserves every rhapsody that has been uttered concerning it, except the common statement that it is a proof of Christophe's genius for power. He conceived it as an impregnable fortress to which he would retire with his army in case Haiti should be reconquered by the whites, and any way you look at it, that was an infantile notion. The place could not have held out indefinitely, for it could have been beleaguered and starved into submission. Actually, it never served the least purpose, never fired a shot. If, on the other hand, as has been said, he built it mainly to cow opposition among his own, the failure was lamentable. Years of forced labor went into the work, many lives were lost, and the people grew to hate him for the price he had made them pay. They rose in revolt, and he killed himself to avoid being murdered.

The general plan is that of a vast rectangular medieval castle covering the leveled top of a peak, but there is one bastion, wedge-shaped, that protrudes from the rest, is cemented to the mountainside, and looks from below like the prow of a monster ship at anchor. This singularly effective freak of architecture is what causes the Citadel to be so imposing. Even without it, the half-dozen linked towers, five stories tall, result in a balanced harmony superior to that of most military piles. The interminable corridors with arched gun embrasure housed three hundred naval cannon of the largest caliber then manufactured. The majority of these are still in place, though their wooden carriages are crumbling. Fig trees and withes, lichens and ferns have taken possession of cracks in the masonry, but only an earthquake would be able seriously to damage the frame as a whole. A central courtyard open to the sky is now choked with jungle, and for once poetic justice has been observed; Christophe lies buried there.

It is time to trace the lurid, bloodstained pattern of Haiti's history. Let us see how this Christophe fitted into it.

There was no history on an international scale, apart from that of Santo Domingo, until the activities of the buccaneers and the French

Crown in the seventeenth century. I must reiterate, as I have done in other books, that although the buccaneers often behaved piratically, they had principles and objectives on a higher level than piracy, and they ended by playing an empire-building role. First they were outlaws of many nationalities—fugitives from persecution in Europe, military deserters, and escaped criminals—who sought refuge on Spain's disregarded northwestern peninsula of Hispaniola. They hunted wild cattle and hogs, smoked the meat, and traded in it with passing ships. Following a Spanish attack, which they repulsed, they built strongholds on the coast and notably on the small island of Tortuga opposite Port-de-Paix. Then they took to the sea as raiders and became the most redoubtable corsairs that the Caribbean has ever known.

In 1640 the buccaneers formed a loose organization that they called the Confederacy of the Brethren of the Coast, headed by an elected admiral. They had taken to operating in groups dominated by Frenchmen, Englishmen, or Hollanders, and each of these vowed that they never attacked the flag of their country of origin. Sometimes they broke their rule, but in a broad sense they did retain national sentiment. When their admiral led a joint expedition it was always against the Spaniard, the common enemy. The year the confederacy was established, the adroit Poincy at St. Kitts sent to Tortuga an agent named Levasseur whom he actually induced the buccaneers to accept as a sort of civil governor and link with France. In 1665 a stronger personality, Bertrand d'Ogeron, made the governorship the predominant factor and set about the colonization of the whole western end of the island. Sir Henry Morgan, meanwhile, had transferred the headquarters of the English element among the Brethren to Port Royal, Jamaica. From then on, buccaneering powerfully served the interests of France, England, and to a lesser extent Holland. It received its deathblow by common consent of the nations at the Peace of Ryswick, 1697, when Spain ceded to France the territory that was thenceforth to be known as St.-Domingue.

The last governor of the old order and the first of the new was the illustrious Jean-Baptiste du Casse, who had himself been a privateer and slaver. He and his successors turned St.-Domingue into the most successful tropical colony of the age. Tobacco, indigo, cotton, coffee, and cocoa were the first crops grown. Of these only coffee remained of major importance. A swing toward sugar occurred, and for nearly one hundred years there was fabulous prosperity based on this greatest of eighteenth-century bonanzas. To meet the labor problem, Negroes were prodigally imported from Africa. Interbreeding between the races took place, and as the offspring were usually manumitted, a class of free persons of color came into existence. Many of the latter acquired land and slaves of their own.

Population statistics for 1789, the year of the Bastille, showed: whites, 40,000; mulattoes (the general term for the free persons of color), 25,000; Negro slaves, 480,000. It is believed that the last figure was too low, because proprietors falsified their reports in order to escape the poll tax on slaves. There probably were not fewer than 500,000 Negro bondsmen in St.-Domingue, or eight to one over whites and mulattoes combined.

The French Revolution was unanimously opposed by the planter and merchant class. When the National Assembly in Paris gave the vote to free mulattoes, the whites refused to accept the reform. As a result there was a preliminary insurrection by three hundred of these men of color. It was brutally repressed, its leaders, Ogé and Chavannes, broken on the rack and wheel in Cap François (now Cap Haitien), and twenty others hanged. The slave revolution itself did not come to a head until the summer of 1791. Every iniquity of torture, mutilation, rape, and massacre was practiced by the blacks, and in return they were slaughtered in great numbers. Years passed before they gained the upper hand, and their success was due largely to the genius of Toussaint l'Ouverture, whose emergence as the chief was slow. He defeated Spanish, English, and mulatto opponents as well as the French whites. By a series of maneuvers too complicated to be detailed here, he won the support of Paris and became governor general of the entire island. He never severed the tie with France, though he was virtually a dictator. Under his liberal regime the planters were invited to return and cultivate their estates. To their sorrow many responded, but the terror that awaited them was not the fault of Toussaint.

Napoleon, having become supreme in France, concluded that he would not tolerate the semi-independence of St.-Domingue. He sent a great army under Leclerc, as I have already told. Leclerc was successful at first and eliminated Toussaint, but could not maintain his position against the worst of all West Indian yellow-fever epidemics and the campaign of vengeance waged by Dessalines, Christophe, and Pétion, the ablest generals developed under Toussaint. When the French got out, Dessalines assumed the chief magistracy and altered the name of the state from St.-Domingue to Haiti, an Arawak word meaning a high, or mountainous, country. He began as governor general, since that was the title familiar to the people. In a few months, however, Napoleon declared himself emperor, and Dessalines decided that he must be one too, to show that the "First of the Blacks" was not inferior to the "First of the Whites." He was proclaimed the Emperor Jacques I.

Dessalines was a full-blooded Negro, almost certainly born in slavery at Grande Rivière in the northeast, though some insist that he was a chief's son from Africa. He had always resisted authority and bore the marks of innumerable floggings. His hatred for the French was abysmal, and because they had white blood in their veins he loathed mulattoes. He had been great in war, but as a ruler he proved a savage despot. He extirpated the last of the whites by means of one mass butchery after another, and then he staged a massacre of mulattoes. Soon he was oppressing the blacks who had elevated him. It was too much. In less than three years revolution broke out, and he died chopped up like a wild beast at the Pont Rouge crossroads. A half-witted old woman collected his remains in a coffee sack; if it had not been for her, they would have been left to the vultures.

Henri Christophe was the logical successor. He, also, was black and had been born a slave, but in the British West Indian island of St. Christopher. He could neither read nor write. How he got to St.-Domingue is not clear. He served as a waiter in a hotel at Cap François and afterward as a steward on a French warship. When a regiment was raised to go to the aid of Lafayette during the American Revolution, Christophe was enrolled, voluntarily or otherwise, as one of eight hundred recruits and fought against the English at the Battle of Savannah. In the slave revolution his role was brilliant. He attained the rank of major general and was second in command under Dessalines.

But the cruelties of Emperor Jacques had made the people of the south suspicious of the equally authoritarian Christophe. The political leadership passed to the highly educated mulatto Alexandre Pétion and he was elected president. Christophe revolted and set up a kingdom in the north, assuming the title of Henri I. He created a nobility of princes, dukes, counts, and barons, a flourish in which Dessalines had not indulged. The partition of the country lasted for thirteen years. Legendary indeed was the reign of the monarch, whose portrait has been colorfully drawn in John Vandercook's *Black Majesty*, and who has been praised by many writers for the administrative efficiency he showed at the start. In my judgment the egomania and stupid wastefulness of the closing period deprive him of real stature as a ruler. The hoarded silver bullet with which he achieved his own *coup de grâce* was a measure of the man.

In Port-au-Prince Pétion governed mildly, at times weakly, and set a standard of democracy in the French spirit that has since, through all vicissitudes, been Haiti's ideal as a nation. When the fortunes of the great Simón Bolívar were at their lowest ebb in 1815, he took refuge in the republic, and Pétion gave him money and arms, asking nothing in return but Bolívar's promise to free the slaves of Venezuela. This first president was known as Papa Bon Coeur. He died two years before Christophe and was succeeded by another mulatto, his faithful lieutenant Jean Pierre Boyer. The latter reunited the south and north as soon as Christophe was dead, and it was he who annexed Santo Domingo.

The combined presidencies of Pétion and Boyer lasted for thirty-six years. They were based upon the support of the literate elements, most of whom were light-colored. This finally caused bitterness among the blacks. Boyer was overthrown and Haiti entered a period of some seventy years of chronic revolution, during which her moral credit sank to zero. There was another emperor, the grotesque Soulouque, who had himself crowned as Faustin I, who took the advice of voodoo priests and whose only important public acts were a succession of disastrous wars with the recently liberated Dominican Republic. There was one president who had himself been a voodoo *papaloi*, or priest. Others were incredibly ignorant, bloodthirsty tyrants. The few men of high principles who rose to power, such as Fabre Geffrard and Boisrond-Canal, have been ignored by an outside world that recalls only the atrocities perpetrated by the rest.

Vilbrun Sam, chief executive in 1915, was a notorious sadist. He had 167 political opponents, for the most part members of good Haitian families, butchered in prison. The mob rose, dragged Sam from the French legation, where he had sought sanctuary, literally cut his body to pieces, and paraded the fragments through the city.

This caused the United States to intervene, and the resulting military protectorate lasted until 1934. The country's finances were reorganized, roads were built, sanitation was put on a modern basis, and many other material benefits were conferred. Haitian sovereignty was never voided, but the presidents elected had to be satisfactory to an American high commissioner. The mulatto elite thus regained control and kept it afterward, at least up till the fall of Lescot in 1946. The new president, Estimé, ostensibly represents the black majority, but is by no means a barbarian of the pre-occupation type. Haiti may safely be said to have reached a phase of adult stability as a republic.

CHAPTER 16

NASSAU AND ITS OUT ISLANDS

NASSAU, on the little island of New Providence, is the pleasure resort of the Bahamas. There is a school of native opinion that holds that this far-flung archipelago of nearly seven hundred units, stretching from a point about halfway up the coast of Florida to the eastern end of Cuba, should not be classified as Caribbean territory. It is in the Atlantic Ocean, the argument runs, and at no point is washed by the Caribbean Sea. Bermudians take the same stand concerning their group and with unanimity. I acknowledged in my foreword that their view was correct, for Bermuda is isolated hundreds of miles to the northeast. But to deny that the Bahamas are part and parcel of the West Indies is geographical quibbling. True, they do not belong to the central volcanic chain. They are low-lying, sandy islands, mostly of coral formation, which have emerged on the windward flank of Cuba in comparatively recent geologic times. Counterparts are to be found off Cuba's southern coast and elsewhere in the region. Possessing a tropical flora and fauna, the Bahamas simply *are* Caribbean.

When I left Haiti, Nassau was the next place on my list. Direct routes by sea or air had not yet been restored. It was necessary to go by Pan American to Miami and transfer there. I boarded a clipper after midday in perfect sunshiny weather. The course lay across the island of La Gonâve, which looms in the gulf between the northern and southern peninsulas like a prey upon which the claws of a scorpion are about to close. Weird stories have been told about the prevalence of voodoo on La Gonâve. Despite its nearness to Port-au-Prince, means of getting there are few and I did not visit it. Now I looked down on its typical jagged surface and wondered what curious life fermented among those dark mountains, in the valleys where so few houses are visible, and on the gleaming, surf-fringed beaches. We skimmed beyond the island and headed straight for Cuba. Remarkably soon, it appeared, we were over the high ranges of Oriente province, but bearing toward the straight coast line with wedge-shaped protrusions that cause the eastern end of Cuba to resemble the front of a hammerhead shark. From a height of about eight thousand feet I presently saw Santiago harbor in its entirety. It was a view such as I had never before had of this or any other great landlocked haven. From the narrow entrance with its morro to the farthest extension of the branching, hill-bordered inlets, all was visible in fine detail.

Within the hour another marvelous scenic effect unrolled. I had often read of the pageantry of sunset clouds in certain combinations when viewed from the air, but had not had the luck to encounter it. Here, at last, was an example of the splendor for which I had hoped. An enormous array of cumulus clouds with flat bases and rounded outlines was massed, tier upon tier, in the west. It bestrode and dwarfed the Sierra Maestra range and seemed as solid as the mountains, but translucent, dyed with shifting colors of which an unearthly rose-red was the most constant. One cannot see cloud banks on such a scale from a prairie or at sea, for then they are in part hidden, I suppose, by the curve of the globe. It should be possible atop some lofty peak, if other summits do not interrupt the view; I have had no personal experience of that. My sunset in the sky over Cuba remains unique in my memory. It was the more impressive as our course altered from due west to north-northwest and I had the illusion that it was the stupendous pile that rotated majestically, rather than the plane that sheered off.

We grounded at Camaguey, where I was to change for Havana. On previous voyages I had made quick connections at this point, but now would have a wait of about three hours. It gave me a chance to look into the facilities of the Camaguey airport, which is one of the best on Pan American's main route through the West Indies. As I wrote in an earlier chapter, the field is located at a considerable distance from the city, a drawback that local conditions often impose. But the building is a well-equipped station with a waiting room, a bar where snacks may be bought, and a shop that carries cigarettes, bottled liquors, and souvenirs. A few hundred yards away, across the railroad tracks, is a company club open to the pub-

lic. Regular meals may be had there, and depending on the requirements of the official personnel, rooms may be rented. This is less
adequate than the accommodations at Piarco Field, Port-of-Spain,
and I imagine the club will soon have to be replaced with a hostel.
Airports isolated as is the Camaguey one must logically develop
into villages of a sort. Many passengers in transit do not want to
make a long trip to the city, yet are on the lookout for entertainment
while they are forced to linger.

I caught a plane of the Cubana Avianca line, affiliated with Pan
American, at eight P.M. It was a pitch-dark night, though calm,
calmer if anything than the afternoon had been. The plunge through
the unvarying blackness had an emotional nuance of its own: a
sense of complete abstraction from this earth, of forward surging in
a space machine so steady that you could write in a notebook rested
on your knee. Then the lights of large towns materialized more
and more frequently, each pattern a checkerboard with straggling
edges. We passed over Matanzas, sixty-four miles from Havana,
and in a mere twenty minutes there was Havana itself, a vast incan-
descence crisscrossed by dun threads of streets. We circled inland
south and west, and the eye could take in the city at one sweep.
I noticed that the lights were not static, as they are when seen from
above, but glittered frostily. This phenomenon was caused by their
overlapping with immeasurable speed as the plane swept past at
a low altitude.

Havana's airport is at Rancho Boyeros, twenty miles out and a
good half hour by car from the capital. This center of plane travel
has an administration and passenger terminus larger than any other
in the West Indies, but it is taxed to capacity. You hear talk about
expansion being urgent. Even as it stands, it is a model of those airports of the future that conditions elsewhere led me to forecast. A
township exists at Rancho Boyeros, with hotels, restaurants, and
night clubs at no great distance from the field. The bus service is
adequate. If you prefer to take a cab to Havana, there are plenty to
be had at the rather high rate of four dollars.

I stopped over for a few days, then returned to Rancho Boyeros
and boarded one of the two-engine clippers leaving for Miami at
intervals so brief that they might be described as maintaining a taxi
service by air. The flight over the Florida Strait, the Florida Keys,
and the lower end of the Everglades was richly pictorial on the order

of scenes I have already described in connection with the islets off the south coast of Cuba. From Miami the Nassau plane made the hop in eighty minutes, sighting on the way Bimini, of rumrunning fame during the prohibition era, as well as the northern tip of Andros Island.

Nassau would have only a roadstead for a harbor if it were not for Hog Island, which lies opposite the city and furnishes protection for the exquisitely blue deep-water anchorage. The latter becomes a little hazardous when the wind blows from certain quarters, but it has sufficed for the trade of the colony for close on two and a half centuries. The city has a long water-front thoroughfare called Bay Street, running east and west, and behind this it mounts a low parallel ridge, the result being a maze of streets and alleys that wind pleasantly. Many of the houses are built of white coral and others of a grayish sandstone. Wooden structures turn to a soft ocher under the weather. Creepers and shrubs with gay foliage and vivid flowers enliven the gardens. There are palms, of course. But a special note is struck by occasional huge silk-cotton trees; one on Bay Street is said to be more than two hundred years old.

It is a small city and it has few historic sights to offer, despite the fact that there have been exciting chapters in its past. Several forts, some old Anglican churches, and a watchtower said to have been used by the pirate Blackbeard complete the list. The forts are called Charlotte, Montagu, and Fincastle. Of these Fort Charlotte has been renovated and gives the visitor an excellent idea of how an eighteenth-century fortress was equipped. Fort Fincastle is on a hill to the rear, and from its tower you get a sweeping view of town and harbor. Blackbeard's Watchtower, now pretty much of a ruin, is probably connected only by legend with the exploits of the notorious Edward Teach, who it will be recalled is supposed with equal vagueness to have had a castle in Charlotte Amalie, St. Thomas.

Government House, where until recently the Duke of Windsor presided, is not much to look at from the outside, but the interior is tastefully furnished and charming. A statue of Christopher Columbus stands in the gardens, a tribute rarely found in an English Caribbean colony. The Bahamas, as we shall see, have a special reason for honoring the Discoverer. The avenue of royal palms at Government House is the finest in Nassau. Windsor left his touch in the form of a water-lily pool.

There is more to be seen along Bay Street and its immediate environs than anywhere else. Rawson Square, really an oval, is at the heart of things. Prince George Wharf, the town's only pier, thrusts out from the square, turns in an L, and creates a basin enclosed on three sides. The Sponge Wharf near by is just a landing place where the luggers and barges used to come when sponging was an active industry. Up from Rawson Square are the public buildings, prettily grouped with landscaping. One of them, neatly octagonal, used to be a jail and is now the public library. The best shops are on Bay Street itself; they offer native handicraft stuff and imported English luxury articles. The bar known as Dirty Dick's is one of the most popular tourist spots in the West Indies.

If Nassau is short on monuments and palaces, it is abundantly supplied with hotels, beach clubs, boating and fishing organizations, and other inducements to healthful pleasures in a holiday atmosphere. The better part of New Providence Island, less than twenty miles long, comes within the scope of this statement, and so does little Hog Island in the bay. Let us start with the town. At the east end of Bay Street is the Fort Montagu Beach Hotel (under military occupancy during the war, but now reopened to guests), and at the west end is the British Colonial Hotel. Midway is the Prince George Hotel, opposite the wharf of the same name. Inland, near Fort Fincastle, we find the Royal Victoria Hotel. All these are first-class caravansaries, and they are not slow about charging first-class prices. The first two get from $20 to $40 a day, American plan, during the winter season; the last two from $6 to $16 a day, European plan. Reductions in summer are considerable.

There are some half-dozen other hotels, of which I shall mention only the Windsor because it is new, agreeably small, and centrally located, and the Roselda and Parliament because they feature two-room apartments. Guest houses are legion; among these do not overlook the Cumberland House, picturesquely located on a narrow, steep street near Government House and famous for its restaurant, where turtle dinners are served alfresco. Wave Crest, out of town, is on a beautiful curve of the shore, and although it disposes of only a few rooms, the charges are modest.

The Fort Montagu Beach Hotel offers the most spectacular setting in Nassau. It is on a fifty-acre estate a little to the southeast of the old fort, has its own beach, a fresh-water swimming pool, tennis courts, an eighteen-hole golf course, archery range, and provisions for every imaginable outdoor and indoor sport. The Jungle Club, the chief night resort of Nassau, is within its grounds, "sufficiently removed from the hotel to eliminate any distraction for those who do not wish to participate," as the management rather primly expresses it. Lavish, this Fort Montagu, and the big-money crowd from Miami revels in it. Running a close second is the British Colonial Hotel.

My personal preference is for the Royal Victoria Hotel, but then I am incurably addicted to spacious, old-fashioned rooms, broad verandas, dreamful gardens, and a general air of lazy comfort. Give me those things, and the other fellow can have the chromium plumbing and the jazz bands. The Royal Victoria decidedly is not so smart as the two caravansaries mentioned in the preceding paragraph. But romantic associations cling about it. The building, which is said to be over a hundred years old, was originally a school for girls. When blockade running during the War between the States brought sudden wealth to Nassau, it was enlarged and converted into a hotel of supreme elegance according to the standards of the day. There English speculators, many a Bahamian sea captain, and the Rhett Butlers of the Confederacy threw their money around. Comely, mysterious ladies in hoop skirts fluttered their fans and made rendezvous that were less trivial than they seemed. A procession of "names" passed through, from Raphael Semmes, the sea raider, on the eve of assuming command of the *Alabama,* to Judah P. Benjamin, former Secretary of State, in flight toward London after the party had been lost by Dixie.

A period of depression followed. As the century waned, however, rich Americans discovered Nassau as a winter resort. The Royal Victoria enjoyed a new period of distinction. Lewis Cleveland, a brother of President Grover Cleveland, managed it for some years. It long remained *the* hotel in Nassau, and at no time since has it failed to hold its own against the mounting competition. Miss V. Lorraine Onderdonk is its capable hostess today. The Royal Victoria Club on Rose Island is a subsidiary of the hotel.

The Emerald Beach Club and the Bahamas Country Club are at the far west end of town near the race track. The names suggest the amusements you will find there: swimming and games at all times of the year, and very good horse racing in the winter season. Eastward, within a stone's throw of Fort Montagu, is the Nassau Yacht Club, which stages many sailing events for local boats, and in normal times holds regattas with entries from Miami. The sea may be said to take precedence over the land in a resort like Nassau. Most of the funmaking centers about the beaches with their white coral sand, or on the water. At Prince George Wharf and other landing places it is always possible to hire a sailing boat with an expert islander to handle it and go exploring the adjacent cays. The fishing is excellent. There are so-called marine gardens between Hog Island and Atholl Island, where a magically rich undersea life is visible in the shallows. Glass-bottom boats can be rented for the purpose, but some trippers content themselves with glass-bottom buckets let over the side. As you look down through the bucket, the kaleidoscope of branched coral and radiant organisms in motion appears to leap to within a few inches of your eyes.

And on Hog Island is the largest and most famous of Nassau's seashore spots, Paradise Beach. It is a semicircle of exceptionally suave sand, fine as powder. The Australian pine trees that fringe the beach and keep up a continuous murmur give the place a special character. There are palms, also, oddly dominated by the exotics that, strictly speaking, are not pines at all. The restaurant and bar at Paradise will serve meals either indoors or at little tables under gaily colored umbrellas beside the surf. I do not rate the beach as equaling Varadero, Cuba. But you are in danger of being shot if you say that on Hog Island, where they regard Paradise as the World's best.

The landward reaches of Nassau are of limited interest. A drive or walk, however, by way of the arch near the curious terraced ramp called the Queen's Staircase is worth the trouble. It leads you to Grant's Town on the ridge. This settlement, founded longer than a century ago by freed slaves, has become the principal Negro quarter of the city. I was told that the local whites never go near the two or three cabarets up there, indeed comdemn forays in that direction as "slumming over the hill." Nassau is more color-conscious than any other British West Indian community. Naturally, I found this a good reason for visiting the cabarets. They proved hilarious without being actually tough, but alas, only now and then were the acts worth watching. By daylight Grant's Town is prosy. It produces domestic servants, seamen, and cabinetmakers. The hand-turned furniture of Nassau is celebrated.

New Providence, the island on which the capital is situated, has a thin soil not very suitable to agriculture, but it does support a certain amount of truck farming. Most of the idle land was bought up in the decade preceding the war by two men: Harold Christie, a native-born Bahamian, and Sir Harry Oakes, a Canadian mining millionaire who had adopted the place as his home. They planned big developments, chiefly in the tourist field and the building of houses for permanent residents from abroad. The American public has a short memory and may have forgotten that Oakes was murdered, his son-in-law, Alfred de Marigny, tried for the sensational crime and acquitted. Christie's projects were suspended in large part during the war, but they are being resumed.

Few visitors ever get beyond New Providence and its near-by cays. The natives themselves regard New Providence as being in effect the colony, since government, wealth, and foreign relations are centered there. They speak of all the other islands—12 that are comparatively large, 17 that are big enough to matter, and 661 mere islets and rocks—as the Out Islands. Yet most of them can be reached by boat or plane. The administration keeps up a mail and passenger service with the chief townships. Regular air trips are made to some. Motor vessels can be engaged to go to any point, and planes operated by Bahama Airways are available for charter.

The geographical position of New Providence is at about the middle of the northern half of the archipelago, between the islands of Andros and Eleuthera. The first-named is by far the largest of the Bahamas, being one hundred miles long and forty miles across at its widest point. But this Andros is one of the least exploited, because of its forbidding terrain: flat, sandy, densely overgrown with scrub for some distance in from the shore, and the whole interior swampy. It suggests a vast lagoon that has recently arrived at the stage of being filled up with vegetable detritus and is now merging with its more solid outer rim. There are some attractive beaches and pockets of coastal land where a population of mixed blood farms or lives from the sea. The people of the bush are virtually wild Negroes whose customs resemble those of the Djukas of Surinam.

Eleuthera, on the eastern side of New Providence, is radically different from Andros. It is curved like a finger, nearly sixty miles long, and not more than four miles across at any point. The soil, though sparse, is surprisingly responsive when it is watered. Pineapples were once an important crop here and were exported in quantity to the United States before Florida went into the business on a grand scale. Tomatoes, corn, and oranges are grown, and there is some dairying. The Christie interests are active on Eleuthera, which does a regular trade with Nassau and is perhaps the most prosperous of the Out Islands.

To the north lie Great Abaco, Little Abaco, Grand Bahama, and a multitude of cays, of which the best known is Bimini. Lumber, including lignum vitae, is cut on the larger units. The surrounding waters are ideal for deep-sea fishing and sportsmen come to them from afar. Bimini is the point closest to the Florida coast. That was why the rumrunners made it their jumping-off place from 1919 to 1933. As against the tens of thousands of dollars that used to change hands monthly on this speck of coral, the doleful inhabitants are glad to collect a few hundreds today from tarpon enthusiasts.

Traveling southeast from Eleuthera, you come to Cat Island, San Salvador (of which more anon), Great Exuma, Long Island, Crooked Island, Mayaguana, Great Inagua, and beyond these the Turks and Caicos Islands, which although geographically part of the Bahamas are a dependency of Jamaica. None of these places is of much economic importance, and the tourist who lands on any one of them is a rare bird. When the United States acquired Caribbean naval and air bases from Britain in 1940, a site on Mayaguana was first chosen. It turned out to be unsatisfactory and a shift was made to Great Exuma. The base is a minor one in the scheme of hemisphere defense. Between Long Island and Crooked Island runs the deep channel commonly used by ships from Atlantic coast ports bound for the Windward Passage and the Caribbean Sea. Great Inagua, forty miles long by twenty miles broad, has possibilities in its rolling terrain with patches of fair soil, but it remains lone and poverty-stricken. Long Island was formerly, like Eleuthera, a pineapple Eden; now sisal hemp is grown by a few, while the majority depend upon fishing.

Two of the Caicos Islands in the Jamaican dependency show traces of attempts made by fugitive Georgia royalists to cultivate plantations there after the American Revolution. They must have been optimists, for no more arid site could be imagined. Yet they lasted for a generation, and scattered relics from their neoclassic houses can still be found amidst the scrub and sea grapes. In both

the Turks and Caicos the panning of salt is the chief means of livelihood. The name Turks, by the way, was derived from a species of
cactus that looked to the early voyagers like a Moslem's fez.

The Bahamas export on a modest scale to the United States,
Canada, and Britain. Tomatoes head the list, with fish next and
salt third, according to the latest statistics available. One of the
large Jamaican rum firms has recently transferred its foreign trade
headquarters to Nassau, but I was unable to get the figures on this
commodity. Sponges were for many years the major product of the
Bahamas and were in demand abroad. Not long before the war a
disease affected the marine animals of the sponging grounds in the
archipelago, Florida, and Cuba, and it was thought best to close
them down. There are indications that diving for sponges may soon
be resumed. Boatbuilding—yachts as well as merchant craft—constitutes a profitable small industry.

Income tax, that specter at every man's shoulder in other parts
of the world, is absent from the Bahamas. A policy of encouraging
rich outsiders to come and settle has been followed, and this particular inducement no doubt had much to do with the decision of the
late Sir Harry Oakes and the Jamaican rum magnate just cited to
move to the "Isles of June," as the natives like to term their Elysium.
The Chamber of Commerce puts it complacently as follows:

"Operating under a system of indirect taxation, consisting chiefly
of duties on imports, the Colony has maintained a very satisfactory
financial condition and it has never been found necessary to intro-
duce income tax. The only direct taxation is a very moderate real
property tax based on the assessed rental value of any building in
New Providence only. Unimproved property is not subject to taxes.
Death duties or inheritance taxes are two percent on personal property only."

The Bahamas were not merely discovered by Columbus; they
were his first discovery in the New World, which he believed to be
the outermost shores of Asia, the domain of the Grand Khan. So that
statue in the Government House grounds at Nassau is the least the
existing British colony could do in recognition of a momentous fact.
The landfall was made on the island of San Salvador, also called
Watling Island, on the eastern edge of the group. It is mostly barren
and low-lying, except for a cliff that rises to 140 feet, an elevation

possessed by none of the neighboring islands, and there is no decent harbor. Yet Columbus, exuberant and eager to magnify his success, wrote this account of it in a letter to his patrons, the King and Queen of Spain:

"I had under my eyes an immense mountainous rock that completely surrounds that island. It forms a hollow and a port capable of holding all the fleets of Europe, but the entrance is very narrow. . . . There are gardens there, the most beautiful I have ever seen in my life, and sweet water in profusion."

He was greeted by singularly innocent savages called Lucayos, a tribe of the Arawak race, who had been raided only by the Caribs and who thought the Spaniards were gods. The Discoverer was so impressed by their mildness and generosity that he did not allow them to be mistreated. He left that for the future, reporting to Spain that they could be easily conquered, and that they would make docile servants and workers in the mines. He sailed on to Rum Cay, Long Island, and one or two more of the group. Of the Long Island people he wrote that the women were vainer about their appearance than those of his earlier acquaintance, for they wore headdresses and "small pieces of cotton" strategically disposed. In fifteen days he was out of the archipelago and cruising along the Cuban coast. He never saw the Bahamas again.

There is a lighthouse today on the hill in San Salvador that Columbus had described as an immense rock. On the slope toward the sea stands a cairn erected by a United States newspaper, and this is the sole marker at the spot where modern American history began. Fishermen and peasant farmers earn a hard living. The one village, Cockburn Town, has a Catholic mission on which the inhabitants rely for many things besides religion.

Spaniards coming from Hispaniola combed the Bahamas for labor, as Columbus had implied that they should and would do. They soon exterminated the gentle Lucayos, but they took no interest in settling such unfertile territory. Charles I of England ignored Spain's claim to sovereignty and included the Bahamas among "all the Caribbees" granted to the Earl of Carlisle in 1627. They were then uninhabited. Twenty years later the Company of Eleutherian Adventurers was organized, taking its name from the island that it thought to be the most valuable, and exploitation started. The colony was placed under the rule of the Lords Proprietors of Carolina in

1670. A new wave of settlers arrived, bringing the white population up to about five hundred. This stirred the enmity of the Spaniards and French, who attacked frequently, plundered, and at last destroyed the colony in 1703. For fifteen years thereafter the Bahamas were the resort of pirates, and it may well have been that Blackbeard was really the dominant figure in Nassau for a time.

In 1718 England sent out Captain Woodes Rogers as governor and a new era began. Rogers was a famous explorer and fighting man. It was he who rescued Alexander Selkirk (the original of Robinson Crusoe) from Juan Fernández Island in the Pacific. He brought one hundred picked soldiers with him to Nassau, hanged the unrepentant pirates he found ashore, and conscripted the rest. Then he proceeded to stamp out piracy and defeat every assault made by the Spaniards and others during the eleven remaining years of his life. He designed the coat of arms of the Bahamas, which shows a regal crown above an oval containing a sailing vessel, and has for motto: *Expulsis Piratis Restituta Commercia*. He set up representative government after the model prevailing in Barbados and Bermuda, and this archaic form is still in force today.

Prosperity, though on no grand scale, developed for half a century after the Woodes Rogers regime. Early in the American Revolution the first foreign raid by an American naval force was made on Nassau by Captain Esek Hopkins, the first of American fleet commanders. He seized Fort Montagu, spent the night there, and then summoned the governor in Fort Nassau (on the site of the modern British Colonial Hotel) to surrender. As he expressed it quaintly in his report, he "caused a Manifesto to be published the Purport of which was that the Inhabitants and their Property should be safe if they did not oppose me in taking possession of the Fort and Kings' Stores, which had the desired effect for the Inhabitants left the Fort and Governor all alone." Hopkins departed with loot and three prisoners, including the governor. Two years later there was a second successful attack by Americans.

In 1782 a Spanish force acting under the directions of Bernardo de Gálvez, governor of Louisiana, who had wrested Florida from the English, captured Nassau and proclaimed that all the Bahamas had been annexed by Spain. A governor named Antonio Claraco was appointed and ruled amiably enough for a year. Then a young Tory daredevil, Colonel Andrew Deveaux of South Carolina, vowed to wipe out the stain. He started from St. Augustine with five small boats and a force that was described as "ragged militia," picked up some recruits in the Out Islands, descended on Nassau, and bluffed Claraco into a capitulation. It proved to be one of those unnecessary affairs that used to occur toward the end of wars when the means of communication were slow. Word came that the Bahamas had already been restored to Britain at the peace conference in Europe.

Armed strife has not taken place since in the coral archipelago, save for clashes with the last of the pirates and with slavers, as well as a certain amount of gunplay during the blockade running of the War between the States and the rumrunning of prohibition. These flurries of excitement have also meant temporary bonanzas to a colony that could not hope to get rich on legitimate commerce. The smuggling of corsairs' loot and black ivory was quite a factor up till the abolition of slavery by Britain in 1834. Figures, of course, are lacking.

But we have facts on the golden period from April 1861 to May 1865, the date of the last arrival of a cargo of cotton from a southern port. Some four hundred round-trip voyages under various flags were made between the Bahamas and Dixie. There were 432 clearances for St. John's, New Brunswick, which had been adopted as the point for seemingly legitimate trading within the British Empire, but which served as a "cover" for the distribution of shiploads from the beleaguered Confederacy. The value of exports from Nassau was thirty times as great in the closing days of the war as it had been at its start, the value of acknowledged imports twenty-two times as great. The Federals sank or captured forty-two ships, while twenty-two others were wrecked in flight or taking desperate chances to enter blockaded harbors under cover of darkness. Profits were so large that the speculators did not mind losing two ships if one got through, and it is plain that their record was much better than that. A certain vessel made eighteen round trips before she was caught. Skippers were paid from $3,000 to $5,000 for one voyage, and a Charleston or Wilmington pilot who succeeded at his assignment received $5,000. As I have written elsewhere, the haul by Nassau interests of all kinds was relatively the greatest in the annals of Caribbean ports since the days of the buccaneers' Port Royal.

Who can tell whether the next, and last, opportunity for easy money—the dry decade—outdid the above? Bookkeeping on the illicit rum business was unreliable, to say the least. Hijacking played a part in the game, and there were terrific losses as well as gains. But it was a much longer period. Certainly Nassau, Bimini, and a number of other ports showed evidence of vast activity. It is recounted that the warehouses and wharves were often jammed so full that cases of liquor had to be stacked along the sidewalks of Bay Street. Most of the civic improvements in the capital were made possible by the revenue that flowed into the coffers of an administration willing to close one eye.

When repeal came, a popular local bartender is said to have put the matter philosophically each time he shook a drink. "Boys," he'd trumpet, "the good times are over. We've got to go to work now."

CHAPTER 17

BERMUDA: UNVEXT AND NEAR

FOR a great many Americans, particularly those living on the eastern seaboard, Bermuda has long been the most accessible port of romance under a foreign flag. This small British colony in the Atlantic could be reached by boat in a couple of days from New York, and when the airplane came along the voyage was reduced to a matter of hours. The number of annual visitors rose steadily from 13,000 in 1920 to 86,000 on the eve of World War II, and the latter figure was just two and a half times that of the resident population. The idle rich, honeymooners, and plain vacationists sought the exotic over the rim of the southeastern horizon, beyond the Gulf Stream, and they found it in rewarding measure. The group of islets, totaling twenty square miles, is a land between two worlds, neither wholly American nor wholly European. Undoubtedly the tip of a submerged peak, it may be a westerly bastion of lost Atlantis. It is the "still-vext Bermoothes" of Shakespeare's *The Tempest*, but while possessed of all the charm that that allusion promises, it offers the lucky modern traveler the precise opposite of remoteness and peril.

My visit for the purposes of this book was distinct from my West Indian tour. Before the war a regular steamship service was maintained between Bermuda and certain British possessions to the south, notably Jamaica. It had not yet been resumed, and no link by air existed. It was necessary to go to New York, where the branch office of the extremely progressive Bermuda Trade Development Board (Tourist Commission) made all arrangements for getting to the islands and hotel accommodations there. I boarded a giant, four-engined plane at La Guardia Field. It was called the *Eclipse;* when it comes to de luxe airliners, the practice of naming planes, as advocated in a previous chapter, has already been adopted. They give you a feeling of mastery of the sky, these thunderbirds that fly at a top speed in excess of 300 miles per hour. Midway of the trip, the captain's report, circulated among the passengers, gave the altitude as 17,000 feet and the speed as 275 miles an hour. The temperature outside the cabin windows was fifteen degrees Fahrenheit, while at sea level it was sixty-five degrees. We had climbed above three strata of clouds. The last one seemed quite close, and it looked like a field of lumpy snow, even and motionless, extending in all directions as far as the eye could reach.

We dove down to Bermuda after exactly three hours aloft. The group appeared tiny indeed until you were right over it, the effect being that of a broken atoll with its southern rim and parts of its two ends salient. The rest of the structure, completing an oval, was traceable as a barrier reef below the surface of the water. Intense colors gleamed: the azure of lagoons and sounds framed by the irregular contours of the islets, emerald green along the line of the reef, and beaches where the sand was golden against the surf. But the land itself was predominantly russet with patches of sage, the tell-tale hues of exclusive dependence on rain water and wells. Clustered at intervals around the shore there were white pleasure boats. The roofs of the houses invariably were white, a circumstance to which I shall return.

The airfield is at the eastern end between St. George's Harbour and Castle Harbour, on made land extending into the latter from St. David's Island. It is the chief feature of the huge United States Army base built during World War II, and it added two square miles to the area of Bermuda. The reservation is Fort Bell and the airfield Kindley, mathematically level and aglare with coral dust, an oblong of utility giving no hint of the loveliness beyond its limits. Entry formalities for the American visitor are reduced here to the nominal. A few painless questions, a glance at baggage that seldom involves even the opening of a suitcase, and the freedom of the colony is yours. No other place, not even Canada, gives the same impression that the ideal of "union now" with Britishers has been achieved in fact if not in name. There are station wagons waiting, which will drop you for a reasonable fare at any hotel or guest house on the islands. If you prefer a carriage or one of the low-power taxis, you will be able to observe the scenery a little more comfortably, but will be charged a price that is not so modest. I settled for a station wagon.

Hamilton, the capital and largest town, was the objective. The drive took the better part of an hour, along a winding road that after leaving the airfield crossed a causeway to the neck of land separating Castle Harbour and Harrington Sound, skirted the western and southern shores of the last-named, and then struck through the widest part of the main island. For about four miles the sea was not visible, though nowhere in narrow and relatively long Bermuda is it possible to be a full mile from the sea. The irregular terrain delighted me with its many hillocks and bluffs of a white, soft stone, its little dells of rich earth and abundant vegetation. By far the commonest tree was the so-called cedar, which is really a variety of juniper not found growing wild in any other country, and is both decorative and incredibly hardy. Other trees common to the subtropical zone were fairly numerous, and I noted some that must have been imported from the West Indies, including a scattering of royal palms. Flowers glowed by doorsteps and on lawns. Noticeable were fields of the famous Bermuda lilies, which are cultivated commercially and shipped to many parts of the world.

But the fullness and charm of human occupancy was what most surprised me, as it does every newcomer. Except in the case of a few cays and rocky flats on the shore, there is no wasteland in Bermuda. Houses have been built with good taste, or ingeniously, on unlikely as well as likely spots, some in sunken nooks and some reached by long flights of steps. The pockets of soil, no matter how small, are carefully farmed. If you come upon a stretch of wildwood, you may be sure that it has been preserved as such by the government, or it is part of a rich man's estate and is tended like a park. Yet the atmosphere is happily not suburban. An air of indolent comfort and independence pervades the place. Few dwellings are without close neighbors, but you dismiss the idea that there'd be much curiosity-mongering over the back fences.

We traversed Hamilton by way of Reid Street, the principal shopping thoroughfare, and I was set down at a guest house called The Anchorage on Pitt's Bay just beyond the town. The view from the windows swept most of Crow Lane Harbour, to use the quaint older name of the inlet on which Hamilton is built, and across it to the shore of Paget Parish. Yachts, fishing craft, and a host of little boats dotted the surface. Deep water lapped against a sea wall that sustained a carpet-sized lawn shadowed by blossoming shrubs. A breeze blowing lightly carried the mingled scent of exotic frangipani and the salt of the ocean. Nothing could have been more relaxing, more typical of Bermuda than this combination of wind and sea and flowers that gently dominated the house. One's impulse was to loll and daydream, certain of slipping off into a luxurious nap. This was exactly how I spent my first couple of hours, and I awoke inoculated with the Bermuda spirit.

Supplementing the hotels, there are scores of private homes where visitors are accommodated for four dollars and less a day, including breakfast. The Anchorage is a small but good one. For people who want to get away from the routine of formal living and international meals, the guest houses are heartily recommended. It is amusing to shop around for lunch and supper, especially if you ride a bicycle, which is the thing to do. Wheels for hire are to be found at all turns.

The important sights of Hamilton can be covered in a day, for the town is roughly only eight long blocks by six in size, with of course many side alleys and intersecting lanes. Easily the loveliest spot is the former Perot estate called Par-la-ville, the residence on which has become Bermuda's public library, while the spacious but informal garden serves as a park. It is on Queen Street within a stone's throw of the water front, and virtually adjoining it is Apothecaries' Hall, better known as Heyl's, a drugstore built in the 1860's by an American from the southern states. William B. Perot and J. B. Heyl were friends, and from this resulted an idea that is of vast interest to stamp collectors. Before reviewing the tale, let us glance at the house and grounds.

Built on stone foundations, the wooden superstructure of the dwelling with its wide first-story verandas has a tropical appearance that strikes a pleasing note. It would have been at its best in the dog days when ships' captains came there to fill armchairs and drink rum punches with their host. By the front entrance is a great rubber tree, which was sent as a sapling to Perot from British Guiana in 1847 and flourished amazingly in view of the change of climate. To the left are beds planted with the old-fashioned flowers of clear, gay hues that do so well in Bermuda: nasturtiums, morning-glories (these two are found wild all over the islands), geraniums, sweet peas, pansies, phlox, and sweet william. Winding paths lead to other sections laid out in grass plots and adorned with trees, prominent among which are examples of the Jamaica pimento, from which allspice is obtained. Par-la-ville has been called one of the most attractive little parks to be found anywhere. It stays much as Perot designed it a century ago.

Now, this Perot was postmaster in the days before the adhesive postage stamp had been adopted by Bermuda. He ran his office in a corner room on the ground floor of the building, and his friend Heyl, who had not yet built the drugstore, used to drop in and help him. If a citizen had letters to mail, it was necessary to bring them to the office and pay the fee in cash, when a postmark would be stamped on each envelope. Perot found it inconvenient to be on duty all the time for this purpose, so he welcomed a suggestion made by Heyl. Why not make up sheets of paper bearing twelve postmarks with his signature across each of the latter, said Heyl, and sell the sheet for a shilling? Buyers could cut them apart and paste them on envelopes, the prepaid envelopes to be dropped at any time in a box outside the office door. Thus was created the "Perot stamp," an item that brings enormous prices at auctions today.

The library at Par-la-ville contains over forty thousand volumes and offers a wide selection of American and English periodicals. Habitués like to tell that the original trustees in the Victorian age were so determined not to be tricked by passing fads that they renounced the purchase of any book until at least one year after its first publication. Modernity is the watchword now. In view of the smallness of the community served, the showing is remarkable.

At the opposite, or eastern, end of town near the harbor the Bermuda Historical Society occupies a house built by a seafaring man in 1809, which is architecturally similar to New England dwellings of the period, though claimed as being pure Bermudian. Here are exhibited many relics from the earliest days of the colony, paintings of bygone worthies, sketches and photographs of island scenes, ancient furniture and silver of local workmanship. Notably interesting are some drawings of the swift, narrow, Bermuda-built craft that engaged in blockade running to Confederate ports during the War between the States. There is a still better collection of these in the museum of the St. George's Historical Society, to which we shall come presently.

The cathedral on Church Street is the most impressive and prom-

inent structure in Hamilton, towering above the town and constitut-
ing the landmark that first catches the eye as you approach by sea or
air. An Anglican church, Trinity, originally stood on the spot, but
after its total destruction by fire in 1884 the citizens decided to build
a cathedral. It took twenty-five years to complete, but had been used
for worship meanwhile. The name Bermuda Cathedral was given
to it by an act of the legislature. It might have been transferred intact from England, so faithfully does it reproduce the visual traditions of Anglo-Catholicism. One or two of the stained-glass memorial
windows are admirable. The most dramatic event the cathedral has
known was probably the lying in state of Ramsay MacDonald,
former prime minister, who was brought there after his sudden death
at sea near Bermuda, and the service held before the transshipment
of the body.

Next to the cathedral the Sessions House is the edifice you cannot
fail to remark. It stands on the highest hill, is of red Bermuda stone
with terra-cotta facings, and has a colonnade and a tall clock tower.
Here the House of Assembly meets on the second floor, taking much
pride in the fact that it was founded in 1620 and is the oldest elected
parliament in the British Empire, after the House of Commons. The
Supreme Court has chambers on the ground floor, where also there
are quarters for the chief justice and law officers. The park in which
the building is set slopes toward the harbor; it contains a few undistinguished monuments. Justly, if not very artistically, Sir William
Reid, governor for seven years beginning in 1839, is commemorated
with an obelisk and portrait in bronze. He is held to have done more
than any other chief executive to develop the colony. He improved
agriculture, built the Gibbs Hill Lighthouse, and deepened navigation channels, and he founded the library. Reid Street is named after
him. An authority on hurricanes, he dealt with this intermittent
scourge of the islands in a book that is still consulted.

The post office stands in a corner of the Sessions House square,
and across the street is a two-story stucture of architectural merit
called in modest and literal fashion the Public Building. Several
government departments function there, and the appointive upper
branch of the legislature has its council chamber on the second
floor. Treasures preserved in the Public Building include a sword of
state, believed to have figured in the Crusades; a silver oar with a
hallmark dated 1697, employed as the badge or mace of the Court

of Vice-Admiralty; and a chair made of Bermuda cedar, dated 1642, which symbolizes the throne when the governor opens and closes Parliament.

Victoria Park, toward the rear of town, is formally laid out with a sunken garden at the center and a bandstand. It lacks the allure of Par-la-ville, but serves the ends for which it was designed, as a breathing spot for the many and the scene of outdoor concerts.

For the rest, Hamilton has its hotels, shops, restaurants, and bars, and its always fascinating water front. The biggest and oldest hostelry, the Hamilton, was located at the heart of things and enjoyed considerable prosperity for longer than half a century. Tourists, however, showed a preference for more picturesque sites, especially on the seashore, and little by little the place became a white elephant. It closed several months before the start of World War II in 1939, came to life as a recreation center for British and American servicemen, then went dark again in 1945. No one knows just what will be the fate of the ponderous bulk on Church and Queen Streets. A short distance away, on Queen, the New Windsor Hotel fills a need as a semicommerical house; it has a good patio restaurant. Other hotels within the city limits of Hamilton are the Imperial, the American House, El Morocco, and the Everest. The rates range from $7 to $12 a day for room and meals.

In normal times, the shops are perhaps the greatest attraction the island capital has to offer. They are thoroughly English, by which is meant conservative in their appearance and methods, and specializing in those manufactured articles at which the British Islands excel. It used to be possible to get the old standbys in Hamilton—from tweeds to brier pipes—of fine quality, cheaply according to the grade, and in any quantity. Only the first recommendation holds good for the moment. The English are turning out first-rate stuff for export, but the tide is not yet flowing in full force, and no matter what anyone tells you to the contrary, prices are high. I did see fairly attractive bargains in doeskin gloves, and French perfumes are less expensive here than in the States. Virtually everything else was tagged in dollars at twice the figures of 1939. Within the sterling bloc the purchasing power of the pound is manifestly down to half. If the United States were to cease supporting the pound at an artificial exchange rate of about four dollars, presumably it would slip to two dollars and English goods would be cheap—to Americans.

As it is, purchases in a place like Bermuda cost more than would their equivalents in the United States.

Liquor is an exception. All brands, but particularly West Indian rums, are low enough to make it worth while to bring back the gallon allowed to pass duty free. Beer, on the other hand, is extremely dear. The cafés retail it at forty-five cents a bottle and up.

Bermuda has one other town, St. George's, and a number of villages, some of which call themselves towns though they do not function as such; outside of the two municipalities, the unit of administration is the parish. There are nine parishes and one could write a chapter about each of them, so rich is their lore and so numerous their beauty spots. I must confine myself, however, to certain highlights. Of these St. George's is conspicuous and unique. It is the earliest settlement in Bermuda, the original capital, and to appreciate the archaic charm that has been preserved there for 336 years we must dig back to the beginnings of Bermuda history.

Discovery of the group is usually credited to the Spanish rover Juan de Bermúdez, who found it uninhabited in 1515, gave it his name, and passed on. But the chronicles of Amerigo Vespucci, the importance of whose role in the New World looms larger the more he is studied, point to his having seen Bermuda in 1497. A century later, a fleet under the command of Admiral Sir George Somers was on its way to the relief of the colony at Jamestown, Virginia, when it was scattered by a terrific storm. The flagship, the *Sea Venture,* went ashore on an uncharted reef, but the company was landed and made its way to a pleasant wilderness of hills and fertile hollows, which with adjacent cays protected a deep-water haven. The Admiral thus became the rediscoverer of Bermuda in July 1609, and declared it an English possession only two years after John Smith's attempt on the mainland and eleven years in advance of the Pilgrims and Plymouth Rock. He continued to Virginia, but returned in a few months to his ocean sanctuary to die. For generations thereafter the group was commonly known as the Somers Islands.

Three survivors of the wreck of the *Sea Venture* had decided to go no farther. They appear to have established themselves on Smith's Island at the southern end of the harbor. But when settlers arrived in 1612 under the command of Richard Moore, the first governor, everyone moved to the larger island to the north and St. George's was founded. It remained the seat of government and the chief port for upwards of two hundred years, the shift of the capital to Hamilton occurring only in 1815.

The old section of town with its narrow, twisting streets is wholly seventeenth century in character, for though nearly all the buildings are of later date a continuity has been lovingly maintained in the architecture. Here we find the true Bermuda house, a one-story affair of blocks cut from the soft native coral, with steeply slanting roof, the chimney as an excrescence rising clear from the ground at one end of the building, small-paned windows, and shutters that swing up and outward in a single piece, the doorway usually at the head of a short flight of steps and approached from the side of the house. There are gutters to catch the rain water and direct it to cisterns. The newer roofs are in a series of terraces a few inches wide, as it has been proved that more water is caught that way. By law the roofs must be frequently painted with a whitewash of lime to keep the water pure; this applies all over Bermuda. In St. George's the walls too are often plastered, white or in pastel shades.

Old structures in King's Square on the port front tend to a weather-beaten gray, however. The State House is thought to be the first stone building erected in Bermuda, and it dates from 1620. The pioneers legislated on the ground floor and used an upper story, since demolished, as a warehouse and gunpowder magazine. The square itself was a market place and used to be bisected by an inlet of the sea at which small boats docked. Near by is a walled park called Somers Garden. The heart and entrails of Admiral Somers had been buried somewhere on the site in 1610, while the rest of the corpse was sent back to England, but the park and monument to the discoverer were not dedicated until the 1870's.

St. Peter's Church, on the slope to the northwest of King's Square, is a gem from the youthful period of Anglicanism. Not that the entire building is so very old. But its core is early eighteenth century, and part of it stands on the foundations of what is claimed to have been the oldest English church in the New World. Reconstruction took place in 1814, when the southern transept was added and the square clock tower built at the western end. Font, altar, and "three-decker" pulpit are from the original structure, the first being of English ironstone and the other two of Bermuda cedar. The rector, Canon Arthur Tucker, has explained in a pamphlet that the pulpit was in tiers because it used to be the custom for the parish clerk to stand at the lowest level, read the responses as leader of the congregation, give out notices, and, when required, pitch the tune for the psalm. "The second tier is the reading desk for the parson and the third is for him to preach his sermons from." The high-backed wooden pews have been darkened and polished by generations of use. A gallery reserved in the old days for slaves is still in service; by custom, though not by rule, the Negro members of the congregation sit there. The walls are covered with memorial tablets, one of which is by John Bacon, the fashionable sculptor whose work abounds in Jamaica.

Gently romantic, St. Peter's churchyard conveys a mood not unlike that of Gray's "Elegy." No one of world fame is buried there, but—to paraphrase—many an island Hampden and many a lovely head. In a large tomb on the eastern side, marked "Mr. William Tucker's Family Vault," lies Hester Louise Tucker, who married William at the age of sixteen and died at thirty-one, and is remembered because Tom Moore called her Nea and wrote love poems to her. The bard of the *Irish Melodies* had been appointed to a sinecure in the Admiralty Court at St. George's. He lived during his short stay next door to the Tuckers in the street now oddly named Old Maid's Lane, though it was then Cumberland Lane. Both houses have been replaced by other buildings. Moore was serious enough in his flirtation, as witness the lines:

> *I saw you blush, you felt me tremble,*
> *In vain would formal art dissemble*
> *All that we wish'd and thought;*
> *'Twas more than tongue could dare reveal,*
> *'Twas more than virtue ought to feel,*
> *But all that passion ought!*

Sad to say, William Tucker forbade him the house. Moore continued to moon over Nea and even sent her some verses about the birth of her first son. In days to come he was to lament airily that his "only books were women's looks, and folly's all they've taught me."

Among the quaint street names to be noted in St. George's are Thread and Needle Street, Shinbone Alley, One Gun Lane, Petticoat Lane, Printer's Alley, and Featherbed Alley. At the corner of the last-mentioned and Kent Street is the perfectly lovely old house known to have been standing in 1700 and now occupied by the St. George's Historical Society. I like this museum better than the one at Hamilton, partly because the building is more attractive but mainly on account of the enthusiastic care given to the displaying of treasures by the curator, Miss Lillian Hayward. The exhibits are of great local interest. Many relate to the blockade runners of 1861–65, which operated chiefly from St. George's Harbour. The Confederate agent John Bourne lived at a house called Rose Hill on the height northwest of the museum, which was Nea's last home and the place where she died. Substantial sums changed hands as a result of the traffic, though Bermuda did not come near equaling Nassau in that respect.

When Rose Hill passed it was to give way to the St. George Hotel, a building that covers the entire summit and enjoys the finest view of any hotel in Bermuda. It is reached by a curving drive from the west and a long flight of stone steps from Old Maid's Lane on the east. The wide terrace in front and the adjoining grounds contrast delightfully with the archaic town below. To the rear is a country club with a private beach. You can pay as much as $20 a day at the St. George, American plan. The juxtaposition of old and new, of the picturesque and the comfortable keyed to a leisurely tempo, causes this end of Bermuda to resemble the French Riviera. The longer I stayed there, the more definite did the feeling become. Bermuda is an extension into the Western Hemisphere of a Mediterranean locale, though in some aspects, particularly at the opposite end of the group, there is also a resemblance to Cornwall.

Between St. George's and Hamilton occur numerous points of interest to the tourist. You are barely over the causeway when you arrive at Tom Moore's House, formerly called Walsingham after a survivor of the *Sea Venture*. The poet was a frequent visitor there, but never a resident. An excuse for attaching his name to it is to be found in the fact that his actual home has disappeared. The place is now used as a tavern. It is regarded as a splendid example of early Bermuda architecture, and a replica of it was once built for an Empire exposition in London.

Castle Harbour Hotel on the lagoon of the same name is one of the colony's noteworthy caravansaries, large and well appointed and with a magnificent garden. It was closed to guests on the outbreak

of the war. Since it lay opposite to the site of the new United States
Army base, it was a natural as military headquarters, was taken
over for this purpose and as a barracks, and was not relinquished
until the completion of Fort Bell. The hotel suffered less deteriora-
tion than if it had lain idle. It will probably be reopened to the public in 1948. Near by is the celebrated Mid-Ocean Club, which boasts
golf links said to equal the best anywhere. They ought to be good,
for they were designed in the 1920's by Charles Macdonald, the
man known as the "father of golf in America."

A number of beautiful caves exists on the neck of land between
Castle Harbour and Harrington Sound. The most visited is the one
that long bore the prosy name of Joyce's Dock Cave, but it recently
has blossomed out as Prospero's Cave and is shown to the credulous
as the scene of *The Tempest*. Shakespeare's story, fanciful though it
be, has grown into a Bermudian myth. There is ample reason for
this, because scholars have endorsed the theory that the master dramatist got his idea and background material from the narrative of William Strachey, a member of the *Sea Venture's* company. Shakespeare may well have seen, also, the account written by Sylvanus
Jourdain, another participant, who styled Bermuda "a most prodi-
gious and inchanted place."

On the west shore of Harrington Sound are an aquarium that
ranks high among American institutions of the sort, a small zoo, and
a natural history museum. The aquarium is very popular with tourists. In addition to the marine life on show, there are facilities for
underwater tours in diving suits. The zoo offers two novelties: a
colony of penguins and a run containing twenty or thirty giant tor-
toises, both species brought originally from the Galápagos Islands
by Vincent Astor, of New York, who has an estate on Bermuda and
has been a liberal patron of the Natural History Society's work. The
penguins here are the first that ever bred in captivity. The Galápagos
tortoise is a prehistoric survival and individuals are believed to live
longer than any other creature on earth. Some are hundreds of years
old. The Bermuda exhibit is considered the best and largest.

As we return to the neighborhood of Hamilton, a look at Government House is obligatory. This official residence is sometimes called
Mount Langton, the name having been attached to it by an early
governor in honor of his family seat in Scotland. The grounds are
decoratively landscaped and dotted with imported trees planted by

celebrities, including members of the royal family. But the building is rather severe. Formal entertaining occurs there frequently, the responsibilities of a chief executive in tranquil Bermuda being largely social and ceremonial.

Pembroke is the name of the parish in which Hamilton is located. It is a peninsula sticking up at an angle from the main body of land and thus protects Crow Lane, otherwise Hamilton, Harbour. Beyond the latter, southward, are the intensively developed parishes of Paget and Warwick, followed by Southampton, where the land narrows to a mere half mile in width and curves north to form the Great Sound. Bermuda proper ends at a thread of a strait traversed by a high bridge, but the curve is continued by Somerset and Ireland Islands, which constitute the parish of Sandys.

Hotels on the outskirts of Hamilton are the large Bermudiana and Princess, both of which were closed during the war, but are expected to resume activities in 1948. The Princess Cottages, attached to the hotel of the same name, were receiving guests at the time of my visit. So were Waterloo House and other smaller places, as well as the Eagle's Nest, not far from Government House on the north shore, one of the few spots in Bermuda that runs a night club. Rates vary between $12 and $20 a day, American plan. The exclusive Royal Bermuda Yacht Club, on Albuoy's Point just outside the city limits, is not open to the public, but courtesy cards are issued to visitors who have the right connections. Boat racing and deep-sea fishing are the two favorite sports in the islands.

In Paget we find the Elbow Beach Hotel and Golf Course, another war casualty, soon to be back in the running. The Inverurie Hotel has been doing business right along, and so have the guest houses Horizons, Buena Vista, and Newstead, and several smaller rivals. Belmont Manor, in Warwick, is the only really large hotel, except the St. George, that opened immediately after the restoration of peace. Cambridge-Beaches and the Summerside Hotel, both on Somerset Island, have been busy too. Rates are similar to those prevailing elsewhere in Bermuda, with Belmont Manor's maximum of $24 a day as tops. There are any number of beaches along the south shore where surf bathing may be enjoyed. Perhaps the most popular is Coral Beach, which adjoins the equally fine Elbow and Simmons Beaches.

Somerset is worth a day's excursion to those travelers who may happen to be staying elsewhere. Despite its remoteness, it is the most thickly settled part of the colony outside of the Pembroke re-region around Hamilton. The discoverer, Sir George Somers, took a fancy to the little island and often trudged the twenty-two miles from St. George's to visit it. According to William Zuill, a native, whose *Bermuda Journey* is a commendable guidebook, the island was known at first as "Sommers-seate," a name that later colonists confused with that of a county in England and modified accordingly. Somerset affords a pleasant combination of rurality and the sea-shore. There is no wonder town of seventeenth- and eighteenth-century houses, as at St. George's, but many fine old country residences and modern cottages may be seen. Felicity Hall, near Long Bay, is where Hervey Allen hid from the world to write his successful picaresque novel, *Anthony Adverse*.

The United States Naval Base is on a peninsula jutting into the Great Sound from Sandys Parish and also utilizes some land opposite in Southampton Parish. Britain's naval base is an ancient establishment with a dockyard on Ireland Island. Off the latter and stretching irregularly toward the barrier reef are the "coral gardens," to which trippers are taken in glass-bottomed boats to view the marvels of undersea life. Here the reefs lie within a few feet of the surface, and you revel in a gorgeous panorama of living coral, bright-colored fish such as the famous Bermuda angel fish, sea horses, sea anemones, and marine vegetation that sways with the currents much as plants are fluttered by the breeze ashore.

Local transportation meets all requirements. It has had some odd historical quirks and is still a controversial and colorful subject. One of the things that most outsiders had heard about Bermuda was that it would not allow the use of automobiles, having chosen to remain in the horse-and-buggy age. Actually there was no prohibition at the start. When motor vehicles became popular a few rich Bermudians imported them. But around 1908 tourism began to shape up as a profitable business, and the deliberate conclusion was reached that banning cars would increase the lure of the islands. Peace and quiet was to be the slogan. The necessary legislation was adopted, the government reimbursing the owners of confiscated machines. A picture showing a policeman directing a stream of horse-drawn and bicycle traffic on the Hamilton water front was for twenty-five years the postcard most often mailed to foreign parts.

The approval of visitors was almost unanimous. Woodrow Wilson, a great lover of Bermuda, once joined in a petition with 112 other Americans to urge that the tempo should never be speeded up.

A pro-automobile faction among the islanders remained active. Horses were an expensive luxury in a country that did not grow enough feed for them and had to import hay and grain. Hack fares were correspondingly high. The moving of freight became a real and increasing problem. Utilitarian arguments only made the anti-automobile party more stubborn. But when the proposition of a railroad was launched, the two sides astonished everyone—including themselves—by agreeing on it. There is said to have been misapprehension in both camps. The pros felt that steam trains would prove an opening wedge for cars. The antis held that though a railroad would be noisy and offensive, it could be endured because localized, and that it would forever do away with the demand for cars. A heavy vote was cast in favor; the railroad was built and commenced operations at the end of 1931, the route being from St. George's to Somerset by way of Hamilton, with countless stops and a time schedule of two and a half hours. It lost money for its backers and had to be taken over by the government. The pro-automobile people cried that now there would have to be motor vehicles. The antis coolly replied that it had merely been demonstrated that Bermuda should stick to horses.

Then World War II broke out and modern efficiency had its way. The United States government specified that it must be allowed to use automobiles, trucks, and jeeps in connection with the new bases. Importation of all supplies for the civilian community was limited by military needs, and fodder was classed as unnecessary. The older and weaker horses had to be killed in preference to letting them starve. Others were barely kept alive. Carriages rotted in the stables. Only those that stayed in service could be repaired, and that with difficulty. Inquiries failed to discover a firm in England or America that was equipped to fill a large order for carriages. When the war ended Burmuda was crowded with army vehicles, and no way in sight of dispensing with them. The anti-motor party ended by capitulating, but they obtained a compromise. Legalized private cars and taxis were restricted to ten horsepower (British measurement), 160 inches over-all, and sixty-four inches in width. Trucks were restricted to twelve horsepower and a length of 162 inches. The speed limit was set at fifteen miles an hour in towns and twenty miles on country roads, violation to be punished by loss of the driver's license, and in some cases imprisonment and a fine. No family or household could own more than one car. A visitor could not obtain a driver's license until he had been in the colony at least thirty days. This conservative policy made—and makes—for undramatic, safe motoring. Bermudians are pleased with the results.

As of April 1947 there were 1,477 motor vehicles on the roads, valued at a total of nearly $2,000,000. These consisted of 510 private cars, 210 taxis, 381 light and heavy trucks, 40 miscellaneous trucks such as station wagons and oil tanks, and 336 motor bicycles. At least another 65 taxis were in prospect when available, 275 having been set as the full quota under the law, and 500 persons had filed orders for motor bicycles.

The railroad is still operating, but it is believed that its end is in sight and that its functions will be taken over by passenger bus lines and a fleet of freight trucks. Still very much in evidence, also, are carriages plying for custom and an immense number of ordinary bicycles propelled by leg power. There are said to be more of the last-named per capita in Bermuda than in any other country. The horses may vanish someday. The bikes never will, for they constitute the cheapest means of getting about, and use of them has become a matter of course to man, woman, and child.

From the standpoint of property interests, Bermuda is all that the Virgin Islands would like to be but show little evidence of achieving. Bermuda has a real economy and the results seep down to even the lowest levels of the population. In addition to the busy shops already mentioned, you find large importing and commission houses, banks and building companies. Farming is done to the full extent of the arable land available. Cattle and poultry are raised. Commercial fishing amounts to a respectable minor business. There is a labor problem, in that unskilled workmen and domestic servants complain that wages are too low, but it certainly is not acute. Men questioned on the street admitted that anyone could get a job, while employers said that help was fairly easy to obtain.

The inhabitants number some 34,000, of whom almost two thirds are Negroes. Visitors invariably are astonished to learn that the proportion of blacks is so high, for the colored element stays pretty much in the background. Bermuda seems preponderantly white, or at the least fifty-fifty, as indeed it may well be at a given time, owing to the presence of tourists. Among the Caucasian residents are a couple of thousand Portuguese, descendants of immigrants who came from the Azores to the colony about a century ago. They make the most reliable workers on the land, and although they tend to cling to their ancestral tongue they are regarded as true Bermudians.

After I had taken everything into account—the tested and stable way of life, the industry of the people, etc.—I still could not figure out how a tiny unit like Bermuda that depended heavily upon imports managed to be so flourishing. The hotels and guest houses I had been surveying proffered an obvious answer. But could local tourism be as big as all that? Surely it was only a contributing factor. The way to find out was to consult an authority. I went to see Mr. Joseph J. Outerbridge, the executive secretary of the Bermuda Trade Development Board, and put the matter up to him.

"Eighty-five per cent of the community's profits today are derived from tourism, in the form of either catering or the sale of goods," he declared, leaning forward, his tone emphatic. "That's no exaggeration. Eighty-five per cent."

"Bermuda's must be relatively the largest 'take' of any tourist region on earth," I commented, a bit dazed.

"It probably is."

"To what do you ascribe your success in attracting visitors?"

"Apart from our favorable geographic location, the climate, the beauty of the islands, and that sort of thing, I ascribe it to the regulations that have kept Bermuda tranquil, clean, and dignified without being austere. We've never stood for gambling houses, or rowdy night life of any kind. Yet we have horse racing and other sports. There are plenty of spots where well-behaved persons can drink and dance. We're against toughs, crooked or otherwise, and the policy has paid."

I asked about the times preceding the tourist boom, which gathered momentum during the 1920's but did not become a monster traffic until the 1930's.

"Ah, yes, there used to be a period when Bermuda was isolated and rather poor," said Outerbridge, growing reminiscent. "You must know that in the really long ago our people built wonderful clippers, an industry that was knocked out by the advent of the steamship. Our modern racing craft prove that the knack for designing has not been lost. Whaling figures in the annals, and they do say a certain amount of wrecking. There was the bonanza of blockade running to Dixie. Following the sixties, we settled down to agriculture and did pretty well at it."

Outerbridge went into details about the famous Bermuda lilies, onions, and potatoes, all of which were long admitted to the United States at low customs rates and were in much demand. But the Hawley-Smoot Tariff Act of 1930 was a deadly blow. The duties fixed were too high to be absorbed and the trade virtually ceased. Lily bulbs and blooms continued to be exported to other countries. Canada took a modest quota of seasonal vegetables. There might have been no escape from bankruptcy, however, if the government and merchants had not concentrated on building up tourism. A tremendous advertising campaign was launched.

"With more lucrative results than dealing in farm products could ever have brought," I ventured.

His eyes twinkled. "Of course. More interesting, too. I, for one, like to meet people—plenty of them."

I remarked that Bermuda has no income tax, yet unlike the Bahamas does not publicize that fact as an attraction.

"There are no inheritance taxes either, and no gift, capital, or personal property taxes," replied Outerbridge. "The only direct levies are the assessments on real estate made by the parishes for administrative purposes, and these are kept as low as possible, varying according to the needs of each parish. There is no public debt. The government gets along on customs duties, which average seventeen and a half per cent. It is a condition that helps to make life agreeable for the citizens of Bermuda. We do not publicize it, because though we are glad to welcome transients we are not in the market for settlers, as is the case with the Bahamas. Our little islands are already thickly populated. If an alien wants to buy a house or land here, he must ask the permission of the governor-in-council. His character and financial standing are discreetly investigated through the British consulate nearest to his home address. Should his application be rejected, no reason is given. If he is allowed to become a property owner, we feel that he has been paid a compliment."

"Hasn't there been some talk of imposing an income tax?"

"Yes. The Labour party now in power in Britain has raised the question of the equity of our system of taxation, arguing that it bears more heavily on the poor than the rich. Certain local people feel that this view is theoretically correct, that the fairest tax would be one on incomes. But Bermuda has never had direct taxation, and the idea is unpopular. Our legislature will act as it sees fit about the matter. It will not be dictated to."

The independence of the House of Assembly is beyond dispute, an attitude on which it has prided itself for three and a quarter centuries. Modern observers find the whole form of government anachronistic (I am no longer citing Outerbridge), but it can be made to work in a midget country where everybody knows everybody else. The Assembly, or lower house, consists of thirty-six elected members, four from each parish. To be qualified for office, a candidate must own freehold property valued at £240 ($960), while the voters must be freeholders who own land valued at sixty pounds ($240); women did not obtain the franchise on this basis until 1944. The Legislative Council, or upper house, is a body of nine members, appointed by the governor and invariably conservative. Only the Assembly may initiate or amend money bills. The Legislative Council may block the acts of the Assembly by refusing to concur, and the governor may veto any law on which both have agreed. But without the Assembly's consent there can be no legislation. True, the Crown has the power to intervene, for in the last analysis Bermuda does not have responsible government. But it would take an extreme emergency to force the Crown to such action. The thirty-six elected freeholders have often been successfully defiant.

The system is similar to the one that prevailed in the thirteen American colonies before the Revolution. As told in previous chapters, Jamaica and other British West Indian colonies had constitutions of the same type up till the 1860's. The structure still exists, with modifications, in Barbados and the Bahamas. Bermuda's ruling class rejoices in having kept the seventeenth-century model intact.

Only the other day the Colonial Office in London advised the Assembly to revise the labor laws and threatened to send out a royal commission of inquiry if this were not done. Up stood several members of the island's ancient parliament to voice the opinion that, if interference were seriously attempted, Bermuda should secede from the Empire. This may seem funny to an outside world distracted by vast issues. But an affirmation of liberty should never be treated as a joke. The Bermudian assemblymen did not come out against social justice. They objected to interference, and that was their privilege. Labor reforms are in the air. I was assured that they would probably be adopted.

The franchise limited by property qualifications is, however, a serious drawback to democracy. There are no laws against Negroes being elected to office. The whites owe their advantage to their control of the greater part of the land. In the general elections of 1945, for instance, one white in eleven voted and one Negro in sixteen. The colored electorate in two parishes outnumbered the white. The property qualifications for officeholding being higher than for voting, only eight Negroes were able to win seats as against twenty-eight whites. When, or if, the franchise is broadened, it would be a pity if race rivalry were to become an issue. Bermudians of all classes and shades aver that they do not want that. But can it be prevented? Time alone will tell.

Stripped of pretenses, the social, commercial, and political setup may be said to be dominated by a hierarchy of old families. Mention the names Trimingham, Tucker, Butterfield, Darrell, Gosling, Outerbridge, Trott, Watlington, Smith, Spurling, and Cox, and you have listed most of those that count. No one could accuse them of running their little Elysium despotically. On the contrary, the chief memory that the traveler takes away from Bermuda is the easygoing character of the life. You realize that a settled order is carefully maintained there, but in the most unobtrusive manner imaginable.

I shall close with the words of two poets. In *The Tempest*, Gonzalo, the king's counselor, declares: "Had I plantation of this isle, my lord . . . I' the commonwealth I would by contraries execute all things; for no kind of traffic would I admit . . . no occupation; all men idle, all; and women, too." Though the sage admonition has not been literally carried out, the visitor feels that he, at least, has been encouraged to be deliciously and refreshingly lazy.

And Edmund Waller wrote of Bermuda in the seventeenth century:

> *So sweet the air, so moderate the clime;*
> *None sickly lives, or dies before his time.*
> *Heav'n sure has kept this spot of earth uncurst,*
> *To show how all things were created first!*

Bibliography

American Guide Series (WPA). *Puerto Rico*. New York, 1940. Comprehensive information.

Arciniegas, Germán. *Caribbean: Sea of the New World*. New York, 1946. A historical survey of the region from the discovery by Columbus to the beginning of the present century.

Aspinall, Sir Algernon. *The Pocket Guide to the West Indies*. New York, 1935. Mainly about the British possessions.

Blanshard, Paul. *Democracy and Empire in the Caribbean*. New York, 1947. Keen analysis of social and political conditions.

Bowman, Heath, and Jefferson. *Crusoe's Island*. Indianapolis, 1939. Account of residence in Tobago.

Bradley, Hugh. *Havana: Cinderella's City*. New York, 1941. Despite title, all Cuba is covered. Historical survey and personal impressions.

Bushell, John J. *Picturesque Bermuda*. Bermuda, 1939. A standard handbook that has had several editions.

Chapman, Charles E. *A History of the Cuban Republic*. New York, 1927. The best general history of Cuba in English up to the Machado period.

Clark, Sydney. *All the Best in Cuba*. New York, 1946. A good up-to-date guide.

Davis, H. P. *Black Democracy*. New York, 1936. The best general history of Haiti in English up to and including the American occupation.

Early, Eleanor. *Ports of the Sun*. Boston, 1937. Travel impressions of various West Indian countries.

————. *Lands of Delight*. Boston, 1940. Travel impressions of some other West Indian countries.

Ferguson, Erna. *Cuba*. New York, 1946. An excellent short history, with personal impressions.

Froude, James Anthony. *The English in the West Indies*. New York, 1888. Political and scenic impressions by a famous historian of the last century.

Hearn, Lafcadio. *Two Years in the French West Indies*. New York, 1890. Word pictures by a great stylist. The best account of Martinique life ever written.

Hergesheimer, Joseph. *San Cristóbal de la Habana*. New York, 1927. Brilliant word pictures of the Cuban capital.

Hermer, Consuelo, and May, Marjorie. *Havana Mañana*. New York, 1941. A chatty, useful guide to the city and environs.

Hiss, Philip Hanson. *Netherlands America*. New York, 1943. A general account of the Dutch territories in the New World.

Kahn, Morton C. *Djuka*. New York, 1931. An account of the Bush Negroes of Surinam.

Leyburn, James G. *The Haitian People*. New Haven, 1942. Admirable presentation of social life and historical influences.

Means, Philip Ainsworth. *The Spanish Main*. New York, 1935. Valuable historical survey from 1492 to the end of the seventeenth century.

Morison, Samuel Eliot. *Admiral of the Ocean Sea*. Boston, 1942. Important recent biography of Christopher Columbus.

Niles, Blair. *Black Haiti*. New York, 1926. Literary vignettes of Haitian life and history.

Olley, Philip P. *Guide to Jamaica*. Kingston, Jamaica, 1937. Comprehensive information.

Roberts, W. Adolphe. *The Caribbean: The Story of Our Sea of Destiny*. Indianapolis, 1940. A historical survey of the region from the discovery by Columbus to World War II.

Smith, Glenville. *Many a Green Isle*. New York, 1941. Travel impressions of Caribbean islands.

Smith, Nicol. *Black Martinique—Red Guiana*. Indianapolis, 1942. Impressions of two French colonies.

Steedman, Mabel. *Unknown to the World—Haiti*. London, 1939. An interesting approach by an Englishwoman to the black republic.

Strode, Hudson. *The Pageant of Cuba*. New York, 1934. A sound analysis of the country's story.

————. *The Story of Bermuda*. New York, 1946. A thorough appraisal of the little island's role in the world.

Tugwell, Rexford Guy. *The Stricken Land*. New York, 1947. Puerto Rico portrayed by its former governor.

Vandercook, John W. *Black Majesty*. New York, 1928. A semifictional presentation of King Christophe of Haiti.

————. *Tom-Tom*. New York, 1926. Travels in the interior of Surinam.

Welles, Sumner. *Naboth's Vineyard: The Dominican Republic*. New York, 1928. The only complete history of the country in English.

White, Trumbull. *Puerto Rico and Its People*. New York, 1938. Good.

Zuill, William. *Bermuda Journey*. New York, 1946. Graphic account by a Bermudian.

Appendix

AREAS AND POPULATIONS

The following statistics would have made for hard reading if they had been scattered through the main text. They are of interest to travelers, however, and are given here for ready reference.

CUBA

Area: 44,164 square miles
Population (1943): 4,777,284

HAITI

Area: 10,204 square miles
Population (1937, estimated): 3,000,000

DOMINICAN REPUBLIC

Area: 19,332 square miles
Population (1943): 1,826,407

United States Possessions

PUERTO RICO

Area: 3,435 square miles
Population (1940): 1,869,255

VIRGIN ISLANDS

Area: 132 square miles
Population (1940): 24,889

British Possessions

JAMAICA

Area: 4,450 square miles
Population (1943): 1,237,063

TRINIDAD AND TOBAGO

Area: 1,980 square miles
Population (1945): 571,446

BARBADOS

Area: 166 square miles
Population (1945): 203,528

BRITISH GUIANA

Area: 89,480 square miles
Population (1942): 361,754

WINDWARD ISLANDS

Area: 821 square miles
Population: 265,715

LEEWARD ISLANDS

Area: 727 square miles
Population: 100,497

THE BAHAMAS

Area: 4,404 square miles
Population (1943): 68,846

BERMUDA

Area: 19½ square miles, plus two square miles of recently made
land
Population (1944): 33,925

Dutch Possessions

NETHERLANDS WEST INDIES

Area: 384 square miles
Population: 119,585

Surinam
Area: 55,143 square miles
Population: 183,730

French Possessions

Martinique
Area: 380 square miles
Population: 304,239

Guadeloupe
Area: 583 square miles
Population: 304,209

French Guiana
Area: 65,041 square miles
Population: 36,975

Chief Cities of the Region

CUBA:
Havana, 573,837 inhabitants in city proper; about 800,000 in metropolitan area
Santiago de Cuba, 143,000 inhabitants
Camaguey, 139,828 inhabitants
Santa Clara, 99,969 inhabitants
Cienfuegos, 93,568 inhabitants
Matanzas, 74,087 inhabitants

HAITI:
Port-au-Prince, 150,000 (estimated) inhabitants

DOMINICAN REPUBLIC:
Ciudad Trujillo, 116,959 inhabitants
Santiago de los Caballeros, 51,689 inhabitants

PUERTO RICO:
San Juan, 169,247 inhabitants
Ponce, 65,182 inhabitants

JAMAICA:
Kingston, 109,056 inhabitants in city proper; 201,911 in metropolitan area

TRINIDAD:
Port-of-Spain, 100,595 inhabitants

BARBADOS:

Bridgetown, 70,000 (estimated) inhabitants

BRITISH GUIANA:

Georgetown, 71,160 inhabitants.

SURINAM:

Paramaribo, 55,480 inhabitants

MARTINIQUE:

Fort-de-France, 52,051 inhabitants

INDEX